Our Western World

From the Dawn of Civilization - The Early Modern Age

VOLUME 1

Zachary Alexander ■ Jeffery B. Howell ■ J. Kyle Irvin ■ Wendy Shuffett ■ Kirk Strawbridge

Second Edition

Kendall Hunt
publishing company

Contents

Contents

About the Authors/Contributors

Co-Author

Zachary Alexander is an Instructor of History at Jefferson State Community College in Birmingham, AL. He has been a faculty member since 2007. He has a B.S. degree in History from the University of Montevallo. He holds an M.A. degree in History from Mississippi State University. He is the co-author of the First Edition of *Our Western World* (2013) and an American History textbook, *The American Road* (2016). His research interests include: Diplomatic, Military, and Political History.

Co-Author

Jeffery B. Howell is an Associate Professor of History at East Georgia State College in Statesboro, GA. He earned his Ph.D. and M.A. in History from Mississippi State University. He earned an M.Div. from Mid America Baptist Theological Seminary in Memphis, TN. He has a B.A. in History from the University of Mississippi. He is the author of the books: *Hazel Brannon Smith: The Female Crusading Scalawag* (2017) and *The American Road: Crossing the American Landscape in the Modern Era* (2016).

Co-Author

Joseph Kyle Irvin is an Instructor of History at Jefferson State Community College where he has been a faculty member since 2000. He holds M.A. degrees in Education and History from The University of Alabama-Birmingham. His primary teaching responsibilities are in the History of Western Civilization. He served as Chairman of the Liberal Arts Department of the Shelby Campus of Jefferson State Community College from 2005 to 2016. He is the co-author of the First Edition of *Our Western World* (2013) and an American History textbook, *The American Road* (2016). Professor Irvin frequently leads overseas student tours of historical points of interest. He and his wife Rebecca have two college age children, Sam and Addie, three dogs and one cat. He enjoys spending time with his family and friends, traveling, going to the gym, reading, smoking ribs, good beer, and food.

Co-Author

Wendy Shuffett is an Instructor of History at Jefferson State Community College in Birmingham, AL. She earned a Master of Arts in History with an emphasis in Church History in 1992 from Western Kentucky University. She earned a Master's of Education 2012 from the University of Alabama-Birmingham. Wendy teaches American History survey courses, Western Civilization survey courses, and World History survey courses. Her previous written works include: *The American Road: Volume 1, Traveling the Early American Byways of a New Nation* (2016) and *The American Road: Volume 2, Crossing the American Landscape into the Modern Era* (2016).

Co-Author

Kirk Strawbridge is a Professor of History at Tyler Junior College in Tyler, TX. He earned a Ph.D. in History in 2011 from Mississippi State University. The focus of his studies was Southern History, the Civil War, and 19th Century America. His previous written works include: *Our Western World, Volume 1: From the Dawn of Civilization-The Early Modern Age, 1st Edition* (2013), *Our Western World, Volume 2: From the Scientific Revolution to the Present, 1st Edition* (2013), *The American Road: Volume 1, Traveling the Early American Byways of a New Nation* (2016), and *The American Road: Volume 2, Crossing the American Landscape into the Modern Era* (2016).

Editorial Contributor: Historical Videos Coordinator

Richard Eller is a Documentary Filmmaker and Historian. He completed a Master of Arts in History, University of North Carolina at Charlotte, (1999). He is the Catawba Valley Community College Historian in Residence at the Historical Museum of Catawba County in Hickory, NC. He is also a Professor of History at Catawba Valley Community College in Hickory, NC. His previous written works include: *The Tarheel Lincoln: NC Origins of "Honest" Abe* (2004), *Piedmont Airlines: A Complete History* (2008), *The American Road: Volume 1, Traveling the Early American Byways of a New Nation* (2016), *The American Road: Volume 2, Crossing the American Landscape into the Modern Era* (2016), *Polio, Pitchforks and Perseverance: How a North Carolina County Named Catawba Created a "Miracle"* (2016–17). His previous documentary works include: Producer/Director—*Back Then . . .* (1994–2002), Producer/Director—*Speedbird, the History of Piedmont Airlines* (2012), and Coordinator/Producer/Director *Miracle: How a North Carolina County Named Catawba Battled Polio and Won* (2016–17).

Editorial Contributor: Historical Images Coordinator/In Focus Essayist

Christina McClellan obtained her B.A. in History and a minor in Anthropology from the University of Alabama. She went on to obtain an M.A. in Early Modern European History from the University of Colorado, Boulder. Her research interests incorporated Tudor and Stuart England, Atlantic World History, as well as iconography and heraldry. While at the University of Colorado, McClellan also obtained an M.S. in Museum and Field Studies with an emphasis in exhibition development. Her internships and graduate assistantships included work in the History Museum of Mobile in Mobile, AL, University of Colorado Museum of Natural History, Handel House Museum in London, UK, and the Birmingham Museum of Art in Birmingham, AL. McClellan currently teaches history at Jefferson State Community College in Birmingham, AL, and works full time as the coordinator of collections, exhibitions, and programs at the Abroms-Engel Institute for the Visual Arts at the University of Alabama at Birmingham. She is passionate about cross-disciplinary approaches to learning and incorporates these methodologies in her work and classes.

Chapter 1

The Earliest Roots of the West: Mesopotamia and Egypt

History is shaped by the rise and fall of civilizations. The first civilizations began around six thousand years ago and were similar in many regards, with overlapping distinctive characteristics. As societies of people morphed into civilizations, certain key aspects developed and created the underlying definition of a civilization. These groups of individuals lived according to evident worldviews that shaped their work, religion, and livelihoods. The study of Western civilizations is built upon the development of these worldviews, as populations lived out their beliefs, occupations, and family lives within these frameworks of life.

Civilizations and Worldviews

Throughout history, civilizations did not automatically emerge from a society of people. A society must have certain characteristics in place before it is defined as a civilization. Historians agree that a civilization is a complex culture that involves scores of people sharing common elements. These shared cultural features include an organized government and a military structure. The government provided leadership for the people while the army provided means of defense and conquest. Social and religious organizations also formed. Social structures allowed a place for all individuals, from the nobility to the commoner to the slave, and religious structure provided a means for the people to engage with their god or gods and the spirit world. Civilizations also include artistic and intellectual activity, some form of writing, and usually an urban focus. As these elements come together and define a noticeable culture, a civilization is born.

Once a civilization emerged, however, it was not guaranteed a long existence unless it was successful in solving significant challenges. The best equipped civilizations resolved these problems and survived. However, those that failed to address these issues often left themselves vulnerable. Civilizations faced a regular challenge maintaining an appropriate level of resources. In the earliest years of human history, these included food acquired from hunting and gathering and a vital water supply. The earliest civilizations formed along major rivers. Moreover, as time progressed and humankind became more adept and advanced, resources expanded and incorporated all the numerous aspects of natural resources, including wind, fire, and metals. Nations also needed to provide an organized social order for its people that allowed for co-existence and respect. The move from anarchy to a structure of laws and punishments created an organized social fabric. To protect against outside threats or internal revolts, nations formed security forces and structures. Indeed, these entities provided the means of existence and peace. The transmission of culture and education was also required to ensure the longevity of future generations. Knowledge had to develop to pass on the most important concepts of the civilization to later generations. As civilizations provided for these challenges, they formed not only the structure of the nations but also helped shape the worldviews of its people.

As civilizations began to emerge, the people living within them developed distinct worldviews. Their ideologies often involved answering deep, philosophical questions. People wrestled with issues such as: Why are humans here? What is their purpose? What can we actually know and how? Is there a purpose and meaning in history? Is there a spiritual world and who/what inhabits it? Civilizations in the Western world have debated these questions for centuries, and many of their answers have formed the distinct characteristics of a Western worldview.

Early Human History

The *Homo sapiens* species first appeared in Africa between two hundred thousand and one hundred thousand years ago. These peoples spread out from Africa as they followed their food and water sources. Scientists refer to this stage of human history as the Paleolithic Age, or Old Stone Age, because people made tools by cracking rocks and using their sharp edges to cut and chop. These early peoples scavenged for wild food and followed migrating herds of animals. As nomads, they traveled to most major continents, including the Americas through the land bridge, known as Beringia, which connected the Asian continent to North America. The discovery and implementation of fire helped immensely and provided them with warmth, light, and the ability to cook food. The early humans also created beautiful works of art by carving bone and painting on cave walls. Through the present day, figurines, rock art, and cave paintings still exist around the world.

The end of the last Ice Age occurred between 11,000 and 10,000 BCE and ushered in an era of significant change: the food-producing revolution, which is typically known as the Neolithic Age (New Stone Age). As the Earth's climate warmed, cereal grasses such as wheat and barley spread over large areas. Hunter-gatherers collected these wild grains and ground them up for food. When people learned that the seeds of diverse grasses could be transplanted and grown in new areas, the cultivation of plants began. Though familiar to modern societies, the invention of agriculture was a huge step in the progression of civilized communities. Harvesting plants and raising animals for food changed how people lived and sparked the Agricultural Revolution.

The transition from the hunting and gathering society to permanent settlements began simply enough. Groups of people soon learned that seeds left on the ground from harvest produced those same plants weeks later. This discovery led some to plant seeds to have a ready supply of food. As farmers harvested crops, food storage began to develop to sustain communities all year long, instead of always wandering in hopes of finding the next source of sustenance. Thus, permanent settlements began to form.

Farming was hard work, but the payoff was enormous. Even simple agricultural methods could produce about fifty times more food than hunting and gathering. Consequently, due to the increased food supply, more newborns survived past infancy. Populations expanded, and so did the number and size of human settlements. The domestication of animals was equally as important as finding the right plants to grow. Goats, cattle, and pigs were tamed, bred, and then slaughtered to provide valuable meat for the community. Dogs began bonding with humans during the Ice Ages. While a few societies considered dogs suitable for food, most have viewed them as companions and useful helpers in the hunt. Thus, people developed herd animals from wild ones like oxen or boars. Because of the critical role of cows to the ancient peoples, the animal soon became revered by several different people groups. Farmers made cows beasts of burden as well as food sources, and in some cases, sources of liquid blood to drink and provide nourishment. Ancient remains include numerous statues and paintings of cows and help modern people understand the important role of the animal as well as the later worship of the beast.

With the domestication of both plants and animals, humans settled down, formed communities, and became dependent on their landholdings to raise food. Farming thus led to a whole range of new occupations beyond tilling the soil. Some people could devote their energy to making clothing. Cooks mixed, baked, and boiled increasing varieties of plants and animal materials into a sustainable diet. Potters baked cookware that preserved food better than before and kept it free from spoilage and vermin. Wagons with wheels transported large loads over long distances. Masons stacked bricks and stone into secure buildings. Due to these advancements, communities gradually expanded into villages where hundreds of families could live. In turn, villages had the potential to grow into towns and cities which might hold a few thousand people. One of the oldest known villages was Jericho, founded around

Image 1.1: The archaeological remains of the city of Jericho. © Shutterstock.com

12,000 BCE. Located in Israel near the Dead Sea, Jericho was a walled city and covered several acres. A fresh water spring carried water from the nearby mountains to the village and provided an oasis in the midst of desert lands. Irrigation allowed for the city to establish and become a fertile ground for food, thus creating a long-standing city.

The results of the Neolithic Revolution included numerous changes to the ancient world. Permanent settlements led to the rise of houses and towns as well as specific jobs within the cities. These changes led to an increase in trade among the cities, especially as new metals began to emerge and the development of new weapons, tools, and goods. Men began to play a more dominant role in society as women provided more involvement in child-rearing and duties around the home. Religious ideas also began to emerge as the ancient populations associated women with the reproduction of life and the earth with the production of food and water to sustain life. Moreover, the need for record keeping sparked the earliest inventions in writing. These results changed the course of the ancient world and led to the real civilizations.

Mesopotamia

The complicated life associated with cities formed the first civilizations. Life in urban settlements brought people into closer contact with more opportunities to share ideas. More free time also persuaded some to think creatively and question the nature of life on Earth. The city-state, the first civilized political organization, was the smallest unit of civilization. It included the city itself (made up of homes, businesses, and public buildings) and the surrounding countryside and farmland that fed and supplied city dwellers. These larger numbers of people confined in a small area required leaders to organize increasingly sophisticated human activities. These events, taken together, propelled human society toward the creation of the civilization.

The first civilizations had several defining characteristics: economies based on agriculture, populous cities with large administrative centers, and different social classes such as free people and slaves. In addition, they had specialization of labor that allowed people to do different jobs. Some people were the rulers, while others served as priests, artisans, soldiers, and farmers. For the most part, civilizations were advanced forms of human society. Citizens came together in one location and agreed to work for the mutual benefit of the group. Here, one can see a full range of human activities, from political and social organization to religious and even scientific/technical ways of thinking and acting.

Mesopotamia and Egypt created the foundation for later civilizations. They built irrigation works and cities, organized governments, constructed large-scale monuments, established bureaucracies and schools, developed systems of writing, and made significant technological improvements. They also wrote literary works that offer glimpses into their lives. Although more often considered a part of the Eastern world, the contributions of both were immeasurably important to the development of Western civilizations.

Mesopotamian civilization formed along the Tigris and Euphrates Rivers in what is modern day Iraq. The area encompassing these river systems is known as the Fertile Crescent and has provided the home for numerous states in the Western world, which rose and fell as they competed for dominance in the area. The flooding from the rivers provided good soil through the regular deposits of silt. Residents also built dikes and used irrigation techniques to collect excess water for the dry seasons. These rivers, however, were unpredictable and sometimes caused violent flooding, with disastrous results for the harvest. In addition to the unpredictable nature of river flooding, the rest of Mesopotamia's environment was harsh and experienced erratic weather patterns and frequent storms.

Image 1.2: Mesopotamia is part of a larger area known as the Fertile Crescent. Nestled between the Tigris and Euphrates, the flood plains from these rivers provided an area of fertile soil for farming.

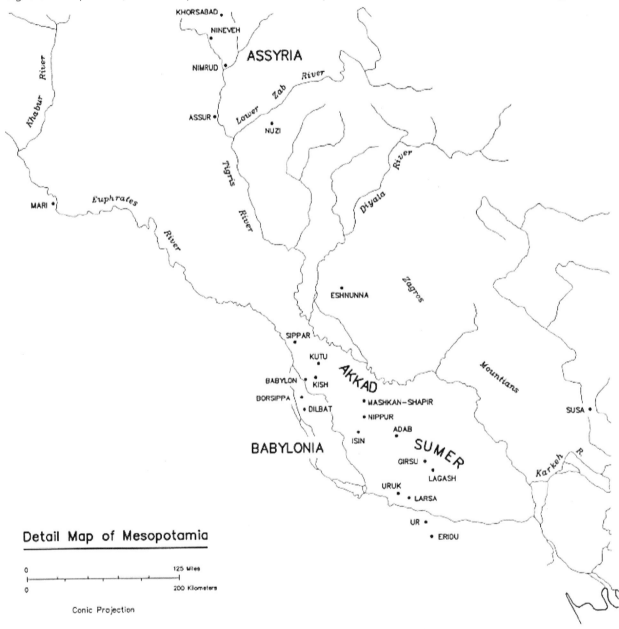

Source: Courtesy of the Oriental Institute of the University of Chicago.

The most prominent people in Mesopotamia were the Sumerians. Sumer was in the southern part of the Tigris and Euphrates rivers, and it included twelve different city-states. These city-states included Eridu, the first settlement, as well as the prominent cities of Uruk and Ur, with populations as high as two hundred thousand people. The cities were mostly made of mud and brick and surrounded by walls, with limits defined by boundary stones or canals.

Each city-state had a king, economy, currency, military, and religious emphasis. Sumerian lives primarily focused on manual labor and religion. They believed in many gods and were thus polytheistic. The sun and stars, the rivers and mountains, the wind and lightning were seen either as gods or the dwelling places of gods. If a river overflowed its banks or a violent wind storm occurred, it was due to the behavior of the gods. Ancient Near East populations attributed all

Image 1.3: The ziggurat of Ur, located in modern day Iraq, built c. 2100 BCE, is the largest and most well preserved remaining ziggurat of ancient Mesopotamia. © Shutterstock.com

natural occurrences to the actions of the gods, whose actions could be erratic and unpredictable.

Residents built Mesopotamian cities in accordance with the worship of one or more divine figures. By honoring traditional rituals and attending religious festivals, people hoped to guarantee they would receive good health, a plentiful harvest, and happiness. Many farmers also offered part of their crops to the gods for the same reasons. Supervised by priests, the temple (ziggurat) was the most prominent location of the city-state. Ziggurats were different from the modern conception of a church, as ancients understood them to be structures where the gods literally resided. Therefore, people honored these structures as places of great importance. Ziggurat priests were more than clerics. They were landlords, tax collectors, and supervisors of different forms of commerce. Temple priests also employed most members of the community as common laborers or servants. Priests were crucial to Mesopotamians, as they were the principal way most people communicated with the gods. In addition to their roles as religious caretakers, priests also coordinated engineering projects that helped irrigate the land and thus provide a means of survival for most Mesopotamians.

Mesopotamia developed theocratic monarchies headed by a king who was thought to have ruled for a god. Kings held most of the power of the city-state, and as they grew, the leaders of these city-states frequently led their people in wars against one another. Although all members of society belonged to one of two primary strata, free or slave, three major social tiers developed in Mesopotamia. Nobles and priests

made up the top level. The next group included farmers and merchants. Slaves made up the bottom unit. Sumerian law also formed and developed into the oldest codification of law in the Western world, the *Code of Ur-Nammu*. It provided regulations for crime and punishment as well as fostered the belief that laws came from the gods. Although death was the penalty for murder and robbery, authorities punished most crimes with a monetary fine. Women had some protections under the Code and could achieve a higher status in Sumer than in other contemporary civilizations.

The economy of the Sumerians was primarily agricultural. However, commerce and textiles developed and helped build trade among the neighboring peoples. Sumerians used a sexagesimal (based on the number 60) mathematical system to track the movement of goods throughout the area. Commerce also led to the creation of record keeping, scribes, and inevitably, writing. Sumerians invented picture hieroglyphs that eventually became a form of cuneiform. They wrote on reeds or clay tablets and kept records, developed literature, poems, and epic tales.

Mesopotamian understanding of death and the afterlife prefigured the attitudes and thoughts of later Western civilizations. Mesopotamians wrestled with various competing views on what happened to people after death. For some, death meant that life just ceased to exist and the soul did not journey onward toward a final destination. Many believed, however, that the afterworld would be much like life as they knew it; basically, a continuation of the hopes and joys of daily living. Therefore, Mesopotamians tended to view philosophical ponderings about the origin of life, man's role on Earth, and the nature of the soul after death together as the same set of questions. One can see all of this come together in what scholars believe is the oldest known literary work, the *Epic of Gilgamesh*.

The Mesopotamian epic features many characters, but the primary two are Gilgamesh and Enkidu. Gilgamesh is a king who departs on a long journey after the death of his friend, Enkidu. He travels to distant lands on a quest to learn how to conquer death while also seeking out the wisdom of the gods. Along the way, Gilgamesh learns how the gods once sent a massive flood to destroy the Earth, and by the end of the tale, he has a better grasp on the limitations of human beings. The *Epic of Gilgamesh* describes man's relationship with the gods as volatile and unpredictable. The story makes it clear that Mesopotamians made it a priority to understand the gods. In turn, they used that knowledge to create a better life on Earth. Therefore, Mesopotamians tended to view questions about the origin of life, man's role on Earth, and the nature of the soul after death together as the same set of queries.

Ancient Egypt

The civilization of Ancient Egypt grew up along the Nile River, which flows four thousand miles north from Lake Victoria and empties into the Mediterranean Sea. Because of this geography, the southern part of the Nile River Valley is called Upper Egypt and the Nile Delta is named Lower Egypt. Most Egyptians lived on the area called "black land." Here, the Nile floods left behind nutrients that replenished the farmland every year. Every summer, heavy rains in central Africa fed into the Nile, causing it to overflow its banks in mid-August. By November, the river receded and left behind rich, black soil providing a nutrient-rich silt. Egyptians created ditches to irrigate the land and then planted their various crops. The annual flood was predictable and necessary to agriculture. In fact, Egypt held the richest agricultural land in the Mediterranean world. In addition to the benefits of having a yearly flood enriching the soil, the deserts east and west of the Nile protected Egypt from invasion. From the time of Egypt's Old Kingdom (2700–2200 BCE) to the end of the era called the New Kingdom (1570–1075 BCE), Egypt was only invaded by one group of outsiders: the Hyksos around 1700 BCE. However, the Egyptians pushed the Hyksos out and reclaimed power by the start of the New Kingdom.

Ancient Egyptian history is divided into kingdoms, the Old, Middle, New, Late, and Hellenistic Kingdoms, with Intermediate periods separating the periods. The kingdom periods were a time of growth, prosperity, peace, and cultural activity while the intermediate periods were times of chaos, weak politics, and threatening movements from outsiders. Dynasties, or powerful families, ruled Egypt for generations. Overall, the nation witnessed over thirty dynasties through the Hellenistic period and eventual rise of the Roman Empire.

The period before the Old Kingdom, or the Predynastic Period, spans the years from 3100 to 2700 BCE. During this era, numerous tribes led by chieftains populated Egypt. These groups settled along the

Nile River and created small, independent societies. King Narmer unified the tribes of Lower and Upper Egypt in 3100 BCE, with Memphis as the capital. During this time, the *Narmer Palette* captured the first formation of Egypt and is the earliest hieroglyphic inscriptions ever found. The hieroglyphs formed in this period became the base of the Egyptian language. This era covers the rule of the first two dynasties of Egyptian history.

The Old Kingdom spanned close to five hundred years. It was a time of prosperity with an increased power of the kings and the construction of the pyramids. This period of Egyptian history created the framework for the nation's history that followed. The king was the most powerful individual in the land, and the rest of society was a stratified one with priests and scribes at the top and peasants at the bottom.

In Egypt, kings called pharaohs, and their power extended to all sectors of society. Pharaohs were considered the descendants of the Ra, the sun god, and the owners of all Egypt. Pharaohs oversaw an army of government officials who collected taxes, supervised construction projects, checked the irrigation works, surveyed the land, and kept records. Foreign trade was a monopoly of the state conducted according to the kingdom's needs, and through these means, the economy of Egypt grew.

Pharaohs also ruled according to Ma'at, or order, justice, and truth. Egyptians believed that obedience to the pharaoh was essential to the spirit of Ma'at and to oppose the pharaoh meant one threatened to disrupt this universal force of Ma'at. Egyptian depicted Ma'at as a goddess who held the concept of justice and injustice in her hands. When opposition arose to the pharaoh, it created the possibility that society would slip into a chaotic state. Egyptians believed that following a pharaoh's lead most likely ensured that the precarious life-giving Ma'at would not become imbalanced. Living in accordance with Ma'at meant honoring all the gods and following traditional practices. There were many cities in Upper and Lower Egypt represented by various deities. It was because the Nile was stable, predictable, and easily navigable that Egyptians, for the most part, felt blessed by higher powers. After all, the Nile not only fertilized farmland but also provided transportation to the various cities and holy places. It was, therefore, important not to disturb the careful harmony that Egyptians thought was needed to guarantee continued success.

The Old Kingdom is also known as the Pyramid Age. These pyramids, or tombs, became an integral

Image 1.4: Map of Egypt showing upper and lower Egypt. © Shutterstock.com

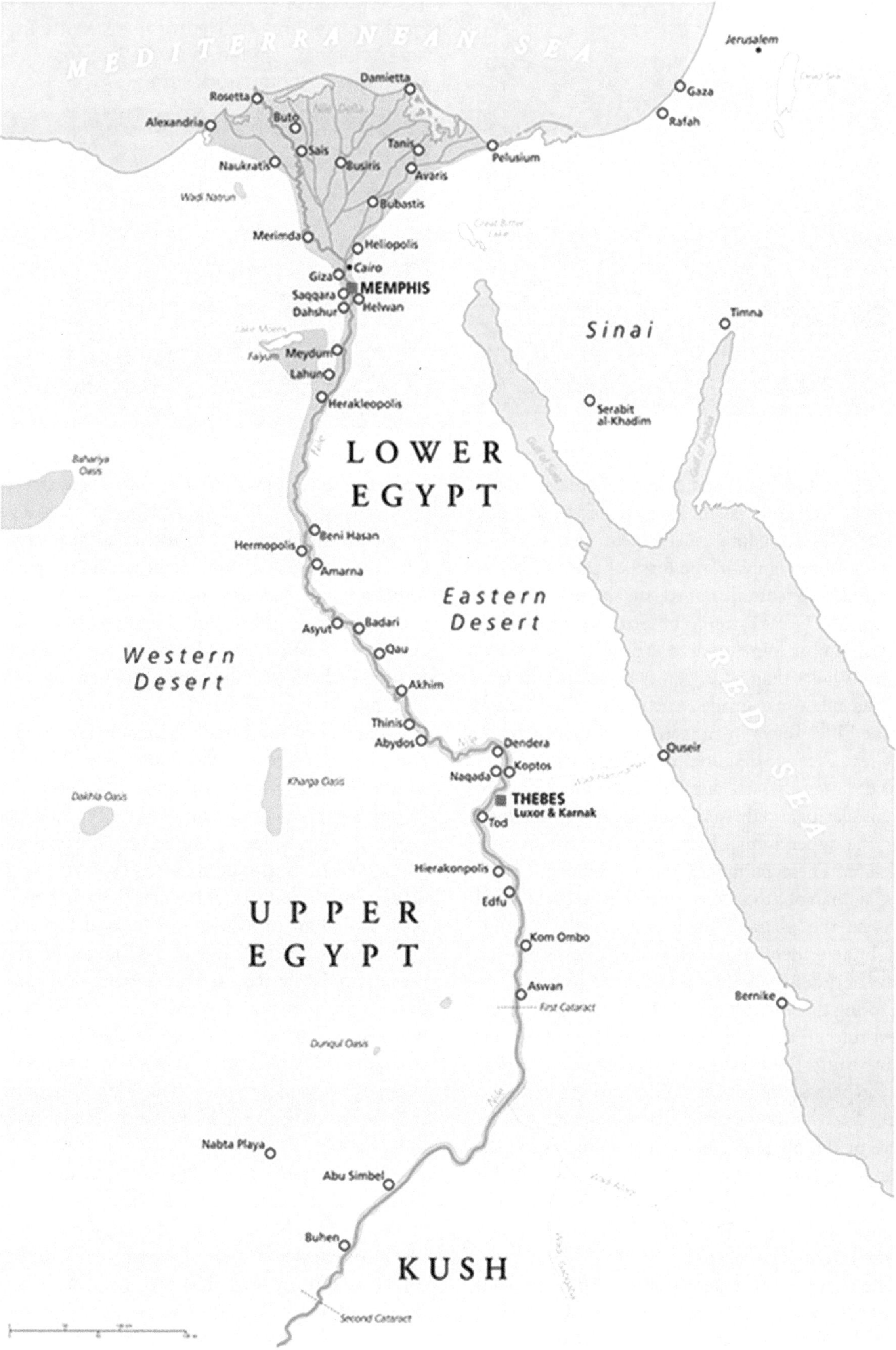

Image 1.5: Stone relief at Temple of Horus, Edfu, Egypt, of Ma'at portrayed in human form as an Egyptian goddess. © Shutterstock.com

Image 1.6: View of the pyramids of Giza, including the Great pyramid, taken from the Giza Plateau. The three smaller pyramids at the front are sometimes referred to as the Queens' Pyramids. © Shutterstock.com

part of Egyptian religion and culture. A crucial feature of Egyptian religion was the concept of the afterlife. Egyptian Old Kingdom rulers spent vast sums of money on huge tombs in the form of pyramids. The Pharaoh Khufu commissioned the largest pyramid ever built, the Great Pyramid of Giza. Standing at the height of almost four hundred eighty feet, the Great Pyramid is taller than a forty-story skyscraper. In fact, it was the tallest man-made structure until the French built the Eiffel Tower in Paris in the 19th century CE. The Great Pyramid required more than two million blocks of limestone, which each weighed up to fifteen tons. Similar pyramids were built nearby at this time under the supervision of the Pharaohs Khafre and Menkaure. These famous pyramids represented the path that pharaohs took to eternity. Egyptians believed that once the pharaoh made a successful journey through the underworld, they ascended to heaven on the rays of the sun from the prism of the pyramid.

During the Old Kingdom, the vizier was the next highest ruler in the land. This role held great administrative control and often ruled alongside the pharaoh. Egypt was broken into nomes during this period as well. Each nome was ruled by a nomarch, under the eye of the pharaoh. As the years progressed, the nomarchs grew in power, and when a drought hit Egypt in the mid-22nd century BCE, the nomarchs revolted and overthrew the pharaoh, thus, ushering in the First Intermediate Period.

The First Intermediate Period was a time of chaos and confusion. It lasted close to seventy-five years and was finally quelled by the rise of the King of Thebes,

who reunited Egypt under his control and started the Middle Kingdom. The Middle Kingdom was a period of wealth and stability. Egyptian culture expanded with an increase in art and literature and people began to believe that, like the pharaoh, they also had a soul and could seek eternal life. Increased trade and the conquest of Nubia brought new types of goods and enlarged their wealth and amplified agricultural holdings.

The fall of the Middle Kingdom came with the rise of the Hyksos in the 1600s BCE. The Hyksos arrived from Syria and Palestine as laborers for the Lower Egyptian/Delta area. As they increased in number, they formed a revolt against the pharaoh and conquered the surrounding area. Their uprising ushered in the Second Intermediate Period. The rise of New Kingdom put down the Second Intermediate Period and started the rule of the Eighteenth through Twentieth Dynasties. It was a period of unprecedented prosperity in Egyptian history. With secure borders and an extended size of the empire, Egypt strengthened diplomatic ties with its neighbors and entered a period of peace. The New Kingdom also saw the rise of the some of the most popular pharaohs in its history.

One of the most famous pharaohs of the Eighteenth Dynasty was Hatshepsut, the longest reigning female pharaoh in Egyptian history. Hatshepsut ruled a total of twenty years during the mid-15th century BCE. She reigned alongside her husband, Thutmose II, and upon his death acted as the regent of her young step-son, Thutmose III. After

Image 1.7: Portrait of Queen Hatshepsut at Temple of Hatshepsut, Luxor, Egypt. © Shutterstock.com

Image 1.8: Stone relief portraying King Amenhotep IV (Akhenaten) with his wife Nefertiti, and their children under rays of the sun god Aten. Tell el-Amarna, Egypt. © Shutterstock.com

several years as a regent, she seized sole power and began her tenure as the lone pharaoh. Hatshepsut depicted herself in traditional male pharaoh kilt and crown, including a fake beard, to assert her authority in Egypt. She built temples, monuments, and ensured economic growth through various means, including a trip to Punt bringing back gold, myrrh trees, and ivory. She also curried the favor of the priests and devised a clever birth story to legitimize her rule that included the role of the gods in her conception. Her rule was a time of growth for Egypt.

The Pharaoh Amenhotep IV (Akhenaten) (ruled: 1353–1336 BCE) was known as the "heretic king." He was married to the beautiful Nefertiti and known for his devotion to his wife and to the sun god, Aten. Amenhotep attempted to alter the time-honored Egyptian belief in polytheism, and he elevated the Egyptian sun god Aten above all the other gods. With his move toward monotheism, he forced his people to abandon the Egyptian gods and many of the old rituals. During his rule, Egyptians removed or altered many representations of other gods, closed numerous temples, and declared all creeds illegal but his own. He also changed his name from Amenhotep to Akhenaten, which means "lover of Aten." This referred to the "sun god." He wrote poems on behalf of Aten, which declared his devotion and love to the sun god.

The process to disrupt the old ways was not as easy as making a decree. Each god had priests and

officials responsible for ministering to the people, and they also collected wealth and prestige from their positions. Many gods had a holy place or even a city where they resided. Therefore, in choosing a different path for the religion of the kingdom, Akhenaten transformed the lifestyles and livelihoods of many of its citizens. Furthermore, Egyptians had difficulty attributing everything in society to one spiritual being. His move toward monotheism resulted in growing anger toward the king.

Akhenaten also moved the capital of Egypt to Amarna. He disliked the hustle and bustle of the capital, Thebes, and moved his palace to the deserted and lonely city of Amarna to provide recluse for his family. This action also garnered resentment from Egyptians as they viewed the pharaoh as disconnected from the nation's concerns and detached from the people. During his rule, the military suffered as Akhenaten spent more time focusing on the arts and literature rather than the domestic and foreign policies needed to run the nation. With many opposed to Akhenaten's decisions, it is not surprising that upon his death the kingdom moved back toward its former ways.

Akhenaten's son, Tutankhamen, (ruled: 1336–1327 BCE) became the next pharaoh and, in his ten-year rule, sought to restore Egypt back to her former glory. Tutankhamen (Tut) took the throne at age nine. He helped Egypt restore its gods to their proper places and moved the capital back to Thebes. These moves were so encouraged during Tut's reign that the religious leaders etched out the name of Akhenaten from historical records to remove the influence of the "heretic king." King Tut's rule became famous through the discovery of his tomb in 1922 CE by Howard Carter. As the first intact pharaoh's tomb discovered, modern historians could ascertain Egyptian religious beliefs of the afterlife as well as the life of the pharaoh.

The most famous pharaoh of the Nineteenth Dynasty was Ramses II (Ramses the Great) (ruled: 1279–1213 BCE). During his reign, Egypt underwent great building campaigns including cities, temples, and monuments. His military exploits included the first non-aggression treaty in history with the Hittites at the Battle of Kadesh and reassertion of Egyptian control over Canaan. He lived to be over ninety years old and had over two hundred wives and concubines with ninety-six sons and sixty daughters. His influence in Egypt shaped the succeeding generations so much so that he was referred to as the "Great Ancestor" for years to come.

Egyptian culture and religion were linked together throughout its history. Religious beliefs were the basis of Egyptian art, medicine, astronomy, literature, and government. The chief function of the pyramids was to ensure the pharaoh's journey into the afterlife. Once the pharaoh died, his body entered the land of the dead, but he would live on in an afterlife reasonably like life as he had known it. His continued life, aided by an embalming process known as mummification, was crucial to the security and prosperity of Egypt. Mummification included the removal of the organs of the deceased, and then, the organs were placed in jars guarded by the god responsible for that organ. All organs but the heart were removed as it was the seat of emotions and intellect. As such, the heart needed to be present for the judgment at the end of the journey through the underworld. Once the organs were taken out, the body was stuffed with linen and sand, wrapped in linen and oils, and placed in the sarcophagus.

The idea of mummification is closely connected to the Egyptian gods, specifically the story of Osiris. According to Egyptian belief, at some point in the distant past, Seth, the god of chaos, murdered his brother Osiris. Seth cut Osiris into pieces and scattered them over the Earth, but Osiris' wife Isis gathered his body parts and used mummification to revive her husband.

Image 1.9: The Great Temple of Ramses II, Abu Simbel, Egypt. Built during the reign of Ramses II, the architecture and imposing statues of Ramses were possibly intended as a symbol of the Pharaoh's power to his people, as well as to Egypt's closest enemy, the Nubians. © Shutterstock.com

Later, Osiris and Isis conceived a son, Horus, who became the next pharaoh. Having accomplished his mission of siring an heir, Osiris went to live among the other gods as the judge of the dead and arbitrated the eternal destination of human souls. At the same time, Horus reigned as the new pharaoh.

The newly dead were thought to travel by night enduring trials and ordeals in the underworld before rising to life. Papyrus (dried reeds used as paper) documents and tomb engravings, typically referred to as the *Book of the Dead*, reveals rituals and codes that guided the deceased into the next life. In addition, the *Book of the Dead* also explains how Egyptians believed people should behave to secure a good afterlife. This is because most felt that one's destination after death largely depended on their actions during life. The heart was weighed against Ma'at at the end of the journey in the underworld. Those whose hearts were just and right went on to eternal life. People whose hearts were found wanting were eaten by the Egyptian god known as Ammut.

Egyptian records, usually found in the form of hieroglyphics, are important because they tell us about the practices, desires, and traditions of these ancient people. The *Tale of Sinuhe* is an early example of literature from Egypt's Middle Kingdom. Like a great deal of Egyptian writing, it was composed for a tomb. The Egyptians spent a large part

Image 1.10: *Bastet,* c. 664–30 BCE, leaded bronze, precious metal, and black bronze inlays. Bastet was a cat-headed goddess that was a powerful protective figure, as well as symbol for fertility.

Source: *The Metropolitan Museum of Art, New York.*

of their time and money preparing for the afterlife, and this often meant constructing tombs to help the deceased prosper in the next life. The story centers on the time of the death of Pharaoh Amenemhat I in 1962 BCE. The story itself has a simple plot: the return of a nobleman from a kind of self-imposed exile to a warm reception by Amenemhat I. The *Tale of Sinuhe* is one of the classic works of ancient literature, and it reveals how Egyptians did not separate the afterworld from their daily lives. For the Egyptians, even more than the Mesopotamians, religion was an ever-present, motivating force that drove them to inquire, build, and achieve.

Egyptians also enjoyed feasts and festivals throughout their lives. Their festivals were often dedicated to the god/goddess of choice and filled with music, dance, and food. Although the typical diet of the Egyptians (bread, onions, dates, figs, and beer) sustained them throughout the year, the festivals were a time for a more variety of foods and time of celebration. Egyptians also valued animals in the role of spirituality. They believed that the balanced relationship between humans and animals was a source of spirituality for the people. Cats played a big part in Egyptian life and became the guardians of the palace and inevitably one of their most prominent goddesses, Bastet.

Religion played an integral part in the lives and cultures of this ancient people. The thousands of gods and goddesses they worshiped held up the belief that the universe was alive with divine power. Ra, the sun god, was of utmost importance to the Egyptians, but so were Osiris and Isis, Horus the falcon god, and Anubis, the Divine Embalmer, leader through the underworld. Overriding all of this was the desire to keep Ma'at and balance within Egyptian society. The interchangeable roles of Egyptian religion and daily living demonstrate the worldview of this ancient people and how they perceived the world around them.

Artistic Influences: Material Culture in Paleolithic Society

By Christina McClellan

While the disciplines of archaeology, art history, and history, may have different methodologies in approaching their discipline, in the grand picture there is in fact a lot of crossover. Archaeologists use written documents and art to synthesize remains and objects found during a dig. Historians, in turn use archaeological findings in conjunction with written documents, as well as art, to better understand people, societies, and culture. In short, the disciplines of the humanities rely on each other to see the full picture.

No greater example of crossover exists, than in the use of archaeological and art historical findings to understand Paleolithic and Neolithic civilizations. While much information can be gleaned from architectural remains or midden pits—areas of accumulated domestic waste that provide details into diet and other habits—information can also be gleaned from what is referred to as material culture. "Material culture" is the physical manifestation of a societal culture beyond tools and other instruments needed to help a human stay alive. In short, material culture is the manifestation of something you want, not something that you need, though it could serve a dual purpose. Some of the earliest manifestations of material culture are beads and pottery, but a more specific example is Venus statuettes.

Venus statuettes of the Paleolithic period are named as such because of their faceless, yet feminine, physique. Their exaggerated sexual characteristics give rise to their association with Venus, the Roman goddess of love and fertility. These figurines still perplex researchers. Some theories conjecture that Venus statuettes denote the importance of women in society, or exist to place an emphasis on women in their religion, while others hypothesize that statuettes were used to represent cultural similarities amongst groups that traded with one another. While we still do not have enough information to know for sure, these statuettes are an example of the importance material culture plays to the society, as well to researchers seeking to understand the pre-writing period of the Paleolithic Era.

Image 1.11: The Venus of Willendorf is a limestone statuette standing at 11.1 centimeters high, and was created sometime between 24,000 BCE and 22,000 BCE. Excavated in Willendorf, Austria. © Shutterstock.com

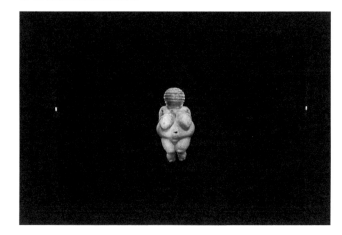

Chapter 2

Near Eastern Peoples: Iron, Trade, God, and Empire

Think about how many daily tasks you perform, almost unthinkingly. You run errands in your car, which has steel components. You pay bills and put your signature on checks using the alphabet. You check your weather app on your cell phone, based on scientific observations of the weather patterns, to see if it is going to rain. Maybe you are religious, and you go to the synagogue, or mosque, or church. Or at least, you are familiar with one or more of the various monotheistic religions. All of these activities are part and parcel with Western societies, yet most people do not know their antecedents flow from a very distant past and a part of the world very distant from Europe or the United States. In this chapter, we are going to look at four great empires in the ancient Near East: the Hittites, the Assyrians, the Babylonians, and the Persians. We are also going to look two smaller groups that had a notable effect on the area, the Phoenicians and the people of Israel. Whether through empire or innovation, all of these not only influenced the ancient Near East, but they also left last imprints that mark our lives in the 21st century.

Hittites

The Hittites were a part of the migration of peoples from Central Europe (known as Indo-Europeans) between 4000 and 2000 BCE. These Indo-Europeans eventually reached as far west as modern day Ireland and India to the east. Included in these eastern migrations were people that eventually came to be known as the Hittites. They arrived in Anatolia (modern day Turkey) around 2000 BCE and intermingled with the natives.

By 1475 BCE, the Hittites had amassed an empire from central Turkey east into northern Mesopotamia and south into the upper Levant (modern Syria). The capital city was called Hattusa. The peak of the Hittite empire lasted until the early 13th century BCE. They rivaled Egypt in power and stature. They, like other groups, assimilated much of the culture around them. Sumerian myths like the *Epic of Gilgamesh* became one of their favorite stories.

Image 2.1: Hattusa, Turkey is an archaeological site in the province of Çorum, Turkey. Hattusa was once the capital of the Hittite Empire, and became a hub for trade and cultural exchange. © Shutterstock.com

What is most important about the Hittites is the innovation they developed around 1400 BCE. Our modern world could not exist without it. What is it? The Hittites were the first people to figure out how to smelt iron. This would lead to the Iron Age and the ending of the Bronze Age. The Hittites kept their iron making technology a closely guarded secret, but eventually this technology spread to the surrounding peoples. Iron weapons, wheels, and tools made bronze technologies obsolete by the 1st millennium BCE.

Like the Egyptians, the Hittites fell under the onslaught of the Sea Peoples during the early 12th century BCE. Many scholars think these were bands of Mycenaeans like the ones that sacked Troy of Homeric fame. The Hittites serve as an example from the ancient world how empires came and went, but many times, the cultural, religious, social, or technological innovations of a civilization remained. Hattusa disappeared after 1180 BCE but not the significance of the Hittites. Their new innovation of iron spread throughout the ancient Near East and transformed the surrounding civilizations.

Phoenicians

Some cultures impacted the ancient Near East not through the creation of empires but through trade and the diffusion of ideas. One such civilization was known as the Phoenicians. Who were these people? Many ancient texts mention them as traders and sailors. The Greeks called them the *phoinikes* which meant "purple people." This is because they traded in Tyrian purple, a purple dye secreted from shellfish. Purple dyed garments meant wealth in the ancient world.

The Phoenicians were native Canaanites, part of the peoples who lived in the Levant, the strip of land on the eastern side of the Mediterranean that includes modern day Syria, Lebanon, Jordan, and Israel. The Phoenicians lived in major coastal trading centers in the northern part of the Levant. Some of their most well-known cities were Tyre, Byblos, and Sidon. The Phoenicians had a flourishing trade network set up by the 2nd millennium BCE, but they came into their own after the Egyptian and the Hittite empires declined in the 12th century BCE. The purple people's civilization reached its peak during the 9th and 6th centuries BCE. They sailed and created trading posts around the Mediterranean. They developed colonies in southern Italy, France, Spain, and Britain. Their greatest colony rested on the shores of North

Image 2.2: Carthage amassed its own networks of trade and control in the Mediterranean until its influence threatened the trade networks and expansion of the Roman Empire. Carthage finally succumbed to Rome in the Third Punic war. © Shutterstock.com

Africa, namely, Carthage. This city would become the greatest rival of Rome during the 2nd and 3rd centuries BCE.

The Phoenicians' importance lay in two areas. The first was trade. These seafaring people not only traded in Tyrian purple, but also in glass, tin, olive oil, wine, and timber. Near East peoples coveted their cedar trees for building purposes. In *1 Kings*, a book of the *Hebrew Bible*, King Solomon imports the Phoenician cedar to build his temple. The Phoenicians bought and traded gold from Africa, tin from Britain, copper from the island of Cyprus, paper from Egypt, and trade goods from the Far East.

The Phoenicians also diffused ideas and technologies throughout the Near East. Myths, religious ideas, science, and mathematical concepts from multiple areas traveled to new lands on Phoenician ships. These peoples did not conquer others and create an empire, but they excelled at something more lasting, the diffusion of culture and innovation. The Phoenicians created the first alphabet based on sounds. Thus, we get our word "phonetics." The alphabet consisted of twenty-two letters, all being consonants. In a Phoenician document, one reads the words from right to left. Developed in the late 2nd century BCE, it was a quantum leap from cuneiform, a pictograph alphabet with hundreds of symbols that originated with the Sumerians. The earliest found Phoenician inscriptions date to around 1000 BCE.

Groups throughout the Mediterranean eventually adopted and adapted the Phoenician script to

Image 2.3: The Phoenician Alphabet was a significant improvement on the pictographic symbols of cuneiform. Instead of an image for each word, an alphabet allows for the spelling of words with a fixed number of characters. © Shutterstock.com

Image 2.4: The Greek alphabet. © Shutterstock.com

meet their needs. The Israelites used the phonetic alphabet to develop Hebrew, the language of the *Jewish Bible*. The Greek alphabet traces its origin back to Phoenician, as did the alphabet of the Etruscans, the peoples who lived in northern Italy and later influenced Rome. From the Romans, we get our modern alphabet. Ironically, there are few Phoenician inscriptions still in existence, but their alphabet continues to affect us to this day. Whether through trade

or their alphabet, the Phoenicians left a lasting imprint on the world of the ancient Near East.

Israelites

The people of Israel did not create a vast empire like the Egyptians or the Hittites. They did not establish a vast trading sphere like the Phoenicians. So what was their importance? This small group, many times conquered by other civilizations, left us a lasting legacy of religious thought. The Israelites gave us the concept of ethical monotheism; the belief in one God who insisted on a proper code of living.

First, we will look at the Israelites as they appear in their narrative known as the *Hebrew Bible*. Christians call this literary work the *Old Testament*. This tome covers the remembered history of Israel from the creation of the world, through the lives of the patriarchs like Abraham, around 2000 BCE, all the way to the return of the Israelites to their homeland from captivity in the 6th century BCE.

The *Hebrew Bible* is basically broken down into three parts. The Torah or "Law" consists of the first five books (*Genesis, Exodus, Leviticus, Numbers,* and *Deuteronomy*). These books describe the creation of the world by one all powerful, all knowing deity named Yahweh. The name Yahweh is noted in most English translations as the word Lord in all uppercase letters, "LORD." According to the book of *Genesis*, Yahweh created the world in six days and placed the first man and woman, Adam and Eve, in the Garden of Eden to tend it and rule over creation. Tempted to disobey by a serpent, Adam and Eve ate from the tree of the knowledge of good and evil and were expelled from the Garden. This disobedience introduced hardship, discord, and death into the world. The next several chapters of *Genesis* details Yahweh's displeasure with humanity resulting in a flood that wiped out every person except one man, Noah, and his family. From Noah's line come all the peoples of the Earth.

The rest of *Genesis* deals with God's choosing of one man, Abraham, and establishing an everlasting covenant him. Yahweh called Abraham out of Mesopotamia and told him to travel to the land of Canaan (modern day Israel), and there God would give his barren wife Sarah a child and the land to his descendants. In return, Abraham would circumcise himself and his male heirs as a sign of covenant with this God. *Genesis* details the lives and struggles of Abraham's son Isaac, and Isaac's son Jacob, later renamed Israel after an encounter with Yahweh. Israel in Hebrew means

Image 2.5: The Torah today is a fixture in every synagogue. A portion is read at every service. The Torah is still handwritten by a specially trained scribe, though printed copies are available for individual study and circulation. © Shutterstock.com

"he who wrestles with God." Jacob, in turn, fathered twelve sons. These men became the heads of the twelve tribes of Israel. By the end of *Genesis*, Jacob, now Israel, and his sons are dwelling in Egypt under the provision of Joseph, a son of Jacob and a major player in the Egyptian government.

Exodus through *Deuteronomy* details the Israelite people's four-hundred-year sojourn in Egypt as slaves, God's miraculous deliverance through miracles, their wandering in the wilderness for forty years after displeasing Yahweh, and their eventual return to the borders of Canaan, known as the promised land. Much of *Exodus* and *Leviticus* give the laws and rituals for ethical conduct and daily living to be carried out by the Israelites in obedience to Yahweh's covenant. These edicts included subjects like circumcision, foods they could and could not eat, and rituals for worship.

Another major section of the *Hebrew Bible* consists of a history of the nation of Israel once they enter the promised land. This corresponds to the historical period of about 1400 BCE to about the 6th century BCE. The book of *Joshua* claims that the Israelites, aided by the miraculous power of Yahweh, entered the land of Canaan and subdued all the Canaanite peoples through conquest. Other books like *1* and *2 Samuel* and *1* and *2 Kings* deal with the development of the Israelite monarchy, first under Saul, then later under David and his son Solomon.

The Israelite monarchy broke up into two kingdoms after the death of Solomon (10th century BCE) and remained at enmity with each other for centuries. Ten tribes came under the title Israel, or the Northern Kingdom. The tribes of Judah (David and Solomon's tribe) and Benjamin became the Kingdom of Judah or the Southern Kingdom. A key theme running through these histories concerns the fact that for the most part, the people of Israel did not keep faith with God (Yahweh), and thus suffered his retribution. In 722 BCE, the Assyrian Empire swept in from northern Mesopotamia and decimated the Northern Kingdom. The ten tribes were taken into captivity and disappeared as an entity. In 586 BCE, the Neo-Babylonians inflicted the same fate on the Southern Kingdom. Many Jews ended up in Babylon. The term Jew comes from the name Judah, which means "to praise." The Jews were not allowed to return to the land of Israel until 538 BCE. This came under the provision of their new masters, the Persians.

It must be noted, that while the *Hebrew Bible* gives a narrative that its readers considered historical, textual scholarship over the last two-hundred years as well as archaeological research over the last century have demonstrated the biblical books to contain a mixture of real events and people, but also myths and fabricated memories. Scholars have used the term convergence to describe much of the biblical record. What does that mean? It means that many times the *Bible* describes political, religious, or social conditions that match the history that has been unearthed or recorded in non-biblical accounts. But like most ancient writers, the creators of the *Bible* also edited accounts and created stories that served their purposes. When you read the *Hebrew Bible*, you are not reading a plain historical account of what happened, say around 1000 BCE. In reality, you are actually reading a theological story (with some real history thrown in at times) that the biblical writers, many times living centuries later, wanted you to think what happened. Let's look at several examples to understand this.

According to stories found in the early books of the *Hebrew Bible*, the Israelite people descended from Abraham, and that he was from Mesopotamia. The later generations of Israel who dwelt in the land of Canaan were different peoples from the native Canaanites. The two groups had nothing in common. One group, the Israelites, served the true God and dedicated themselves to moral and righteous behavior. The Canaanites, on the other hand, worshiped a litany of gods and reveled in debauchery and

Image 2.6: Map of Israeli territory during Biblical times and in modern day through 1967. *Courtesy of the University of Texas Libraries, The University of Texas Austin.*

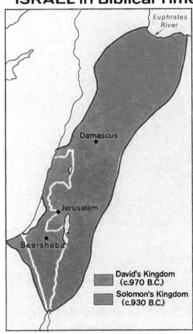

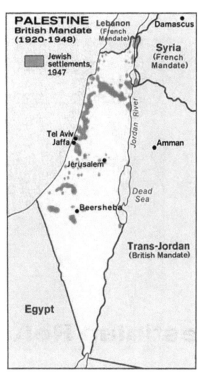

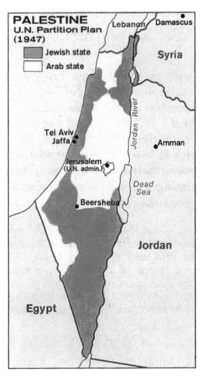

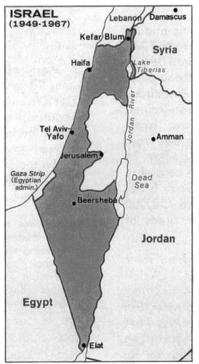

The Parliament of Israel proclaimed Jerusalem as its national capital in 1950. The US Government has not recognized this proclamation and its embassy remains in Tel Aviv-Yafo.

Image 2.7: Lorenzo Monaco, *Abraham*, c. 1408–1410, tempera on wood and gold ground. The symbolic kneeling of his son Isaac at his left, and the holding of a knife in his right hand signify Abraham as the subject of the painting. In the Bible, Abraham was going to sacrifice his son Isaac until an angel of God intervened.

Source: *The Metropolitan Museum of Art, New York.*

Image 2.8: Gustave Doré, *Noah Released a Dove*, engraving, 1866. © Shutterstock.com

evil. Thus, Yahweh gave the Israelites the moral justification for annihilating the Canaanites during the conquest of Joshua.

Upon deeper study over the last two centuries, textual scholars and archaeologists have found a much different story. First, there are clues found in digs (like similarities in pottery) all over the Levant that point out the people of Israel did not come from outside the land of Canaan, but were indigenous to it. In other words, the archaeological consensus today is that the Israelites did develop a separate identity over time, but originally they were Canaanite in origin.

The archaeological record does not support a mass evacuation of over three million Israelites from Egypt as the book of *Exodus* promotes. Neither does the archaeological record support a massive invasion of Israelites into the land. According to the book of *Joshua*, the Israelites razed to the ground the city of Jericho. The archaeological evidence demonstrates that the city had long been in ruins and uninhabited during the time of the supposed conquest.

One of the central events of the *Hebrew Bible* is Noah's flood in *Genesis* 6–8. According to the biblical account, God sent a flood lasting one-hundred-fifty days over all the Earth, wiping out all humanity except Noah and his family. Modern science does not support such a catastrophe, especially not in the last ten-thousand years. Since the 19th century, textual scholars have pored over the findings from multiple ruins dating back to the time of the ancient Near East. Whether in cuneiform tablets found in the library of Ashurbanipal, a king of the Assyrians in Northern Mesopotamia (6th century BCE), fragments from Hittite texts, or small tablets dating back to 2000 BCE, all of these artifacts tell of flood myths that date centuries before the biblical record was created. Most scholars today believe that *Genesis* stories of Adam and Eve and the Noah flood borrowed elements from Sumerian stories like the *Epic of Gilgamesh* and the Babylonian flood story, the *Enuma Elish*. Biblical writers were not independent of their cultural context. Instead, they assimilated many ideas and stories and then shaped narratives to fit their own theological purposes.

A final example concerns the concept of Jewish monotheism itself. The *Hebrew Bible* declares in a vital text, *Deuteronomy* 6:4, that Israel worships one God. It reads, "Here O Israel, the LORD (Yahweh) our God, the LORD is one!" But a closer reading of many biblical texts demonstrates that for a great length of time the Israelites were either polytheistic or at least henotheistic. Polytheism refers to the belief in many gods. Henotheism means there might be many gods, but one god is supreme. In ancient Egypt, Akhenaten praised the Aten as the supreme god. In ancient Babylon, Hammurabi praised the supremacy of the god Marduk. Many passages in the *Hebrew Bible* insinuate that while Yahweh was supreme, he may not have been alone. This is seen in passages like *Genesis* 1:26 where God decides to create humanity. It reads, "Then God said, 'Let us make man in our image, in our likeness." Who is the us in this text? Many scholars believe it refers to a divine council of beings. Thus, early in its history, many Israelites believed that there was a plurality of gods.

The foundational moral code of the *Hebrew Bible*, the *Ten Commandments* demonstrates the concept of henotheism. In *Exodus* 20:2, Yahweh reveals himself to Moses and hands down his moral codes that Moses was to teach to the people of Israel. The text reads, "I am the LORD your God, who brought you out of the land of Egypt, out of the land of slavery. You shall have no other gods before me." An alternate translation of the word before is "besides." Yahweh tells Moses and the Israelites that he was supreme, but not that he was alone. Thus, while the *Hebrew Bible* makes claims about its uniqueness and the supremacy of Yahweh, it also contains evidence that points to it being a piece of literature that underwent a slow process of development where stories were compiled, assimilated, edited, and even fabricated to make a theological point.

While the historical or theological veracity of the *Hebrew Bible* may be debated between religious adherent and skeptic, its cultural value certainly cannot. The Israelites have left us with a collection of stories, poems, and reflections that have left an indelible imprint on Western Civilization. Let's look at some examples.

The concept of monotheism has influenced Western thought for over two thousand years. After being banished to exile in Babylon in the 6th century BCE, Jewish thinkers were forced to re-evaluate their understanding of God. In many places in the early books of the *Bible*, Yahweh comes off as a territorial deity, much like the gods of the surrounding nations. Exile from their homeland, the destruction of Solomon's temple, the loss of their way life, and questions concerning the power and purposes of Yahweh forced the Jews into exile to think more deeply about the God to whom they claimed allegiance. It is during this exile that the *Hebrew Scriptures* were first collected and the long process of editing started.

During the exile, many Jews came to see Yahweh in a much larger context. It is during this time that works like the latter half of book of *Isaiah* was written. In *Isaiah* 45, the reader sees Yahweh as the majestic creator of the universe, even the exile is under his sovereign hand. The prophet notes that Yahweh promised to raise up a rescuer for the people of Israel. *Isaiah* 45:12–13 says, "It is I who made the earth, and created mankind upon it. My own hands stretched out the heavens; I marshaled the starry host. I will raise up Cyrus in my righteousness: I will make all his ways straight. He will rebuild my city (Jerusalem, my addition) and set my exiles free, but not for a price or reward says the LORD Almighty." The Cyrus mentioned is Cyrus the Great, the first great ruler of the

Image 2.9: Lorenzo Monaco, *Moses*, c. 1408–1410, tempera on wood and gold ground.

Source: The Metropolitan Museum of Art, New York.

Image 2.10: Remains of the Second Temple, Jerusalem, Israel. The destroyed Solomon's Temple was replaced with the Second Temple under the reign of Herod c. 515 BCE, and was destroyed in 70 CE. © Shutterstock.com

Persian Empire. He allowed the Jews to return to Israel in 538 BCE. Obviously, *Isaiah* is written at a later date, looking backward, and making a prophecy as if it was a telling of the future. But the concept it is teaching is clear. Yahweh is the sovereign creator and ruler of the universe. Isaiah goes on in Chapter 45 and has Yahweh say, "Turn to me and be saved, all you ends of the earth; for I am God, and there is no other" (45:22). Thus by the time Isaiah is written, Jews were looking at their God as the god of all.

Jews spread all over the ancient world after the exile. Centuries later, there were large Jewish communities in most major cities of the Roman Empire. These Jews took their traditions and their god with them. Monotheism was attractive to many non-Jews (Gentiles) as well. Later, Christians assimilated the ideas of the *Hebrew Bible* and developed a new faith. They, in turn, spread their version of monotheism and biblical traditions throughout Western Europe.

This belief in one God was more than intellectual assent. It had moral content. Scholars call this ethical monotheism. Yahweh demanded his adherents not only reverence him and partake in sacred rituals, but they were also to treat their fellow human beings with respect. The *Ten Commandments*, literally the *Ten Words*, call for children to honor their parents, for people to refrain from murder, adultery, lying, and selfishly craving for the possession of others. Many of the Hebrew prophets like Isaiah and Micah call for the Israelites to defend the widow, protect the fatherless, feed the poor, and to do justly by one's neighbor. *Micah* 6:8 says, "He has shown you, O man, what is good. And what does the LORD require of you? To act justly, and to love mercy and to walk humbly with your God." While the *Hebrew Bible* has many rituals that will not be followed by non-Jews, for example, the refusal to eat pork, passages like these have impacted countless generations of people.

The cultural influence of Israel has lasted throughout the centuries. The assimilation of *Hebrew Bible* stories and ideas by Christians meant that these concepts spread even further. Stories like David and Goliath, Adam and Eve, the poetry of the *Psalms*, and the reflections on the nature of life in *Ecclesiastes* have generated countless songs, poems, stories, paintings, statues, cathedrals, and lessons. As a kingdom, the Israelites could not compare with Egypt, the Hittites, or later Rome. But as a developer of religious ideas and heart-stirring faith, the Jewish people had almost no equals.

Assyrians

The Assyrians are known as one of the most brutal empires of the ancient Near East during the early part of the 1st millennium BCE. Ironically, their greatest contribution came through cultural preservation. Located in northern Mesopotamia, the Assyrians got their name from their capital city of Ashur. The Assyrians had developed a small empire during the Bronze Age of the 2nd millennium BCE, but they continued to grow and reached their zenith during the 9th and 7th centuries BCE. At its peak, the Assyrians ruled directly or through client kings the entire Fertile Crescent including Egypt. They were known for their brutality in war. They developed siege ramp equipment and iron-tipped battering rams for piercing thick city walls. They were known for ruthlessly annihilating those who resisted. Upon taking a rebellious city, one Assyrian ruler boasted of his slaughter. "I cut off their heads and like heaps of grain, I piled them up." In other Assyrian accounts, kings gloated over skinning alive all the prominent men of a conquered city and burning alive the young men and women. What stands out about the Assyrians was their policy of taking a portion of the people they conquered, usually the most skilled and the elite, and transporting them in small groups to live permanently in other conquered lands. This happened to many in the ten northern tribes of Israel during the Assyrian conquest of 722 BCE. These Israelites disappeared entirely from the historical record. From a practical standpoint, this Assyrian policy of conquest and relocation of their enemies created a more cosmopolitan society across the Fertile Crescent.

Israel is an example of how Assyrian influence affected other peoples. The Assyrians spoke a Semitic dialect known as Aramaic. Through their long domination of Canaan, more and more people began to speak Aramaic instead of Hebrew. Aramaic was also used during the Persian Empire. By the 1st century CE, Jews living in the Roman province of Judea (modern day Israel) spoke Aramaic as their primary language. This would have included an itinerant preacher named Jesus of Nazareth.

While the Assyrians are well known for the military prowess and brutality, their ultimate legacy came through their cultural pursuits. Ashurbanipal (ruled: 668–627 BCE) was an Assyrian king. He built what is known as the first library of the ancient world in his capital city of Nineveh. This is near the modern day

Image 2.11: The Assyrian Empire and the region about the Eastern Mediterranean, 750–625 BCE. *Courtesy of the University of Texas Libraries, The University of Texas Austin.*

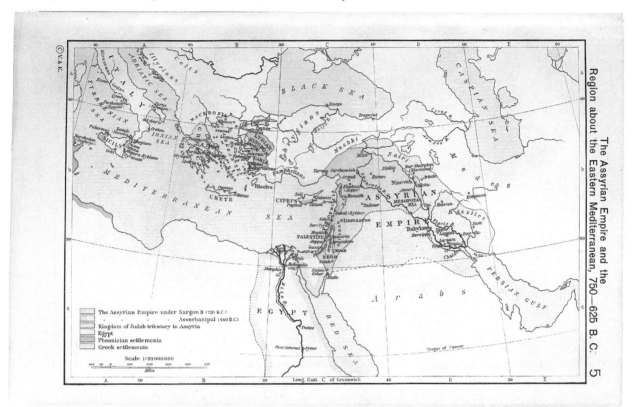

Iraqi city of Mosul on the Tigris River. This organized library held not only government records but also tablets containing information about the law, medicine, science, mathematics, magic, and legends. The Babylonians destroyed the city of Nineveh in 612 BCE. But while the fire decimated the city, the conflagration only further baked and hardened the tablets. Archaeologists discovered the library, which contained over thirty-thousand cuneiform tablets in the mid-19th century.

The importance of the library of Ashurbanipal cannot be missed. Through conquest, Ashurbanipal acquired ancient texts from all over the Near East. Amongst the tablets, archaeologists found a complete copy of the *Enuma Elish*. This is the Babylonian creation and flood myth, which scholars believed greatly influenced the *Genesis* account in the *Hebrew Bible*. The discovery of the great library helped scholars not only understand the nature of Assyrian life, but also insight into beliefs and customs of the ancient Near East. It also helped textual specialists to understand the context that produced one of the most influential works of literature in world history, the *Hebrew Bible*.

Image 2.12: King Ashurbanipal on a lion hunt, 645–640 BCE, gypsum wall relief. © Shutterstock.com

Babylonians

Like the Assyrians, the Babylonians played a major role in the legal, intellectual, and social development of the ancient Near East. Like many ancient peoples,

Image 2.13: The Code of Hammurabi, now housed at the Louvre in Paris, is one of the earliest known written law codes, carved into a basalt stele with cuneiform script. The law and punishment for a crime, according to the Code of Hammurabi varied depending on which class or to which gender the accused belonged. © Shutterstock.com

the Babylonians had periods where they were prominent, but also periods of decline. Babylonian history stretches back to the early 2nd millennium BCE. They emerged from Amorite nomads who invaded Mesopotamia around 2000 BCE. On the Euphrates River, these migrants created a village, which evolved into a great city named Babel, which means "gate of God."

The Babylonian king Hammurabi (ruled: 1792–1750 BCE) conquered for himself an empire that stretched the entire length of Mesopotamia. An enlightened ruler, Hammurabi created one of the oldest existing law codes in world history. The Babylonian king declared that his desire was to create a system of mandates in order "to cause justice to prevail in the land, to destroy the wicked and the evil, to prevent the strong from oppressing the weak, and to further the welfare of the people." Hammurabi's two hundred eighty-two laws dealt with issues such as trade, family relations, business, and the purchasing and ownership of property. The code is most known for the principle "an eye for an eye and a tooth for a tooth." While sounding harsh, the idea was that the punishment should fit the crime. Thus, the code created a standard for major and minor transgressions. After Hammurabi's death, the Babylonian empire went into a long decline, and its power was usurped by groups like the Hittites and later the Assyrians. Babylon would not return to prominence for centuries.

Babylon reached great heights once again in the 7th century BCE. These new Babylonians were

originally called Chaldeans. They started out as nomadic peoples who moved into southern Mesopotamia sometime around 1000 BCE. In the 8th century BCE, the Chaldeans conquered the native Babylonians and became client rulers under the Assyrians. In 612 BCE, these Neo-Babylonians teamed up with the Medes, another people tired of Assyrian rule, and successfully overthrew the Assyrians. The new Babylonian empire quickly encompassed the entire area of Mesopotamia. The greatest of the Babylonian kings was Nebuchadnezzar II (ruled: 605–562 BCE).

Nebuchadnezzar II left his mark in several areas. He built one of the seven great wonders of the ancient world, the Hanging Gardens of Babylon. To be fair, many scholars doubt whether this structure was ever constructed. Supposedly, one of the king's wives, Amytis of Media (Iran), missed her homeland with its verdant hills, so Nebuchadnezzar had a ziggurat temple built with terraced sections of lush vegetation.

Nebuchadnezzar II conquered the Southern Kingdom of Judah, destroyed the temple of Yahweh built by King Solomon, and sent thousands of Jews into captivity throughout Babylon. It was during the Babylonian captivity that Jewish writers began to collect and narrate what eventually became the *Hebrew Bible*. Jewish anger and humiliation over the destruction of their homeland and culture found its way into this work. In *Genesis* 11, there is an account of the first humans who pridefully try to build a structure to make it to heaven, and thus be equal with God.

According to the story, Yahweh confuses the language of these peoples, and the building is not completed. Thus, according to *Genesis*, this is the origin of the variety of human languages. What was the name of this tower? Of course, it was the Tower of Babel. Remember, Babel means "gate of God."

Image 2.14: Artistic rendering of what the Hanging Gardens of Babylon may have looked like. The Hanging Gardens of Babylon are the only wonder of the world for which the location has not been verified. © Shutterstock.com

The Babylonians contributed tremendously to the study of mathematics and astronomy. They believed that they could tell the future story of individuals and nations through charting the paths of the sun, the planets, and the stars. While this belief was fallacious, it did allow these Babylonian thinkers to develop concrete knowledge in an array of scientific areas. Scholars credit Babylonians with determining the correct length of one year.

Babylon began to decline after the death of Nebuchadnezzar II. Like the Assyrians before them, the Babylonians met people who would better them in battle and take their empire. This group was known as the Persians. They conquered the Babylonians in 539 BCE. The Persian Empire became the first great world empire, spanning from Asia to Africa, and for a while, to the European mainland.

Persian Empire

Like the Hittites, the Persians originated from Indo-Europeans who left central Europe and traveled east into Asia. By 1200 BCE, the forerunners of the Persians arrived in Iran. Three centuries later, two groups had evolved from these Indo-Europeans, the Medes, and the Persians. The Medes dominated northern Iran and called it Media. The Persians dominated southern Iran and called their territory Persia.

Image 2.15: Map of the Persian Empire, c. 500 BCE. *Courtesy of the University of Texas Libraries, The University of Texas Austin.*

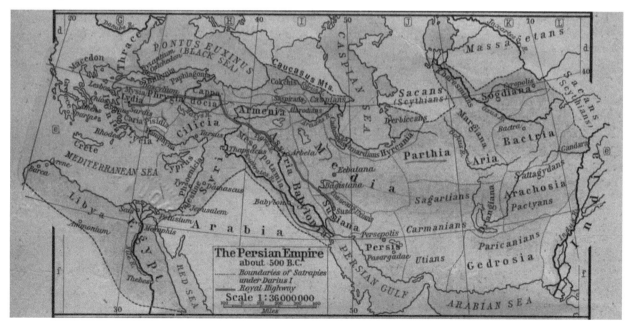

By 700 BCE, King Achaemenes came to power in Persia. His descendants created the Achaemenid Dynasty. Cyrus II (ruled: 560–530 BCE), known as "Cyrus the Great," is considered the founder of the Persian Empire. In 550 BCE, Cyrus revolted against the Medes, and by 530 BCE, he had conquered most of the Fertile Crescent and Anatolia (modern day Turkey). Under later Persian kings, the empire incorporated Egypt, Northern India, and Afghanistan.

Cyrus was an enlightened ruler whose policies eventually proved enticing to the people he conquered. Under the Persian Empire, local peoples were allowed a measure of self-government and could continue their local customs and worship their own gods. Under Cyrus's rule, Jews were allowed to return to their homeland in 538 BCE. While many decided to stay in Babylon, others migrated back. The books of *Nehemiah* and *Ezra* in the *Hebrew Bible* document this matter. As seen earlier, the prophet Isaiah claimed that Yahweh had selected Cyrus to release the people of Israel from their captivity. In *Isaiah* 45:1, the prophet calls Cyrus Yahweh's "anointed." The Hebrew word for anointed is *messiach* from which we get the word messiah. The Greek word for messiah is Christ. Thus, Isaiah ascribed to Cyrus the same title later given to Jesus of Nazareth in the 1st century CE.

Darius the Great (ruled: 522–486 BCE), the son-in-law of Cyrus, developed an efficient government infrastructure. He broke up the empire into twenty districts or satrapies. A satrap, or governor, ruled each province and answered directly to the king. The satrap not only watched over the province but also directed tax collection and the execution of laws.

A vast empire stretching from Turkey to Egypt to Iran needed to be connected to enhance communication and facilitate the movement of troops. In this, the Persians also excelled. The empire consisted of four capital cities stretching from Iran west into Anatolia (Turkey). Their names were Persepolis, Susa, Babylon, and Sardis. To connect these cities, the Persians constructed the Great Royal Road. Spanning sixteen-hundred miles, royal messengers could travel this route in about ten days.

As we have seen, peoples and empires came and went in the ancient Near East, but what continued were innovations, whether an idea or invention. The Hittites disappeared, but their new invention of iron continued to spread throughout the Mediterranean world. The Phoenicians did not create an empire, but through trade, they diffused ideas, technology, and culture throughout the Near Eastern world. The

people of Israel were never a major political entity and left us no significant technologies, but they did leave us the belief in a righteous omnipotent God who is concerned about humanity and expects moral conduct. Ironically, the Persians did carve out a tremendous empire, but that is not what has impacted people's lives for the last two thousand years. Most people today have no idea that the main cultural ingredient left to us by the Persians also consisted of religious ideas.

Let's take a test. At the end of these questions, answer what religion fits these parameters? What religion first taught dualism, that there is a constant battle between a righteous creator god and evil force? What religion first explained that a virgin-born savior would one day come to the world of men and vanquish the evil force? What religion first taught that the righteous creator god would raise all people from the dead and conduct final judgment? Ultimately, the righteous will enjoy bliss in the eternal presence of God. What is your answer? If it was Christianity, then you would have answered incorrectly. All of these doctrines were first taught by a religion adopted by the Persians and came to be known as Zoroastrianism.

Zoroastrianism is the religion preached by the prophet Zarathustra, better known by the Greek name Zoroaster. Zoroaster lived in Iran between 1100 and 600 BCE. Like most areas during this period, the people were polytheistic, worshiping many gods. Zoroaster claimed to receive revelation from Ahura Mazda. Ahura Mazda means Wise Lord, and he was the supreme god. He was in a struggle with an evil,

Image 2.16: Stone carved relief of Ardashir I of the Sasanian Empire in Persia, receiving his crown from Ahura Mazda, at Persepolis, Iran.
© Shutterstock.com

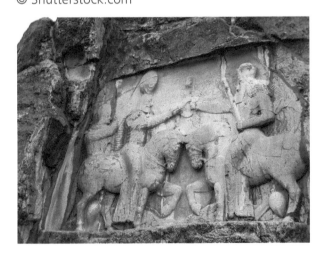

lying, and destructive being known as Ahriman or Angra Mainyu. Humans had to make a choice whether they were going to follow the force of good and truth, or follow the destructive and evil spirit of darkness. Thus, all of life concerned this dualism. According to Zoroaster, one's choice determined one's destination after death. Those that followed Ahura Mazda and goodness and truth ended up in paradise. Those that followed the lie of Ahriman, known as the druj, ended up in a form of burning hell. At the end of time, Ahura Mazda will send a virgin-born savior known as the Saoshyant. He will overthrow Ahriman and institute final judgment. Everyone will be resurrected and embraced by Ahura Mazda. Even those who did evil will go through a fiery purge and be reconciled to the Wise Lord.

Many of the Achaemenid dynasty kings embraced the God of Zoroaster. During the reign of Darius the Great, the king had the Behistun Inscription created on the side of Mount Behistun in Western Iran. Etched one hundred meters from the ground, fifteen meters high, and twenty-five meters wide, the inscription tells of the history of Darius and previous Persian kings. In this inscription, Darius praises Ahura Mazda. The inscription reads, "By the grace of Ahura Mazda am I king, Ahura Mazda has granted me the kingdom." Thus, we can see that for the Persian kings, Ahura Mazda was the supreme god. The Behistun Monument was also important because it was written in three languages using cuneiform script. One of the languages was Babylonian, and scholars were familiar with it. This allowed later archaeologists and linguists to decipher cuneiform like the Rosetta Stone allowed scholars to decipher Egyptian hieroglyphics.

Image 2.17: Stone carved relief of King Darius of the Persian Empire at Persepolis, Iran.
© Shutterstock.com

Why is this important? Zoroastrianism influenced the religion of the Jews. The Babylonians took thousands of Jews captive and transported them to Babylon in the early 6th century BCE. Even after the Persians conquered the Babylonians, and Cyrus the Great allowed many Jews to return to their homeland in 538 BCE, a large number decided to stay in Babylon or one of the other Persian capital cities. Zoroastrianism and Judaism were very similar in that both declared the supremacy of one God who demanded righteous conduct. Jews also found support from the Persian kings. Many scholars believe an exchange of ideas took place between the two faiths.

Jews before the exile held to the Mesopotamian view of the afterlife. The message of the *Hebrew Scriptures* is that there is no heaven or hell, and death is basically the end. There is no satanic figure who dominates the world and leads men astray. Pre-exilic Judaism knew nothing of a final judgment. Yet, between the time of the exile in the 6th century and the 2nd century BCE, a number of Jews changed many of their views. Life after the exile forced a re-evaluation of God and the Jewish place in the world. Many Jewish thinkers began to adopt and adapt many of these Zoroastrian concepts. In the Jewish writings of the 2nd and 1st century BCE, one sees mention of a war between the sons of light and darkness, and angelic spirits who support or try to destroy men. A final resurrection and a final reckoning are mentioned in many sources.

A prime example is the book of *Daniel*, which scholars think was written around 160 BCE as the Jews in Israel were trying to overthrow their Greek masters, the Seleucids. This is the last composition of the *Hebrew Bible*. In this book, Daniel talks about the coming of a divine figure called the Son of Man who will be sent by God (the Ancient of Days) to overthrow evil, bring about the resurrection of the just and unjust, and establish an everlasting kingdom (*Daniel* 7: 9–14, 12:1–3). Thus, the Persian influence on post-exilic Judaism is clearly evident.

The kind of theology that focuses on the end of the world (or the age) and God's rectifying all evil and ruling forever is called apocalypticism. Apocalypse is a Greek word that means to uncover or reveal something. Persian apocalypticism clearly affected Jewish thinkers and influenced them to develop their own version of apocalypticism. This thinking later affected two other religious teachers, Jesus of Nazareth and Mohammed. Jesus, a Jew, and Mohammed, an Arab, both founded monotheistic religions that were offshoots of

Judaism. Both also taught a version of apocalypticism where God or Allah is going to overthrow all evil doers and usher in a paradise where righteousness reigns. There is an apparent continuity between Judaism, Christianity, and Islam. What most people today do not know is that continuity goes all the back to the Persian religion of Zoroastrianism. While Zoroastrianism today is a very small religion with less than two-hundred thousand adherents, its influence on the world's largest monotheistic faiths is colossal.

When we think of Western civilization, we recall its emphasis on scientific inquiry and technological innovation. We also remember principles like religious and intellectual freedom. We recollect the free flow of trade and ideas. Ironically, when you look for the roots for what created the West, then you will find them stretching back to the ancient Near East! Whether through the Hittite innovation of smelting iron, the Phoenician diffusion of technologies (like their alphabet), the Assyrian preservation of knowledge, Babylonian science, Israelite monotheism, or Persian apocalypticism, what we think of as Western civilization is the results of borrowing and adapting from the past.

Chapter 3

The Development and Influence of Ancient Greece

In his epic poem, *The Iliad*, the poet Homer gave a description of the goddess Athena blessing the warrior Achilles. According to Homer, "She made weariless fire blaze from his shield and helmet like that star of the waning summer who beyond all stars rises bathed in the ocean stream to glitter in brilliance." Though he was referring to one Mycenaean warrior, the words of Homer can be applied to ancient Greece itself. In numerous ways, ancient Greece stood as a "star . . . beyond all stars" in the ancient world. From this small peninsula and islands located on the Mediterranean Sea in southeastern Europe, we get the foundation stones for Western civilization. The Greeks gave us philosophy, democracy, the Olympics, tragedies and comedies, Spartan military prowess, as well as Athenian thought, sculpture, and architecture. The Greeks gave us the beginnings of science and history. Moreover yet like Achilles, who had a fatal weakness, so did Greece. With all their innovations, their pride led them to batter each other into weakness, and this weakened state allowed them to be conquered by outside forces. But while the Greeks lost their autonomy and military strength, they left us a lasting cultural legacy that informs the Western mind to this day.

Image 3.1: Statue of Achilles, Athens, Greece. Achilles was shot through the heel in his tendon during the siege of Troy, rendering him unable to walk. The heel cord through which he was punctured is now called the Achilles tendon. © Shutterstock.com

The Forerunners of Greece: Minoans and Mycenaeans

When the average person thinks of ancient Greece, they usually gravitate to Athens and Sparta. In reality, two major Bronze Age civilizations predate these well-known city-states by several centuries. They were the Minoans and the Mycenaeans. The Minoans lived on the island of Crete, south of the Greek mainland. Their antecedents are traced back as far as 2700 BCE. The peak of the Minoan civilization came between 2000 and 1500 BCE. The society got its name from the legendary King Minos and the legendary beast that supposedly lived there. It was known as the Minotaur. This being had the body of a man and the head of a bull and dwelt in the labyrinth, a maze-like structure in one of the palaces of King Minos. There were several large palaces on the island with hundreds of rooms, Knossos being the biggest and most important.

Living on the sea, the Minoans earned a reputation as a trading people. They trafficked in goods such as wine, olive oil, precious stones, and grain. Minoan ruins have revealed evidence that point to Near Eastern and Egyptian influences. Minoan religion revolved around a mother goddess and an infatuation with bulls, thus the Minotaur myth. Being an advanced civilization, the Minoans were literate people. They used hieroglyphics and later a script found on pottery known as Linear A. To this day, it is indecipherable. The Minoans went into decline between the 16th and 15th centuries BCE. Historians and archaeologists have proposed a variety of theories concerning why including outside invasion, deforestation, earthquakes, and a nearby volcanic eruption on the island of Thera. The decline more than likely involved a combination of all or some of these factors. The Minoans were replaced as the dominant kingdom in the region by the mainland civilization known as the Mycenaeans.

The Mycenaeans were a part of the Indo-European movement of peoples out of Central Europe. The people that eventually evolved into the Mycenaeans arrived on the Greek mainland around 2000 BCE. They too were a literate people. Linguists call their script Linear B which was an early form of Greek. By 1400 BCE, the Mycenaeans controlled Minos. The Mycenaean kingdom consisted of cities, and a powerful warrior king ruled each one. It was a well-to-do society. Archaeologists to this day are still discovering tombs filled with gold and other treasures.

We know about the Mycenaeans through the epic poetry of the blind sage Homer, but his most notable creations, the *Iliad* and the *Odyssey*, came centuries later. In the *Iliad*, the Mycenaean Kings joined forces to sail east across the Aegean to take vengeance on Troy located in Asia Minor (Western Turkey). In the poem, the Trojan Prince Paris wooed away Helen, the wife of Menelaus, the King of Sparta. Menelaus joined with his brother Agamemnon, King of Mycenae and invaded Troy. The great warrior Achilles led the Mycenaean forces. Archaeologists have found evidence that Troy fought a war and experienced destruction around 1180 BCE. Instead of a battle over the lovely Helen, scholars argue for a more mundane cause, namely that Troy was more than likely fighting a war over the Aegean trade routes. The Aegean is part of the Mediterranean that separates Greece from Turkey. The eclipse of Mycenae triggered a three century long dark age of chaos, which included the loss writing and sophisticated pottery, depopulation, and tremendous poverty.

Image 3.2: The ruins of the Minoan Palace of King Minos of Minoan Crete, located at the archaeological site of Knossos in modern day Heraklion, Crete.Excavation has revealed the layout of the palace was a labyrinth in of itself. © Shutterstock.com

Image 3.3: Map of Mycenaean Greece and the Orient, c. 1450 BCE. *Courtesy of the University of Texas Libraries, The University of Texas at Austin.*

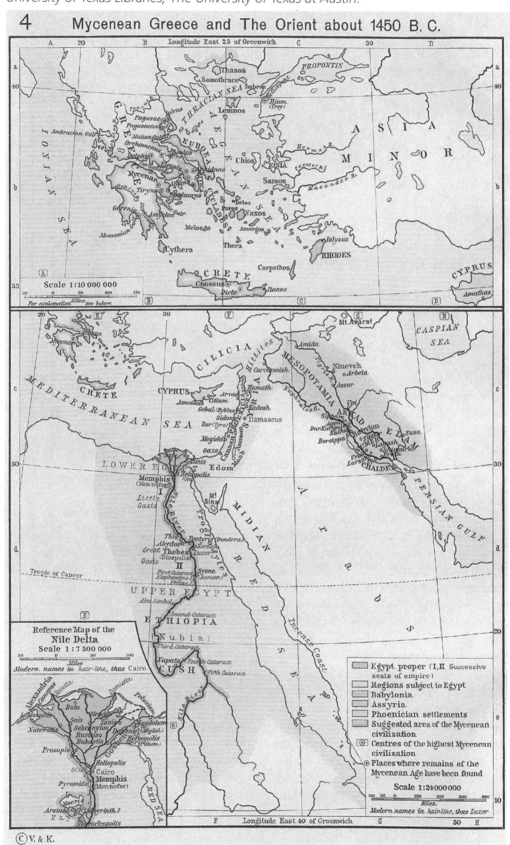

Image 3.4: Sebald Beham, *Achilles and Hector*, 1518–30, engraving. In the *Iliad*, Achilles kills Hector in battle in Book 12.

Source: *The Metropolitan Museum of Art, New York.*

Dark Ages and Archaic Greece

The Greek Dark Ages were not without some light. While people did endure poorer existences on scattered farms, there were some cultural improvements toward the end of the period. One of the contributions of this time revolved around athletic competition. In 776 BCE, the Olympic games were initiated. It was part of a religious festival held in honor of the chief of the Greek gods, Zeus, at the base of Mount Olympia. The Greeks considered the mountain to be the home for the Greek pantheon of gods. Athletes met at Olympus and competed every four years. Male athletes, from all over the area, competed in the nude and took part in endeavors including, running, boxing, jumping, wrestling, horseback riding, chariot racing, and discuss throwing. The various kinds of events evolved from an initial footrace to the full-array of events in a century and a half. The Olympics later spawned other competitions including the Isthmian Games at Corinth and the Pythian Games near Delphi. Greeks conducted the Olympic Games for a thousand years before being discontinued by Roman Christian Emperor Theodosius in 393 CE.

As mentioned before, the blind poet Homer lived during this era. Most scholars think he lived around the 9th or 8th century BCE. His most famous works were the *Iliad* and the *Odyssey*. Both take place in the context of the Trojan War. The former dealt with the war, and the latter dealt with a Mycenaean soldier, Odysseus, and his perilous journey to get back home after the war. Originally oral poems, they were later

Image 3.5: Terracotta Panathenaic prize amphora, attributed to Euphiletos, c. 530 BCE. The pottery depicts a foot-race during the Panatheanic Games, a version of the Olympic Games. The Panathenaic Games were held every four years in Athens from the 6th century BCE to the 3rd century CE. Unlike the Olympics, some of the events in the Panatheanic games were only open to Athenians.

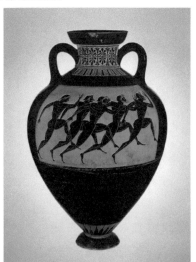

Source: *The Metropolitan Museum of Art, New York.*

written down. Homer revealed much of the historical context of the era as well as information about the Greek pantheon of gods. In the *Iliad*, one can see the beginning of limited government favored by many later Greeks. The Mycenaean Kings had to take into consideration the desires and feelings of their soldiers. This is seen in the conflict between King Agamemnon and his champion, Achilles. In addition, in these poems one can see the values that Greek warriors appreciated; namely those of bravery, personal honor, fighting skill, and manliness. The Greek word *arete* described these concepts, and for that matter, the overall Greek concept of excellence. Homer's poems are considered foundation stones for Western literature.

Hesiod, though not considered on the same level as Homer, also stood out as a skilled poet of this era. Two of his works have survived, the *Theogony* and *Works and Days*. *Theogony* is an epic poem that deals with the creation of the Greek gods. It details Zeus's struggle with his father Cronus and how Zeus and his brothers, Poseidon—god of the sea, and Hades—god of the underworld, became the chief deities. The poem also tells of the god Prometheus and his disobeying Zeus by giving human beings fire. *Theogony* also describes the birth and exploits of the half god half man figure, *Herakles*, better known to us as Hercules. *Works and Days* is the lesser of the two works and deals with common peasant life. While composed toward the end of the Dark Ages, both Homer and Hesiod set the stage for a renaissance of Greek culture.

While Greece underwent this three-hundred-year period of cultural stagnation, a linguistic change occurred that would revolutionize Greek thought. As we have seen, the Minoans used an alphabet known as Linear A. It is a script that is dead and cannot be deciphered. The Mycenaeans used Linear B which was the forerunner of Greek. Where did the Greek alphabet, as we now know it, come from? Sometime near the end of the Dark Ages, Greeks adopted the Phoenician alphabet. Using this template, they came up with innovations including vowels. As we will see later, the Greek language and alphabet became the lingua franca of much of the ancient world by the 1st century CE.

It was during the Archaic Age, the age of the rulers or archons, that the characteristics that defined ancient Greece mostly came into being. During this period, the polis or city-state fully evolved, and the hoplite soldier and the phalanx formation came to represent Greek armies. Greeks formed colonies across the Mediterranean and Aegean, Athens saw the birth of democracy, and Sparta developed its hyper-military state.

Between the mid-8th and 6th centuries BCE, the Greek polis took shape.

The word polis means "city-state," but it meant more than that. During the Dark Ages, people lived in scattered farms, but by the late 9th century BCE, they started to develop communities, usually around a high rock formation for defense known as an acropolis. The word means "high city" or the highest point in a city. The polis consisted of people with a common heritage including religion, language, and customs. Usually, the polis was tied to a god. For example, Athens got its name from their patron deity, Athena. She was the daughter of Zeus and was the goddess of logic, reason, and artistic achievement. These kinds of attributes characterized the Athenian people. The polis usually had an open market known as the agora. However, most of these poleis also built defensive walls around their cities. The members of the polis were considered citizens and expected to defend their homeland.

The creation of the polis led to military innovations. The citizens of the polis were expected to fight when the community was threatened. Hoplite, from the Greek word meaning tool or equipment, became the name for the Greek soldier. Citizen soldiers, or hoplites, provided their own equipment that included a helmet, shield, breast and leg armor, and an eight to nine-foot-long pike or spear. Hoplite soldiers fought in a phalanx formation. This formation went back to the Sumerians, but the Greeks perfected it. Hoplite soldiers grouped in a tight formation, at least eight

Image 3.6: The acropolis of Athens held the Parthenon and other major religious temples. Pericles initiated renovations and building of these temples on the acropolis after Greek victory in the Persian war. © Shutterstock.com

across and eight deep. Each man was protected by his colleague's shield. The column moved as one. The shields protected the soldier from arrows and flying missiles, and the long spears were used to kill or wound the approaching enemy. It took great strength, training, and discipline to fight successfully. The phalanx became the military formation used by armies in Europe for centuries.

The Archaic Age not only saw military innovations, but colonization also stood out as another key characterization of the period. What spurred on this great movement of people? Agriculture was the mainstay of the polis. In the mountainous geography of Greece, land was at a premium. The old system of the kings had died out, but a wealthy elite evolved during this period, and they controlled most of the land. This put many Greeks at a disadvantage. In many poleis, people fell into debt and were sold as slaves. Conflict simmered between the poor and the aristocracy. Between the 8th and 6th centuries BCE, colonization proved to be a release valve for some of the conflict. Usually, a polis would send out some of its citizens to colonize a new area. During this period, well over one thousand poleis were founded. Greek poleis developed around the Black Sea, Asia Minor, North Africa, southern Italy, and as far west as Spain. This ignited trade, new technologies, and fresh ideas flowing into Greece and its colonies from all over the Mediterranean. These colonies transplanted the culture of their home colonies including building styles, worship of the same gods, and farming practices. They bred what came to be known as a Panhellenic (All Greek) spirit.

Throughout much of the 7th century BCE, aristocratic rule defined Athens. Toward the end of the century and throughout the 6th century BCE, Athens saw the rise of the tyrants. The word then had a slightly different meaning that what it does today. Who were these men? Tyrants were members of the aristocracy who grabbed power for themselves, usually to address pressing problems of the day. Many tyrants were considered heroes of the people. While there were downsides to tyrannical rule, many of the tyrants sought to implement reforms, and these changes eventually led to direct participation in the government of Athens. Historians have noted that the many tyrants of the 6th century BCE broke the power of the aristocracy and unleashed the creative power of Athens to flow.

Athens is located on the Attica Peninsula in Eastern Greece. During the early part of the 7th century BCE, nine aristocratic rulers known as Archons (rulers) ruled the polis. They served alongside a council of nobles known as the Areopagus. The name Areopagus means "Hill of Ares." Ares was the Greek god of war. Since the council met on this hill, the name stuck. As noted before, conflict between the aristocracy and the landless majority led to slavery but also violence and social unrest. To address these problems, some aristocratic men either were given power or seized it and became known as tyrants.

Draco was one of the first of the Athenian tyrants. The early 7th century saw Athens in chaos as many people did not own land, and there were no laws to prevent murder or provide justice for victims of crime. In 621 BCE, Draco issued a code of mandates to restore order and cement the power of the aristocracy. His decrees were so harsh the word draconian has come down to us meaning laws that are unusually strict and harsh. The law contained death offenses for what many thought were minor crimes. Historians consider Draco's statutes as being the first written law code in Greek history. Draco's edicts did bring some measure of order, but they did not help the majority of poor Athenians.

Solon earned a reputation as one of the greatest of the tyrants as well as one of the wisest. He was already an Archon, but was given unlimited power in 594 BCE and became a tyrant. Unlike the modern use of the term, Solon tried to bring reforms for the majority of Athenians. He limited the amount of land an aristocrat could own, thus providing opportunities for non-aristocrats to acquire land. He limited the amount of grain sold outside of Athens, thus assuring that fewer people went hungry. Solon ended the debt enslavement of Athenians, and he set up a Council of Four Hundred to be organized alongside the Areopagus. While historians are not exactly sure of the Council's powers, they believe it was the forerunner of the democratic Council of Five Hundred created in the 6th century BCE under the tyrant Cleisthenes. Solon also did something unheard of for the time. He went so far as to give up power and leave Athens for several years to see if Athenians could govern themselves. In reality, Athens still had challenges on the horizon.

Pisistratus had a long history in Athens. He attempted to take power around 560 BCE but was driven into exile. He traveled for the next decade and acquired wealth through trade. Pisistratus returned to Athens and seized power in 547 BCE. He brought

Image 3.7: Map of Ancient Greece and the Peloponnesian peninsula.

Source: The University of *Texas at Austin*.

about lasting changes in his twenty-year reign. Pisistratus limited the power of the aristocracy and sought to curry favor with the common people. He is known for unifying Attica under Athenian rule. Pisistratus brought religious unity by making Athena the chief deity of the city. One of his key contributions was the urging of Athenian farmers to grow cash crops such as olives. Pisistratus also established a public works program. While a tyrant who held absolute sway, he contributed to the growing status of Athens.

Cleisthenes is known for introducing *demokratia*, or democracy to the people of Athens. Like many in the aristocracy, Cleisthenes ran afoul of other elite families vying for power. He was exiled by Hippias, the son of Pisistratus and tyrant in power in Athens, around 525 BCE. Cleisthenes returned to power and was made an Archon by 508 BCE. Many in the aristocracy opposed him, but like his predecessors, he worked to maintain power by sharing it with the common people. His enemies worked with Sparta to drive out Cleisthenes for a brief period, but Cleisthenes soon returned to power and introduced a wide array of reforms. *Demokratia* means "the people rule." Cleisthenes gave power to all citizens of Athens. Both landowners and the landless took part in the Assembly. He created the Council of Five Hundred which made the laws. Citizens thirty years old and over served on the Council. On average, individuals served on the Council of Five Hundred about twice in a lifetime. Thus, all ten thousand male citizens

played a role in making decisions. What about trouble makers? The democracy carried out the practice of ostracism. Every year the citizens would write on broken pieces of pottery known as *ostraka* the names of citizens who were a detriment to the polis. If a miscreant received a sixty percent vote (six thousand people), then they were banished for a decade.

This move to democracy had profound effects. As the supreme legislative body, the Assembly included all male citizens over eighteen, and this represented approximately twenty-five percent of the population. In addition, anyone was allowed to speak and vote. A simple majority decided most issues. The Assembly declared war, made peace, spent tax money, chose magistrates, and even heard judicial cases. Thus, theoretically, every citizen was involved in political decision making.

Certainly, there were many flaws in Athenian democracy. Women were not allowed a vote, and slavery still existed for those who were not citizens, but those shortcomings should not cause us to undervalue its extraordinary achievements. The idea that the state represents a community of free and self-governing citizens remains a crucial principle of Western Civilization. Athenian democracy embodied the principle of a government based not on force, but instead, on free citizens debating, devising, altering, and obeying laws. This participatory citizenship not only involved voting but also other aspects as well. Athenian men were expected to learn how to read and speak well. They were to be well-versed in religious ideas and a capable hoplite soldier. While the democratic experiment would eventually disappear under constant war and internal strife, it left a legacy that would revive a thousand years later at the end of the European Middle Ages.

Other poleis developed during the Archaic Period, and one stood out as the polar opposite to Athens. To quote the movie *300*, "This is Sparta!" By the 8th century BCE, hunger and the need for land sparked a war with Sparta and the neighboring group known as the Messenians. The Spartans enslaved the Messenians and called them *helots*, which meant a state-owned serf or slave. The constant fear of a slave uprising forced the Spartans to revamp their society by the 7th century BCE.

Sparta became a hyper-military state. Two kings from two royal families ruled the polis. One king almost always led the Spartan army into battle. Preparation for war started at birth. A Spartan king

Image 3.9: Reference Map: Ancient Greece, Southern Part. *Courtesy of the University of Texas Libraries, The University of Texas at Austin.*

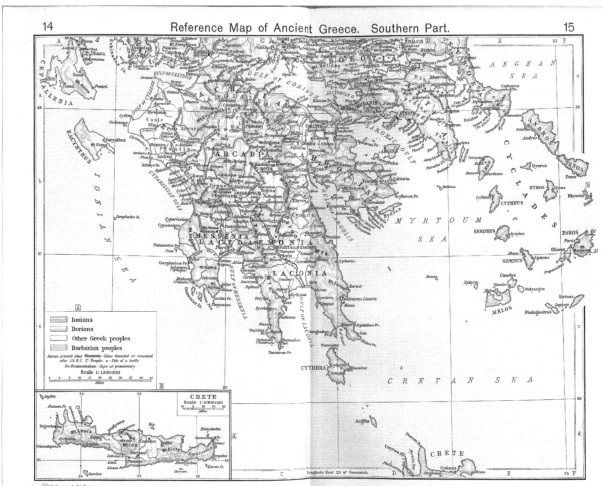

decided the fitness of newborns. They disposed of those they deemed unfit. Boys were taken from their mothers at age seven. They began a decade's long period of harsh training, which included fighting, surviving the elements, and learning to adapt to adverse situations. At age twenty, these young men became soldiers. They became full citizens at age thirty and served in the army through age sixty (if they survived that long). For the Spartan warrior, nothing proved greater than serving the state and showing oneself courageous and skilled in battle. The old story goes that a Spartan wife told her husband on the way to battle, "Return with your shield (thus in victory) or on your shield (having died doing your duty)." A Spartan man married and produced children, but mostly he lived in the military barracks with his comrades. Even Spartan women and girls were expected to be physically fit.

While two kings ruled Sparta, it was a limited monarchy. Before acting, the kings had to get the approval of the Council of Twenty-Eight, which consisted of twenty-eight men sixty years and older. All Spartan men over the age of thirty belonged to the Assembly of Citizens. They usually rubber stamped the decrees of the kings and the Council of Twenty-Eight. For the Spartans, the state was everything. Unlike the Athenians who promoted individuality and introspection, Spartans were expected to obey and serve with unquestioning loyalty. As Greece entered into the 6th century BCE, these poleis had to band together to face an outside threat. The threat came from the Persian Empire.

The Persian Wars

By 500 BCE, the Persian Empire extended from the Indus Valley to the Mediterranean Sea and from Central Asia to Egypt. To Persia, conquest of the small and divided city-states of Greece must have seemed like a minor challenge. Over the previous two centuries, the Greeks had taken up residence on the western coast of Asia Minor, also known as Ionia. Through rapid expansion of its empire from east to west, the Persians began to encroach on the Greek lands in Ionia by the early 5th century BCE. Persia eventually demanded that the Ionian Greeks pay tribute to their king, and the independent-minded Greeks resisted.

In 490 BCE, the Ionian Greeks initiated a rebellion aided by a flotilla of Athenian ships and soldiers. The operation was largely a failure, but the Persians could not allow this challenge to their growing authority and power to go unanswered. During the same year, Persia decided to attack the Greece mainland in hopes of quelling any future resistance. The Persians landed not far from Athens near the village of Marathon. They were met by a small but determined Athenian hoplite army, which won the day. A great empire like Persia could not allow a small, regional state like Athens challenge its authority nor humiliate the great empire with a defeat. But internal problems within the Empire put off immediate Persian action for a decade. In 480 BCE, the Persian King Xerxes invaded Greece by land and by sea. The Persian army descended the Greek mainland with Athens in its cross hairs. At a mountain pass called Thermopylae, a combined Greek force under the leadership of Sparta stood firm. After several days of fighting, only three hundred Spartan hoplites remained. The Spartan troops fought valiantly even after their Persian victory was assured. When told that Persian arrows would darken the sky in battle, one Spartan warrior supposedly responded, "That is good news for we shall fight in the shade." The legendary stand of the three hundred soldiers was a military setback for Sparta, but the story about Greek bravery echoed throughout the ages.

After the costly victory at Thermopylae, Xerxes entered Central Greece and burned down the temples and monumental buildings of Athens. Citizens fled from the city, and despite its destruction, Athenians continued the fight at sea. Led by their fast and sleek warship, the trireme, the Athenian

Image 3.10: Monument to the Battle of Thermopylae at Thermopylae, Greece. Detail of the monument depicts Leonidas and others of the 300 during the battle. © Shutterstock.com

navy lured the massive Persian fleet into the narrow bay at Salamis. Unable to maneuver, the mighty Persians fell prey to the smaller but faster Greek ships. The next year, in 479 BCE, the Greeks defeated the Persian army at Plataea, which ended further threats of invasion.

The Persian Wars had tremendous consequences for the Greeks. For the rest of the 5th century BCE, Sparta and Athens, which had distinguished themselves militarily, used their fame to command the respect and gratitude of the other Greek city-states. Success against a significant power brightened the Greek tendency to want to improve their lives and institutions. A sense of superiority permeated political, social, and cultural life, and the Greeks came to believe that they were the only people capable of achieving real freedom.

Peloponnesian Wars

The Greeks coined a term, *hubris*, which means excessive pride or self-confidence. The cooperation in defeating Persia quickly dissipated in the years after the war. What took its place was *hubris*. Beginning with the arrogance of Athens, the Greek poleis began to bicker and fall into rival camps. The alliance against Persia unraveled and resulted with a century of on again off again civil war and unrest.

In the aftermath of the war with Persia, the city-states met on the island of Delos in 478 BCE and created the Delian League. The purpose of the league was twofold. The main goal was continued

Image 3.11: Greece at the beginning of the Peloponnesian Wars. *Courtesy of the University of Texas Libraries, The University of Texas at Austin.*

cooperation to protect each other from Persian retaliation. The second goal involved helping the Ionian Greeks break away from Persian control. Over three hundred city-states joined the League. For about a decade, the League succeeded in driving the Persians out of much of Asia Minor. But, the League also became the tool by which Athens developed hegemony over much of Greece. Athens led with its navy, collected tribute from the other city-states, and devised plans of action. Eventually, the Athenians

moved the treasury from Delos to Athens. Athens used the money to finance its golden age in the 5th century BCE. Athenian arrogance led to its running roughshod over many city-states in the following decades and bred resentment among the weaker city-states.

Civil war defined Greece for much of the 5th century BCE. Conflict broke out between Corinth and Athens and ran from 460 to 444 BCE. Sparta intervened on the side of Corinth on several occasions. This was what historians call the First Peloponnesian War. Resentment between the city-states simmered for the next three decades and the Second Peloponnesian War broke out in 431 BCE. This conflict lasted twenty-seven years. Ironically, Persia intervened and gave aid to Sparta. This war devastated much of Greece. Entire citizen groups were wiped out. Sparta held the advantage on the land and Athens the sea. During these terrible years, both sides invaded each other's lands and inflicted great damage. In 429 BCE, Sparta invaded Athens. Pericles, the leader of Athens, decided to depend on the navy and ushered all Athenians inside the city's impenetrable walls. This strategy backfired as a plague hit Athens and killed many of its citizens, including Pericles. With the financing of Persia, the Spartans built a fleet of two hundred ships and defeated the Athenian navy in 405 BCE. The Spartans showed no mercy and annihilated three thousand Athenian captives. By 404 BCE, Athens sued for peace. The Spartan terms of surrender proved devastating. Athens had to pay a substantial financial tribute. The city lost almost all its fleet, and the Spartans destroyed the five miles of defensive walls that ran from the port of Piraeus to Athens. Sparta became the leading city-state, but the price of victory came at a high price. None of the city states ever attained the level of strength they held before the wars.

Image 3.12: Marble bust of Pericles (494–429 BCE). © Shutterstock.com

The Golden Age of Greece

Ironically, Greece reached its cultural and political peak in the same century it was ripped apart by civil war. During the 5th century BCE, Athens and other parts of Greece excelled in sculpture, pottery painting, drama, and architecture. Like in other aspects of life, Greek art reflected the desire to seek the potentiality of human creativity. Artists carefully observed nature and people and tried to achieve an exact knowledge of human anatomy. Then, they attempted to accurately portray the body at rest and in motion. The Greeks noticed how the muscles contracted, sometimes twisted, and then relaxed all based on action and reaction of the body. Artists succeeded in transforming marble or bronze into an accurate human likeness. Greek art was also idealistic, aspiring to a finer, more perfect representation of what was seen while depicting the essence and form of a thing as beautiful. Thus, the typical Greek statue resembled no particular individual and instead revealed a flawless human form, without wrinkles, warts, scars, or other imperfections.

Greek sculpture passed through two major phases—the Archaic Period (800–500 BCE) and the aforementioned Classical Age. During the Archaic Period, sculptors created statues that are discernible as animals or humans, but their black-like or columnar shape is not naturalistic. The most popular and recognizable statues from this period are the highly formalized, free-standing human figures. *Kouros* is the Archaic Period name for statues of young males. These sculpted works appear rigid and tense, and they are reminiscent of earlier Egyptian sculptures. Although the Egyptians did not sculpt nude male figures, the pose of a *Kouros* statue evidences Egyptian influence: stiff arms, clenched fists, forward positioning of the left leg, and an unnatural, stilted styling of the hair.

The transition from the Archaic to the Classical Age is shown in the sculpture *Kritios Boy*, which dates from the late 5th century BCE. Instead of the rigid symmetry of the *Kouros*, the *Kritios Boy* has a human like, non-symmetrical stance, and demonstrates a sense of real movement. Henceforth, subsequent sculptors felt free to create even more flexible, non-mechanical figures that are more true to life. Greek artists proclaimed the importance and creative

Image 3.13: As the Romans borrowed from the most influential culture in the Mediterranean before them, the Greeks, so too did the Greeks, borrowing artistic styles from Ancient Egypt. The *Kouros* (young male statue) and the *Kore* (young female statue) are symmetrically and stiffly proportioned, a style appropriated from the Ancient Egyptians. © Shutterstock.com

Image 3.14: Portion of the Elgin Marbles—the portion of the Parthenon frieze taken from the ruins of the Parthenon, Athens, Greece, and now displayed at the British Museum, London, United Kingdom. Statues of the Classical era sought to truly understand and convey human form and movement, just as the Greek philosophers were seeking at the same time to understand humanity. © Shutterstock.com

capacity of the individual. They exemplified the humanist spirit that characterized all aspects of Greek culture. Classical sculptures placed people in their natural environment, made the human form the focal point of attention, and exalted the nobility, dignity, self-assurance, and beauty of the human being.

The Greeks contributed a great deal to the evolution of drama. Greek dramatic plots investigated a range of issues. Tragedies typically dealt with human suffering and hard-learned wisdom that only comes from experiencing pain and loss. One of the best known of the Greek tragedies is *Oedipus the King* by Sophocles, first performed around 430 BCE. In common with almost all Greek drama, it retells a traditional story. Like other tragedies, the play's subtext is about humans trying to understand and control their lives amid potential limitations and pitfalls. With *Oedipus the King*, Sophocles' audience knew that the house of Oedipus was cursed, and his parents had been told that he would murder his father and marry his mother. The significance of the play was how Sophocles used this ancient and disturbing story to examine what it meant to be human.

Classical Age Greece also developed comedy as another innovative form of public art. Written in

Image 3.15: Gustav Moreau, *Oedipus and the Sphinx*, 1864, oil on canvas.

Source: *The Metropolitan Museum of Art, New York.*

verse and performed at religious festivals, comedies directly commented on public policy, criticized politicians and intellectuals by name, and devised plots and scenes of outrageous fantasy to make a point. For example, actors flew to the gods on a giant beetle, and dancers in the chorus dressed as talking birds or dancing clouds. Comic playwrights hoped to win critical acclaim for their work while also entertaining the audience and parodying prominent people. The humor was bawdy, and many of the themes concerned sexual escapades or bodily functions. No matter the topic, comedic plays were sprinkled with plenty of imaginative profanity. Often, plays targeted well-known male citizens who were typically mocked as cowardly or sexually effeminate. The comedy's remarkable freedom of speech promoted frank, indeed brutal, commentary on current issues and personalities.

Even during the Peloponnesian War, comedic playwrights presented works aimed at governmental policy and called for an end to the fighting. It was no accident that this energetic and critical art form emerged in Athens at the same time a radical democracy was taking shape. The principle that all voters should have a stake in determining government policies fueled a passion for using biting humor to keep the community's leaders from becoming arrogant and aloof. Athenian comedies often blamed particular political figures for government policies that had been approved by the Assembly. The most famous of the Athenian comedy playwrights was Aristophanes (446–386 BCE). He proved a master at presenting comedy as social commentary. No person, god, or institution escaped his mockery. Audiences howled at the fun, but these plays always contained a thought-provoking message. His comedy *Lysistrata* presents women acting out against a male dominated society. In the work, Athenian women commandeered government funds and engaged in a sex strike toward ending the Peloponnesian War. Teaming with the women of Sparta on the sexual relations matter, the females of each society managed to convince the male populations of Athens and Sparta to agree to a peace treaty.

Another notable cultural development during the Golden Age was to see the goal of history as the description and interpretation of the past based on a critical analysis of sources. Herodotus' (485–425 BCE) *Histories* ("inquiries") stood as a groundbreaking

work that explained the Persian Wars as a clash between East and West. Later Roman writers christened him as the "Father of History." Herodotus achieved an unprecedented originality by giving his work an investigative approach to evidence, a wide interest in human diversity, and a lively story. In several ways, Herodotus was a historian rather than a teller of tales. First, he asked questions about the past instead of merely repeating ancient legends. Thus, Herodotus tried to discover what happened and the motivations behind the actions. Second, he demonstrated, at times, a cautious and critical attitude toward his sources of information. Third, although the gods appeared in his narrative, they played a far less vital role than they did in Greek popular mythology.

Nevertheless, by retaining a belief in the significance of dreams and divine intervention, Herodotus fell short of being a rationalist. It was Thucydides (455–399 BCE) who took the work of Herodotus and made it something more unique. His brilliant *The History of the Peloponnesian War* is a very influential work of history. It provides a model for analyzing the causes of human events and the outcomes of individual decisions. In Thucydides' analysis, humans, not the gods, are entirely responsible for their triumphs and defeats. He also provides remarkable insight into how humans act. Thucydides believed humans not

Image 3.16: Statue of Herodotus, Vienna, Italy. Herodotus is often credited as the first historian because of his investigative approach toward chronicling the Persian Wars. © Shutterstock.com

only acted in predictable ways but also thought outcomes were contingent on many variables unique to any given situation. Nonetheless, he noted that similar political intrigues recurred over the years and believed that the study of history was therefore of great value for understanding the present.

The creativity and greatness of the Greeks could also be seen in their architectural and painted vase innovations. A prime architectural example was the Parthenon built on the Acropolis in Athens. Persian troops burned the original Parthenon in 479 BCE, but it was rebuilt under the guidance of Athenian statesman Pericles. Reconstruction started in 447 BCE and was completed in 438 BCE. Athens' control of the Delian League treasury gave them the means to build this amazing temple. It was constructed with plain Doric columns and housed a gold and ivory statue of the patron goddess Athena. The structure is the perfect example of harmony and symmetry, and it has set the standard for much of Western architecture to this present day. Greek vase paintings also took on the humanistic spirit. The red painted vases displayed realistic human figures ranging from representations of the gods to Olympic athletes. These vessels also ran the gamut from somber religious rituals to bawdy sexual scenes. In all of these works of art, Greek innovation and creativity stood out.

Image 3.17: Ruins of the Parthenon on the acropolis in Athens, Greece. Many sculptures from the Parthenon's facade, known as the Elgin Marbles, remain at the British Museum, while others can be viewed at the Acropolis Museum in Athens.

Source: http://www.metmuseum.org/art/collection/search/437153?sortBy=Relevance&ft=oedipus&offset=0&rpp=20&pos=1

Greek Philosophy (From Thales to Aristotle)

The Greeks did not invent philosophy, but they certainly took it further than most ancient peoples. They even coined the term that we use today. *Philos* means love and *Sophia* means wisdom. A philosopher is one who earnestly pursues wisdom. As with other ancient civilizations, traditional Greek wisdom held that the world was a product of divine forces. As such, the root causes of all things in the universe were mysteries hidden among the gods. The explanation for earthly phenomena lay, therefore, in a realm that human beings could not explore. During the 6th century BCE, some Greek thinkers from Ionia began to question if individuals could, in fact, attain a deeper understanding of reality. These Greek intellectuals believed that the rational human mind could observe the world and learn about its inner workings. They found it hard to believe that Zeus produced lightning or that Poseidon caused the storms that often sunk their ships. The Greeks called the first thinkers to seek rational alternatives to the mythic view of nature "lovers of wisdom." History ultimately called the early Greek thinkers Pre-Socratics, because they first sought sensible answers to the simplest questions; the origin of lightning, sea storms, etc. This desire to find a rational understanding of all things has driven much of Western thinking ever since.

Thales of Miletus (624–547 BCE) lived in the Asia Minor city of Miletus and is considered the first the Pre-Socratics. He is the founder of natural philosophy. Thales wanted to understand what was the basic substance of life. He promulgated the idea that everything is made of water. According to the Greek historian Herodotus, Thales predicted a solar eclipse in 585 BCE. He and other contemporaries began the process of questioning traditions and seeking answers to life's most difficult questions.

Pythagoras of Samos (570–490 BCE) lived on the island of Samos just off the Ionian coast. He is mostly known for his mathematical contributions, though much of the information recorded about him came much later. He came to believe all connections in life could be reduced to mathematical relationships. For example, he figured out how to put musical notes on a mathematical scale. Every school child knows the Pythagorean Theorem, which states that in right triangles, the square of the hypotenuse, the opposite side of the right triangle, is equal to the sum of the squares of the other two angles. Whether it is actually him, or his later followers, Pythagoras contributed to our modern understanding of math.

Xenophanes of Colophon (570–478 BCE) grew up in Asia Minor. He is most known for his views toward the gods. In a day when people saw everything as a part of a divine drama where humans interact with the gods, Xenophanes dismissed most of this speculation as sheer nonsense. He claimed that only one god existed, was nothing like frail humans, and basically could not be known in much detail by humans. For Xenophanes, humans mostly created the gods in their image. His famous quote on the subject went like this, "Mortals suppose that the gods are born and have clothes and voices and shapes like their own. But if oxen, horses, and lions had hands or could paint with their hands and fashion works as men do, horses would paint horse-like images of gods and oxen oxen-like ones, and each would fashion bodies like their own. The Ethiopians consider the gods flat-nosed and black; the Thracians blue-eyed and red-haired. There is one god, among gods and men the greatest, not at all like mortals in body or mind." For his time, Xenophanes was radical. His importance lies in the ideas that humans anthropomorphize their deities and that natural phenomenon is just that, natural. Thus, nature can be studied and quantified.

The Pre-Socratic thinkers influenced a group of professional philosopher-teachers called Sophists. They took their name from the Greek word for wise (*Sophia*). An intellectual named Protagoras stood out as one of the greatest Sophists. He is famous for having declared, "Man is the measure of all things, of what is and of what is not." Sophist philosophers could create standards of behavior that were always true for every individual. This was especially true, the sophists said, about the principles of right and wrong behavior. Such doctrines do not exist eternally, nor are they creations of the gods. Rather, human beings produce standards of right and wrong. Moreover, disparate nations held conflicting notions about how individuals should and should not act, so how could one ever arrive at what was always "right?" Sophists believed the query had no answer because the question was based on a faulty assumption that there is one uniform set of human

ethics. In other words, there were no truths except those people chose to see as valid.

Therefore, wisdom, for the sophists, could not be a matter of knowing some fundamental reality or unity. What was left? For the sophists, wisdom meant understanding how to persuade others to accept a reality that one believed in as valid without concern for the "truth" or "falsity" of one way of viewing the world. Aristotle, one of their better critics, observed that the sophists taught how to make "the word argument seem the better." Sophists, then, taught the art of persuasive speech. This technique was known as rhetoric and it had as much staying power as philosophy or most other disciplines. In their prime, the sophists were important because they had the power and ability to persuade people to one side or another. The sophists were certainly popular in Athens, but their relativist perspectives drew opposition from some who sought a revival of absolutist standards of right and wrong. In time, a new group of Athenian thinkers set a different standard for considering ethics and human action.

Socrates (469–399 BCE) argued against the relativism of the Sophists. While walking through the streets and main gathering areas of Athens, Socrates constantly asked questions of his fellow citizens. Through questioning, he hoped that others would engage him in conversation and ultimately learn. This called the Socratic Method. Athenians struggled with self-doubt after a long, protracted war against

Image 3.18: Jacques-Louis David, *The Death of Socrates*, 1787, oil on canvas.

Source: *The Metropolitan Museum of Art, New York*.

Sparta. When Athens flourished, the people congratulated themselves, but when it blundered, they looked for someone to blame. Socrates was an easy target. He did not view Athenian institutions like democratic government as anything sacred and delighted in attacking commonly held opinions of the people. Athenians indicted, tried, and convicted Socrates on a charge of corrupting the youth of Athens by inciting them to question their faith in the gods and the wisdom of their elders. In Athens, the condemned were allowed to suggest an alternative punishment. Socrates sarcastically replied he should be given an award for bringing enlightenment to the city. Unamused, the jury ordered him to death by drinking a deadly poison called hemlock that causes gradual paralysis of the central nervous system. His friends suggested a plot to get him out of town, but Socrates refused. He said he was a citizen of Athens and would abide by its laws, even a law that condemned him to death. He drank the hemlock and died in 399 BCE.

Socrates' pupil Plato (427–347 BCE) explored new philosophical directions. Returning to the controversies of earlier Greek thinkers about the nature of the universe, Plato asserted the unity of things. This position is evident in Plato's theory of the "forms," also sometimes called "ideas." Consider, for example, trees. One can see short or tall trees; they appear as oaks, maples, and endless other varieties. Yet they are all trees. Why? Because, according to Plato, they all reflect a single "form": the essence of what it means to be a tree. The form of a tree makes it

Image 3.19: Statue of Plato, Academy of Athens, Athens, Greece. © Shutterstock.com

a thing unlike any other object. In addition, Plato believed the forms are perfect. Trees can be cut down, deformed, and burned. However, the form of a tree is not physical, and so it is invulnerable. The senses can detect physical matter but cannot be relied on to know the forms.

Only the mind, relying on reason, can get beyond the senses to perceive the forms, and therefore reality itself. Plato's forms were not only exercises of the mind and but also had a practical application. Plato experienced the ruinous Peloponnesian War and witnessed Socrates' trial and execution. This decision was carried out by the democratic government of Athens, and it was clearly an unjust act. A just state, in his view, had to conform to universally valid principles and aim at the moral improvement of its citizens. Plato believed that it was foolish to expect the common man to think intelligently about foreign policy, economics, or other vital matters of state. Yet, the common man was permitted to speak in the Assembly and to vote, and he could also be selected to an executive office. These elected leaders were chosen and followed for non-essential reasons, such as persuasive speech, good looks, wealth, and family background. Plato's vision for how the state should be properly organized is outlined in his work *The Republic*. Plato thought that a correct and just state could be realized only when all social classes worked together for the good of the whole, where each class performed its assigned tasks. Due to the importance of the mind in grasping reality, social status should be determined by the ability to reason and not by wealth or inheritance. Plato's ideal state would be run by a small elite group of philosopher-kings and queens who understood the forms and were most qualified to lead the government.

Plato's student Aristotle (384–322 BCE) believed in universal principles or forms, but he believed that Plato had been unclear about the relationships between the forms and physical objects. Plato might say that a physical tree "reflects" or "participates in" the form of a tree, but what exactly, asked Aristotle, does that mean? How can one say that a form produces a physical instance of that form, or that the form of a tree produces a physical tree? Aristotle asserted that Plato had no good answer to these questions, and went on to produce a different account of forms. Aristotle believed that forms do not exist without the matter, the stuff, in which they appear in individual instances. Moreover so, the form of a tree

Image 3.20: Statue of Aristotle, Stageira, Greece. © Shutterstock.com

does not exist unless there is a physical tree. Forms are not independent of the material world, and so the material world is as important to existence as forms or essences. Therefore, the forms are not the source of reality. Moreover, because existence is based on the physical manifestation—there are only trees, not some pre-existing form of tree—the senses are the key to discovering the knowledge the real world. Form and matter were inseparable. By examining individual objects, we can perceive their essence and arrive at universal principles, but they do not exist in a separate plane of reality beyond the material. Rather, forms are a part of the thing, itself.

In his influential treatise *Nicomachean Ethics*, Aristotle theorized that humans needed to apply their knowledge relevantly to life, and govern their behavior by reason, not on whim, tradition, or authority. In most activities, each person should find, through trial and self-criticism, the desired mean between extremes. This has come to be called the Golden Mean—the best performance of mind and body working together in harmony. This, according to Aristotle, is both virtuous and how humans are designed to live. Aristotle believed that communities, too, had a purpose. Their function was to create the conditions in which virtue would flourish, but there was no single way of reaching this goal. In his classic work *Politics*, Aristotle examined existing city-states, and in doing so, evaluated the major types of political organizations. He considered any government, whether a democracy or not, legitimate that was devoted to the general welfare of the people. Aristotle believed that any type of government goes astray when the rulers pursue their own interest alone.

Where would we be without the Greeks? We value forms of democratic government, invented by the Greeks, where the common man has a voice. We appreciate the contributions of science, and the Greeks paved the way through philosophical inquiry. To this day, militaries around the world appreciate and emulate the standards set by Spartan warriors. You are reading this history book, and the Greeks gave us the first standards for critically understanding the past. When one travels to Athens, one sees the ruins of great architecture like the Parthenon, and yet the Greeks still inform and shape our present. What a debt we owe to the Greeks!

Chapter 4

Hellenistic Greece and the Roman Republic

The Rise of Hellenistic Greece

If a major Greek gift to Western civilization was democracy, Rome's was a republic. Both systems include citizens who participate in the political process, but while majority rules in a pure democracy, a republic places limits on government by law, which has important implications for those in the minority. However, before examining the World of Rome, it is important to understand the world that the Romans would later absorb and essentially claim as their own. That world was one that resembled that of the Greeks but had undergone considerable changes.

Macedonia sat along the mountainous northern reaches of Greek civilization. While technically Greeks, the Macedonians had not achieved some of the cornerstones of classical Greek civilization and were typically looked down on. Another likely reason for this attitude was that tribal kings ruled the Macedonians, while most of the Greek city-states had embraced some form of democratic government. The Macedonians though admired the Greeks and longed to build an alliance with them.

In 359 BCE, Macedonia came under the rule of King Philip II. He was a ruler of broad vision and was determined to gain control of the Greek city-states. In addition, he envisioned that the Greeks could come together as one to face their rivals. Not all Greeks embraced Philip as offering the only real hope of ending the Greek civil wars. One such individual was Demosthenes, a great Athenian orator, and champion of democracy. He warned in vain that "democracies and dictators cannot exist together." He too encouraged the Athenians and other Greeks to stop Philip before it was too late. Ultimately, Athens and Thebes did act to stop Philip's advance, but their combined forces were shattered at Chaeronea in 338 BCE. At Philip's urging, the Greeks formed a military alliance where each city, while retaining self-government, pledged to "make war upon him who violates the general peace," and to furnish Philip with men and supplies to invade Persia. Most Greeks looked forward to punishing Persia for their destruction of Greek temples and other public buildings and spaces. However, before Philip could set out on his revenge campaign, he was assassinated, possibly by someone who held a personal grudge. The ensuing war against the Eastern power would be taken over by his gifted twenty-year-old son Alexander.

Alexander the Great: Conqueror of Lands and Cultural Innovator

Alexander was one of history's most remarkable individuals. Of average height and looks for a Macedonians, he nevertheless impressed his contemporaries as a fit athlete, a charismatic personality, and a natural born leader. Both his father, Philip, and his mother, Olympias, were strong influences in his life. He garnered his military prowess from his father, and from Olympias a sense of destiny as she constantly assured her son that his true father was not Philip but Zeus.

Image 4.1: Map of the Empire of Alexander the Great. © Shutterstock.com

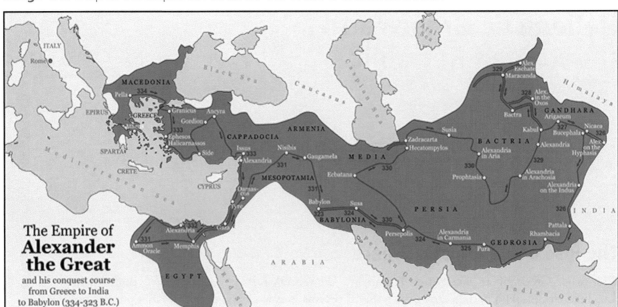

Having been tutored by Aristotle, Alexander was aware of the rich history and accomplishments of the Greeks, and he clearly wanted to succeed as a type of Greek hero. Reveling in the heroic deeds of the Iliad, which he always kept at his bedside, Alexander was the new Achilles, striking out against barbarians that readers of Homer's famous work would most appreciate. In 334 BCE, Alexander invaded the Persian Empire with approximately thirty-five thousand Macedonian and Greek soldiers. Almost immediately, he conquered Asia Minor, Syria, and Palestine, defeating the Persians in two great battles. He marched into Egypt, where the Egyptians welcomed him as a deliverer from their Persian master and recognized him as pharaoh, the living god-king of Egypt.

Greatly impressed with Egypt and its tradition, Alexander wished to spend more time in the ancient land. But Persian King Darius III was gathering one more great army to oppose the invasion, and Alexander marched into Mesopotamia to meet him. In 331 BCE, at Gaugamela, near the ancient city of Nineveh, the Macedonians defeated the Persians. Darius was executed by his relatives as he fled, and Alexander became the Great King of the Persian Empire. He next led his army north through Media, then south and east into present day Afghanistan, finally venturing as far east as the rich river valleys of India. There his weary and frightened soldiers, many of whom had been away from home for more than ten years, forced him to turn back.

In 323 BCE, Alexander fell ill with a mysterious fever. He may have contracted malaria in India; it is also possible that he fell victim to his accumulated battle wounds; it is even believed that years of heavy drinking had taken its toll. Whatever the case, after a short illness, and without designating an heir to his empire, Alexander died at the age of thirty-two years in the famous city of Babylon.

It seems that Alexander wanted to unify the lands he conquered. In fact, he referred to his endeavor as bringing, "concord and partnership in the empire." He included Persians with Greco-Macedonian army and administration; Alexander founded approximately seventy cities throughout the Near and Middle East, and many of his followers settled there. In addition, he encouraged his troops to take foreign wives.

The conquered territories acquired a unique cosmopolitan persona. Historians call this cultural period the Hellenistic ("Greek-like") Age. For several decades following Alexander's death, his generals rivaled each other for the spoils of empire. Eventually, three major kingdoms arose, and they maintained a restless balance of power until Rome subdued them in the 2nd and 1st centuries BCE. Egypt came to be ruled by Ptolemy, a general and friend of Alexander. Asia, which included most of the areas of the old Persian Empire, was ruled by Seleucus, another one of Alexander's generals. Lastly, Macedonia and Greece were ruled by the descendants of Antigonus the One-Eyed.

In addition to changing politically, the Hellenistic Age was a time of great changes. In the wake of Alexander's conquests, thousands of Greeks began to colonize the Near and Middle East. As a result, these areas' economies boomed. The sudden expansion was also stimulated by Alexander's introduction of large amounts of Persian gold and silver, which permitted a uniform coinage. A larger and more affluent middle class developed and this boded well for urban areas. The condition of the poor, however, was made worse by rising prices.

Of all the new cities, Alexandria, Egypt outdistanced them all as a commercial and culture center. Trade routes linked Arabia, East Africa, and Central Asia, bringing great wealth to the cities of Alexandria, Antioch, Pergamon, and Rhoades. Alexandria, which replaced Athens as a cultural center, boasted a population of more than one million people. It became home to the world's most impressive library that was part of a cultural complex known as the Temple of the Muses (for "Museum"). The nine Muses (goddesses) were thought to inspire the various academic disciplines then recognized. It was built to gather together all the world's knowledge. In addition to housing written works, it also served as a research institution where scholars made significant academic and intellectual advances from developing what today we call the scientific method (making observations, collecting data, forming hypotheses, and testing them) to analyzing and critiquing ancient texts. Unfortunately, the library was destroyed. The details of its destruction are conflicting, but the weight of evidence suggests that it did not succumb to one event. Instead, the structure suffered several crises from the civil wars surrounding Julius Caesar to those that would later trouble the Roman Empire.

Alexander's death spurred upheaval in his kingdom and indirectly led to the dispersal of Greek people and culture. Even before the Greek city-states of Athens and Sparta emerged as significant urban centers, Greeks had emigrated westward across the Mediterranean. Now, summoned by Alexander's successors who needed them as soldiers, officials, and traders, they migrated eastward as well. By 200 BCE, Hellenic culture touched many areas between Western Europe and Central Asia. Greek became the international language of business and government, and ambitious people of all ethnicities learned it to get ahead in those fields. Ancient and local traditions, however, continued to flourish. In Egypt, for example, temples were built and decorated. Conquest by the Greeks thus did not mean people were forced to abandon the gods who had, in some case, been worshiped for thousands of years.

Hellenistic Cultural Contributions

Developments in philosophical thought reflected the changed conditions of the Hellenistic Age. With the growing loss of political freedom as monarchs took control, philosophers turned away from creating the perfect society, as was the case with Plato and Aristotle, to only searching for individual contentment. Thus, four schools of philosophy emerged. Of the four, Cynicism had the least impact on Hellenistic civilization. The Cynics, believing that society diverted the individual from the more vital goals of personal independence and freedom, denounced all religions and governments. They shunned physical comfort and advocated the avoidance of personal pleasure. To prepare themselves for life's misfortunes, they exercised rigorously, walked around shoeless, and wore dirty and ragged clothes. One famous Cynic, Diogenes once stated, "Look at me, I am without a home, a city, property, a slave; I sleep on the ground. I have neither wife nor children, no miserable governor's mansion, but only earth and sky and one rough cloak. Yet what do I lack? Am I not free from pain and fear, am I not free?" The basic point of the Cynics was to see that true freedom arises from realizing that if one wants nothing, then one will never lack

Image 4.2: Turan Baş, *Statue of Diogenes*, 2006, marble, Sinop, Turkey. © Shutterstock.com

anything. Total self-sufficiency is the goal. Their program, however, was too austere to attract a large following.

The advocates of Skepticism argued that nothing could be known for certain. This view stemmed from questioning the value that the senses played in attaining absolute knowledge. Thinking that everything was relative, the Skeptics maintained that all ideas must be examined and that no single philosophy or religion was correct. Inquiring into the origin of things and clever reasoning would not clarify truth or happiness so, they argued, why should one bother with it? Some of the more sophisticated Skeptics did not simply turn away from reason and reflection; they instead insisted that all ideas should not be treated as absolutes. Reflecting on nature might cause one to embrace the view that the world was orderly, but that does not mean a divine being created it. Since one could not be sure of absolute moral principles, it was better to live one's life by practical experience.

Epicureanism and Stoicism were more practical and popular philosophies. The Athenian Epicurus (342–270 BCE) taught that a person who could avoid disturbances was free, and since fear and desire are the principal sources of trouble, they need to be eliminated. Neither the fear of death, the gods, or pain nor the desire for unnecessary things should concern us.

The object of life accordingly was pleasure. But for the Epicureans, happiness was more about avoiding pain than pursuing self-indulgence. In total, moderation was the best policy.

Zeno (333–262 BCE), from the island of Cyprus, founded the most influential philosophical school of the Hellenistic Age. Late in the 4th century BCE, he opened his school in a building known as the Painted Stoa. From this gathering place, his philosophy was called Stoicism. Zeno's position was simple: one needed to follow natural law to experience true happiness regardless of circumstance. The good Stoic was to accept everything that happened without rebellion or complaint, and in turn, they maintained inner calm and tranquility.

While traditional Greek religious practices overall focused on the success of the city and its inhabitants, Hellenistic religion was more experiential and nuanced. Ancient bonds and loyalties that connected people with their traditional city-states faded, and in turn, a more individualized approach to religion developed. This found expression in a variety of religious and ethical ideas that stressed personal fulfillment or personal salvation rather than community success. As the Greeks retreated physically and spiritually away from their traditional cities, they ventured more into themselves. More Greeks tended to turn away from the old Olympic gods to seek solace and meaning in more personal religious experiences.

The Hellenistic world was soon awash in mystery and salvation religions. They tended to center on the death and resurrection of a god who promised a better life on Earth and eternal salvation later. From Egypt came the cult of Isis who was seen by many as the mother of salvation since she was responsible for bringing her husband Osiris back to life. The same fate awaited those who embraced her as their deliverer. From Persia, and somewhat later, came the worship of Mithras, a variant of Zoroastrianism that incorporated the latter's vision of a cosmic struggle between good and evil with a savior-hero who redeemed his male worshippers. The Mithras faith would later become popular with Roman legionnaires.

The scientific contributions during the Hellenistic Age was significant. By 300 BCE, the mathematician Euclid summed up the two preceding centuries of Greek geometry by organizing it all into a systematic series of axioms and proofs that are still taught today. The wide-ranging military campaigns of Alexander and the subsequent cultural interchange among

Image 4.3: Marble head of Epikouros (Epicurus), 2nd century CE.

Source: *The Metropolitan Museum of Art, New York.*

Image 4.4: Bronze plaque of Mithras slaying the bull, c. mid-2nd—early 3rd century, bronze. The Roman cult of Mithras was predominantly followed by the Roman army, and was appropriated into the Roman pantheon via trade and control throughout the growing Roman Empire in the wake of the *pax Romana*, the Roman Peace.

Source: *The Metropolitan Museum of Art, New York.*

Image 4.5: Bronze statuette of Aphrodite, c. 150–100 BCE. Aphrodite of Knidos by Praxiteles was considered one of the most famous statues of the Ancient Greek and Roman world. Because of its popularity, many copies or variants were made by artists, such as this one.

Source: *The Metropolitan Museum of Art, New York.*

many areas of the ancient world led to vast increases in Greek geographical knowledge. Eratosthenes, the head of the Alexandrian library in the later 3rd century BCE, produced the most accurate and thorough world maps to date, complete with lines of longitude and latitude and climatic zones. Recognizing that the Earth was a sphere, he calculated its circumference with considerable accuracy. The greatest scientist and engineer of the ancient world, Archimedes of Syracuse, made original contributions in both pure and applied mathematics. He developed the science of hydrostatics, experimented successfully with levers and pulleys to lift tremendous weights, invented a system for expressing large numbers, and came very close to discovering integral calculus.

Hellenistic art, like Hellenistic philosophy and religion, became more individualized and focused on the human world of experience. Nowhere is this new humanizing spirit plainer than in the statue of *Aphrodite of Knidos* by Praxiteles, a well-known artist of the 4th century BCE. In his works, gods and goddesses lost some of their esteemed grandeur as and featured

sharper human characteristics. Praxiteles took the unprecedented step of representing the goddess of love completely nude. Female nudity was rare in earlier Greek art and had been confined almost exclusively to vase paintings. Certainly, no one had dared fashion for a temple a statue of a goddess without her clothes. Although shocking in its day, the *Aphrodite of Knidos* is not openly erotic, but remains sensual nonetheless.

Although Hellenistic sculptors tackled an expanded range of subjects, they did not abandon traditional themes like the Greek athlete. However, they often rendered the old subjects in new ways. This is certainly true of the magnificent bronze statue of a seated boxer, a Hellenistic original discovered in Rome. The boxer is no longer the victorious young athlete with a perfect face and body, but a heavily beaten, defeated veteran. He seems to gaze upward to the man who put him down, with his face distorted by his opponent's repeated blows.

Realism is revealed in statues of old men and women who came from the lowest levels of society. Shepherds, fishermen, and drunken beggars are common. A good example of this style presents an old woman bringing her wares to market. She clearly shows the marks of old age: wrinkled face, bent over body, all showing signs of a hard life. However, she seems to carry on, maybe because she had no other choice. No one knows the purpose of such statues, but they attest to an interest in a kind of realism that earlier artists had little interest.

The Rise of the Roman Republic

From about 200 BCE onward, the Greeks began to lose their position as rulers of the known world. First to fall were the lands stretching eastward from Mesopotamia to the borders of India. These areas were taken over by invaders from the steppes, most notably the Parthians, who formed a formidable empire in what is the present day nation of Iran. Unsuccessful Egyptian rebellions and a successful Jewish one further weakened Greek rule. The Romans gradually gained control of Greece, Anatolia, and other Eastern Mediterranean territories, and in 30 BCE they conquered Egypt. Even so, Hellenistic culture lived on under Roman rule. In fact, Greek advances in philosophy, science, literature, and art found fertile ground among the Romans. While Rome embraced a republican form of government for roughly its first five hundred years, the Hellenistic belief in divinely-sanctioned dictatorial rulers did not die. Within the Roman Empire, the eastern Mediterranean remained a distinct region dominated by Greek civilization. When that empire finally divided, its eastern half continued for several centuries until the Muslim conquest. Even then, the empire of Byzantium, acquired by Arab conquerors and ultimately taken over by Christian Europe, continued the Greek legacy.

The Romans sought to create a distinct legacy. Around 25 BCE, the historian Livy authored an extensive treatise on the Roman Empire called *History of Rome*. In the work, he created a narrative about how Romans developed their place as the world's superior kingdom. Livy theorized that the extraordinary integrity of its people played a chief role in attaining this position. Indeed, the Romans demonstrated many outstanding qualities as an industrious and innovative people. However, Rome did not come to prominence overnight. It was only after several centuries of forward thinking leadership, and perseverance that the Romans took their place as one of the world's greatest civilizations. Over time, Rome evolved from a monarchy to a republican style of government. Because of this development, various levels of social classes

achieved greater levels of political and economic influence. Military success strengthened the Roman Republic but at the same time planted the seeds for potential problems. Indeed, Rome's military campaigns brought not only tremendous glory but also precipitated internal violence and political intrigue. Eventually, the republican form of government degenerated into bloody power struggles, and chaos came to define the political process.

The glory that was Rome began as a collection of migrating tribes. They arrived in a Mediterranean land with good resources that enabled them to support a big population, and in time, larger armies. In addition to the good farmland, easy access to the Mediterranean made sea travel trade attractive pursuits. The Indo-European settlers formed various tribal groups including the Latin people of central Italy. Some settled near the mouth of the Tiber River, choosing to build a cluster of dwellings on low-lying hills along the water. These settlements became known as the "Seven Hills of Rome." Around 750 BCE, these communities joined to form a single city-state: Rome.

The Romans borrowed directly from the Greeks and any other peoples who had something to offer them. Beginning around the 8th century BCE, the Greeks established settlements in various areas of Southern Italy. These villages spread northward up the coast and close to the borders of Latium. In the early days, kings ruled the Romans. A council of elders, called the Senate, advised the king, and he appointed their members. Usually, a king chose from among the patricians (aristocrats). However, the Latin people, through their neighbors, learned the Greek alphabet and gained knowledge of the life in its city-states. In part because of this, the Romans resisted their controlling government and overthrew the monarchy around 500 BCE. With this event, Rome became a republic.

Even after the Romans secured a republican form of government, plebeians (commoners) struggled for social and political equality with patricians. The patricians belonged to old, influential families, and many of them could trace their lineage to Rome's initial founding. It is easy to guess that tension would arise between those who claimed superiority due to their birth and those who hoped to climb the social ladder. Plebeians were everyone who did not belong to patrician families: including workers, merchants, and small farmers. Even wealthy people, without long-standing connections to the origins of Rome, could be plebeians.

Image 4.6: Map of the Seven Hills of Rome and the Servian Wall that surrounded the hills. The seven hills were the Quirinal Hill, Viminal Hill, Esquiline Hill, Capitoline Hill, Palatine Hill, Caelian Hill, and the Aventine Hill.

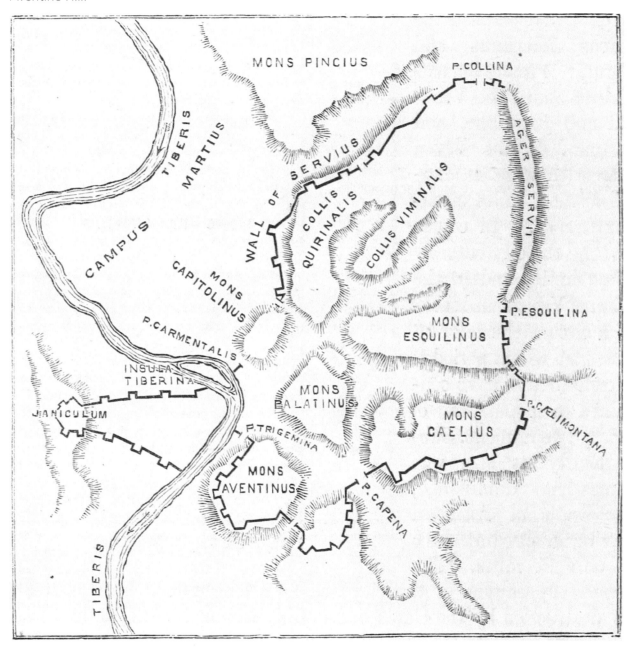

Source: Library of Congress.

Ultimately, a system of government developed that was neither a Greek-style democracy nor an oligarchy. Instead, Roman governance became a mix of authoritarian and democratic systems. In the early days of the Roman monarchy, it also had a Senate comprising about three hundred powerful patricians. While the king ran the state, the Senate was there to ensure other voices carried weight. When the monarchy was abolished, Rome kept the senatorial arm of its initial government. The Senate ruled over the practical concerns of the average Roman. It also offered advice to assemblies of the people who passed the laws of the state. In addition, the Senate was responsible for the state's foreign policy and played the most important role in deciding to go to war.

Two consuls headed the chief executive offices of the Roman Republic. Chosen annually from the Senate, one executed laws at home while the other consul commanded the army. Each could veto the decisions of the other, as Romans feared that any one person should gain too much power. In fact, all government magistrates, the name for Roman elected officials, served one-year terms. In the year 366 BCE, the Romans created the office of praetor. The praetor typically carried out the administrative functions of government when the consuls were away from the city, and in unusual circumstances, could lead the army. The expansion of Rome created all manner of new disputes, and thus, there became a need for a larger number of judges. As such, Rome implemented a new plan to dispense justice throughout the provinces. Former consuls or praetors received new titles and authority to govern in the newly acquired lands. As seen here, the ability to come up with a practical solution to an immediate problem was one of the defining characteristics of the Roman Republic. It was reasonable to assume that officials with governing experience would make good administrators. However, the ideal did not always meet the reality as corruption and scandals plagued some provincial governments.

One of the most pressing problems, Rome faced in its early days was the division between plebeians and patricians. Initially, plebeians deferred to the patricians, but as Rome grew and the plebeians expanded in numbers and wealth, they began to resent their second-class status. Rome relied on its citizens to fight as soldiers. The plebeians were far more numerous than the patricians, and the state would be unable to prosecute wars without them. As such, plebeians used their significant population advantage and the need for them to take part in military service to gain political concessions from the patricians.

The plebeians complained most bitterly about their lack of legal protection. Before the 5th century BCE, there was no written code of laws in Rome. Instead, patrician judges acted on an oral legal tradition that was subject to change and open to interpretation. Around 450 BCE, in response to plebeian demands, the laws of Rome were codified in writing. Reportedly, the new code was engraved on twelve slabs of bronze and mounted in the chief public square (the Forum) for all to see. These *Twelve Tables* served as the foundation for the elaborate system of Roman law that evolved in later centuries. No longer could patricians manipulate the law in their favor. In addition, plebeians attained the right to organize their own policy-making assemblies.

Within these bodies, plebeians formulated and passed laws with the advice and consent of the Roman Senate. Moreover, plebeians gained the right to elect their own leaders called tribunes. The tribunes could veto legislative efforts they viewed as harmful or regressive to plebeian rights. The struggles and compromises between patricians and plebeians produced a system of government that was complicated in its design and operation. Roman government was certainly flawed, but it also was likely the most forward-thinking and just system of its time. It was Rome that gave Western nations the inspiration to create progressive governments. The idea has been to invest authority in multiple branches of government so that one does not assume too much power. Although the Roman government was often less than this in practice, in theory its reach extended far beyond the ancient world.

The unique peculiarities of the Roman government fostered a climate where patricians and plebeians tended to work together. Both groups profited through the patron-client system. Plebeians could be elected to magistrate offices, but patricians occupied the most important positions. In addition, public elections via the assemblies determined most of these roles. Winning an election, as is the case today, required a candidate to receive more votes than his competitor. Candidates then, as now, spent large sums of money trying to win votes. Patrician patrons running for office typically held important positions within Roman society. They might be a lawyer, a great landowner, a former military general, or a combination of these things. Clients were plebeians who looked to patrons to provide them with assistance. For example, plebeians charged with a crime needed legal representation from someone of the upper class. Or, another might be in economic straits and need a loan to satisfy his financial obligations. It seemed the needs of each class were both served in this type of environment. Ultimately, the patron-client system involved a mutually beneficial relationship. The patron needed political support in the form of votes.

Clients needed assistance in the form of money, goods, or a professional service. This exchange made the alliance a viable one for both entities.

Religious beliefs were important and served to strengthen the common values of most Romans. By the birth of the Roman Republic, individuals had developed a special relationship with three deities. Their joint temple stood on the city's fortified citadel Capitoline Hill. The first deity was the sky god Jupiter, whom the Romans believed was the same as the god the Greeks referred to as Zeus. The second deity was Jupiter's consort, the fertility goddess Juno (Hera in the Greek tradition). Finally, the third one was the goddess of skill and wisdom Minerva (Athena in the Greek tradition).

Responsibility for maintaining Rome's good relationship with these and many other deities belonged to the pontiffs. They were a group of priests headed by the supreme pontiff (Pontifex Maximus), who were also leading magistrates. The Romans believed that their success depended on respecting their deities and offering appropriate sacrifices to them. A sacrifice could consist of a single drop of wine, a piece of cake, or an animal, but whatever the case, the Romans believed that proper observation of religious rituals ensured prosperity. In this way, Roman appreciation of their gods made them like the Mesopotamians, Egyptians, Hebrews, and Greeks.

In the Roman tradition, the concept of good citizenship began at home. Instead of devoting his life directly to the city-state, a Roman man belonged first to a family and a clan (a group of families descended from a real or mythical ancestor). Men who had the status of paterfamilias (head of the family), wielded unlimited power over everyone in his household. In addition, this authority even included sons and daughters who left his household upon marriage. Furthermore, a head of the family's wife might not be completely subject to him if she was considered still beholden to the will of her father. The dominion of fatherly figures helped create a masculine culture that limited the activity of women.

The Romans were, above all, a military people. Their first wars were against neighboring tribes and barbarian invaders. As they secured their position at home, Romans began to expand outward, fighting territorial wars. While Rome successfully engaged many peoples, they were shrewdly generous toward the enemy. Often, defeated peoples became allies, and they kept their local laws and traditions. In fact,

Roman colonists enjoyed rights of citizenship that were almost equal to those citizens who lived in Rome itself. In time, the allies requested and were denied full Roman citizenship, and early in the 1st century BCE, some of them took up arms. Following these Social Wars (Wars of the Allies) most non-Romans in Italy gained Roman citizenship, and the status of an ally, separate from the Romans, disappeared. Simply stated, Rome put into practice effective strategies to expand and sustain an empire.

The Challenges of War and Politics

Founded about 700 BCE by Phoenician colonists, Carthage was an oligarchic and empire-building nation like Rome, and its influence spread across North Africa, Sardinia, Corsica, and Sicily. In their initial clash, Carthage and Rome fought over the island of Sicily. The Greek city-states had for centuries struggled with Carthage for control of the Mediterranean island, and the Romans inherited the fight when they assumed responsibility for protecting their Hellenistic allies. Ultimately, however, at stake was the command of the whole Western Mediterranean.

The Punic Wars were the conflicts pitting Rome versus Carthage on both land and sea. The two powers waged war in three vicious rounds between 264 and 146 BCE. In the first phase of the struggle, Rome forced Carthage out of Sicily, but the North African city kept the rest of its empire. In the second occurrence, the brilliant Carthaginian military commander Hannibal invaded Italy and defeated several Roman armies. However, he did not capture to city of Rome. As such, the Romans survived to fight another day.

Rome invaded Africa in 203 BCE, and Hannibal felt compelled to return to Carthage to defend his capital city. One year later, the two great Mediterranean powers fought at Zama, not far from Carthage itself. In the end, Rome defeated Carthage. Eventually, fearing a Carthaginian revival, Rome provoked a third war. In 146 BCE, Rome forced another Carthage surrender. This was a war of annihilation in which Rome either killed or captured the Carthaginians. Rome wanted to exterminate their rival and prevent any future wars with them. Due to the unlimited plundering of the conquered land, Rome increased its collective wealth. In a final act of vengeance, the Senate ordered Carthage leveled, its people sold into slavery, and even the ground on which it had stood to be forever cursed. The

Image 4.7: Rome and Carthage at the Beginning of the Second Punic War, 218 BCE. *Courtesy of the University of Texas Libraries, The University of Texas at Austin.*

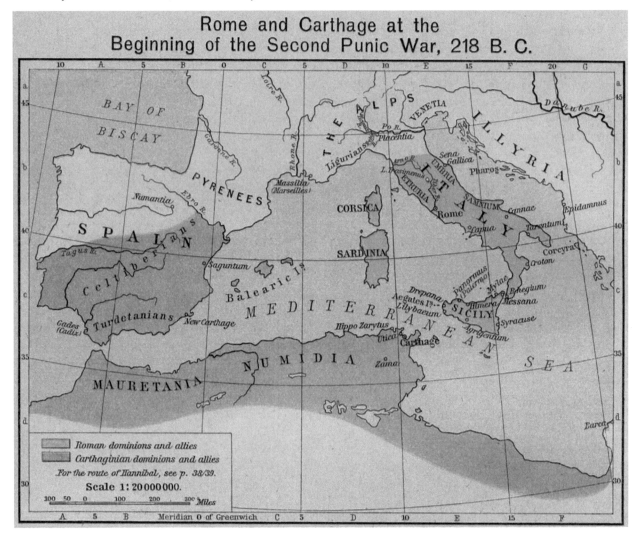

Punic War trilogy occurred during a spectacular period of Roman expansion. In the previous two hundred fifty years, from 500 BCE to the outbreak of the Punic Wars, Rome had unified most of Italy. In the next two hundred fifty years, they would spread their rule from the eastern Mediterranean to the British Isles.

Already by the end of the Punic Wars, Rome ruled an empire far larger than that of any earlier city-state. The Senate, the people's assemblies, and the magistrates they chose now wielded unchecked power over millions of people. Roman law protected many of the provincials, but they typically had no voting rights. Furthermore, war and conquest had disrupted the traditional social order in Italy, the heartland of the newly arisen empire. The political leaders and ordinary voters in Rome used acquired power to

advance their own self-interests. As a result, Rome's city-state government system gradually broke down, and a state in which an emperor would exercise absolute power lay in the future.

Roman imperial expansion shaped life on the home front. In former days, the farmer-soldier had been the backbone of the state. The social and economic revolution, however, that followed the Punic Wars changed things. The Punic Wars and the endless conquests increased the burden of military service on the Roman farmer-soldiers. Drafted soldiers served for several years at a time. Many never returned home. Those who did come back often found their farms spoiled by neglect. Some farmers remained stubbornly on their land, but most gave up, sank to the status of proletarians (the lowest class of Roman

Image 4.8: Henri Motte, *Hannibal's army crossing the Rhone*, 1878, engraving.

Source: Library of Congress.

citizens) and drifted into the cities. These people received free food and public entertainment at the expense of prominent citizens who thereby won prestige and power. Meanwhile, a new group of war profiteers rose to prominence in Italy. These individuals became contractors to the armed forces and dealers in loot and slaves. They purchased ruined farms, restocked them, and turned these estates into agricultural factories of enormous profit and human exploitation. Where former independent farmers had raised grain, these new holdings were turned into large estates for use as vineyards, olive groves, or pasture lands for livestock. The new owners, who were somewhat resembling Roman entrepreneurs, had little interest in compensating displaced farmers either as tenants or as hired hands. Instead, they used gangs of slaves captured during wars. In the cities, slaves worked in the households of the rich and powerful as secretaries, tutors, domestic servants, and workers in every kind of business. Others even worked as prostitutes. Owners lawfully could take all a slave's earnings but often allowed him or her to keep a portion of the wages. By this means, some slaves saved enough money to purchase their freedom, and sometimes, Roman citizenship. Either during their lifetimes or in

their wills, owners often freed valued slaves as a reward for loyal service. Once freed, they were expected to continue in the service of the former owners or their families. However, ex-slaves sometimes succeeded in business and became founders of wealthy families.

Political leader Tiberius Gracchus hoped to make society more just and fair for all, and he was punished for his efforts. Caught up in the scramble for the spoils of empire, the wealthy aristocrats in the Senate had little interest in finding ways to solve the Roman Republic's problems. On the contrary, toward the end of the 2nd century BCE, the Senate put a violent end to the Roman Republic's most determined reform effort. Tiberius, the son of a prominent Roman family, initiated a partial solution to Rome's troubles. His plan was to resettle many of the city's poor and discharged army veterans on small farms. Tiberius also sought to create programs to offer food to citizens who chose to stay in Rome. The intention was to help the poor and give them a chance to create independent, sustainable farms.

Unable to win Senate support for these measures, Tiberius proposed them directly to the plebeian assembly. In 133 BCE, Tiberius was elected tribune of the people and initiated the reform effort. Tradition, however, limited his term as tribune to one year, so he was not given sufficient time to carry through the long-range program. Moreover, the Senate attacked him as a dangerous troublemaker. Tiberius decided to stand for re-election as a tribune. His opponents used this as an excuse to instigate and condone Tiberius' murder, along with the killing of hundreds of his supporters. These enemies publicly beat Tiberius and around three hundred of his allies to death with clubs and stones. Their bodies were thrown into the Tiber River. By doing this, the opposition mob denied Tiberius and his followers appropriate burials. As such, scholars have cited the tragic incident as an important negative turning point in Roman political discourse.

During the Republic, the composition of Roman armies and the character of its leaders began to change. This new type of soldier proved just as courageous and tough as the old one, and throughout the 1st century BCE, Rome's imperial holdings expanded faster than ever. Rome's citizen-soldiers, however, were now professionals. They fought largely in the hope of materially bettering themselves. Some were more interested in looting than fulfilling their responsibilities, and others simply hoped to serve long enough to be awarded land. Army commanders thus became more than military strategists, as troops began to look to them for financial favors. Many leading military officers turned into what could be accurately called independent warlords. Moreover, antagonism between mercenaries developed into numerous violent battles. The situation was bleak and offered the potential of near-constant armed conflict. Victorious mercenaries became the tyrant-rulers of Rome and put an end to any of those aligned against him. However, the right to rule as a tyrant, gained by sheer will and brutality, was almost guaranteed to end in death and tragedy. It was one thing to control and another thing to govern by the popular will.

As one might imagine, the Roman Republic staggered from one bloody crisis to another. It seemed that only the establishment of an absolutist government could resolve Rome's political and social crisis. One politician and general, Julius Caesar (100–44 BCE), almost succeeded in achieving that status. In 62 BCE, he formed a three-man coalition with two other powerful Romans, Pompey, and Crassus, called the First Triumvirate. They briefly restored peace to Rome. Caesar's ambition was to surpass his two partners who had both gained sterling reputations as generals.

Image 4.9: Amethyst intaglio portrait of a man believed to be Julius Caesar, c. 50–40 BCE, amethyst.

Source: *The Metropolitan Museum of Art, New York.*

Pompey already had a solid reputation as a commander. His list of conquests was very long, and it included Hellenized lands and many of those in the Near East. Crassus earned fame after he crushed a rebellion led by the charismatic Spartacus; a former soldier once free who had been made a slave and forced to fight as a gladiator. Between 73 and 71 BCE, Spartacus and his army of rebel gladiators and slaves killed their masters and escaped their bonds. After their defeat, Crassus crucified more than six thousand of them along the Appian Way, as this was one of the most traveled highways connecting Rome to other important cities.

Caesar sought to surpass his two colleagues by conquering northern Gaul: the land that today comprises most of France. Since their near conquest of the city in 390 BCE, the Gauls had done little to threaten the Romans for several centuries. The Celtic and Germanic people who lived in the Gaul of Caesar's time were not uncivilized tribesmen. They had long interacted with the Greco-Roman Mediterranean culture, as they supplied the Republic with agricultural products and slaves captured in various wars. Several tribes had even agreed to defense treaties with Rome.

When the Gauls were threatened by an invading tribe, they asked for help from Rome, and this became Caesar's chance at glory. Caesar was a man of tremendous ambition unlike very few in the history of

Western civilization. For him, war meant the opportunity to expand Roman dominion, enhance his reputation, and win wealth for himself and his supporters. For several years, Caesar exploited the fighting among different Celtic tribes and engaged in a series of campaigns to conquer Gaul, and he finally accomplished this goal in 50 BCE. With his fame established, Caesar turned to his real aim: dominating Rome itself. He declared his intentions of becoming sole dictator of Rome by leading his army from Gaul into Italy in 49 BCE.

By 46 BCE, Caesar had defeated all his rivals. By forging an alliance with Queen Cleopatra, Caesar also controlled the breadbasket of the Mediterranean, Egypt. Like the better Greek tyrants, Julius Caesar did more than tighten his powerful grip on Rome, as he sought to address real problems among the people. He carried out land reform, rewarded his veterans with confiscated property, and extended Roman citizenship to conquered peoples in Gaul and present day Spain. Caesar improved the administration, lowered taxes, and built public utilities such as aqueducts, baths, and temples. He even made modifications to the annual calendar, which with a few alterations over the years, is our basic twelve-month calendar.

A group of senators plotted to assassinate Caesar and permanently end his rise toward potential dynastic ambitions. During the Ides (middle of a month) of March in 44 BCE, as he entered the Senate chamber, the conspirators fell on Caesar and stabbed him twenty-three times. Contenders stepped forward to take Caesar's place. Mark Antony was once a commander under Caesar and then later became a consul. He, Caesar's grandnephew and adopted son Octavian Caesar, and a lesser warlord named Marcus Lepidus formed an alliance called the Second Triumvirate. Furthermore, the Second Triumvirate pursued and defeated Caesar's primary assassins. The Second Triumvirate declared their intent to restore the government, and had the Senate proclaim Julius Caesar a "Divine Being." The murdered dictator became a founding hero whose memory inspired other rulers of Rome.

The partners then divided the Roman world, with Octavian based in Rome, Lepidus in North Africa, and Mark Antony in Alexandria. However, the Second Triumvirate's cooperation soon turned to rivalry, and the balance of power seemed destined to turn toward Octavian. Antony's passionate love affair with Cleopatra made him unpopular in Rome, and his efforts to win prestige by making conquest on the eastern frontier ended in failure. Meanwhile, Octavian

Image 4.10: Guido Cagnacci, *The Death of Cleopatra*, c. 1645–55, oil on canvas. Fascination with the story of Cleopatra and Mark Anthony emerged during the Renaissance and Early Modern eras, glorifying their doomed love story in art. Here, the subject conveys the moment of Cleopatra's suicide by asp bite after Mark Anthony's loss in the Battle of Actium.

Source: *The Metropolitan Museum of Art, New York.*

pushed Lepidus out of power and began expanding Rome's borders northward toward the Danube River. In 31 BCE, Octavian and Mark Antony went to war against each other. Octavian's forces achieved victory, and he became the supreme leader of Rome. Moreover, his rise as Augustus Caesar in 27 BCE marked an end to the Roman Republic and the arrival of a powerful and often controversial Roman Empire.

By the ascendancy of Octavian as the sole ruler of Rome, the small city-state on the banks of the Tiber River had transformed into the mighty capitol of an empire. Its holdings included most of Western Europe, the Mediterranean, and the Near East. In the earlier years of the Republic, Rome had developed a form of government with appropriate checks and balances. Over time, patricians and plebeians both developed a great foothold within the society. The patron-client system tied disparate parts of a community together in a more symbiotic whole. Roman society also benefited from a very dedicated and committed body of citizens. Having defeated all opponents near and far, Rome gave them a stake in the continued growth of

Roman power. While provincials typically could not vote, they benefited in other ways. The provinces enjoyed the uniformity of Roman law, a trade network that brought economic benefits, and a Roman army that provided defense and security.

Everyone seemed to share in the fruits of an expanding empire. However, excessive wars brought great changes. A huge influx of slaves made the acquisition of large estates profitable, at the expense of Italy's peasant farmers. The result was a growing and dangerous social instability with military and political ramifications. Ultimately, Romans saw an end to their Republic and the start of a new age: The Roman Empire.

Cultural Influences: The Iconography of Athena and Minerva

By Christina McClellan

Roman art, as defined when distinguished from its forerunner—Etruscan art—appropriates whole styles and bodies of work of Greek art. Prior to the rise of the Roman Empire, Greek society was the most influential in the Mediterranean. It was something to be emulated, mastered, and surpassed—a challenge worthy of the Romans. As we see throughout Roman history, trade and contact with other societies led to the appropriation of cultures and religious elements into the Roman pantheon, as well as Roman language, culture, and religion into the society and culture of which they conquered.

However, before the rise of the Roman empire, the Roman religion and its Pantheon of deities, was subject to the influence of a stronger and more influential culture, that of the Greeks. Most Greek gods and goddesses ended up with a Roman equivalent, and their similarities did not simply manifest in mythology, but also visually.

In Ancient Greek mythology, Athena is the goddess of handicrafts, practical reason or wisdom, and of war, amongst other various patronages. Sculptures of Athena often depict her with a spear, shield, and some sort of military headdress or crown denoting wisdom. In the famous Athena Parthenos, now lost to time, she holds the female personification of victory, the winged Nike. Similarly, Minerva, in Ancient Roman mythology, was the goddess of handicrafts, professions, arts, and war. She is often portrayed in her sculptures with a spear, shield, and some form of military headdress as well. While Minerva was likely a direct holdover of the ancient Greek goddess Athena, the similarities in dress over the course of not just one, but multiple iterations, signify not just a characteristic of that goddess, but also of what the sculptor and his society felt most important to highlight. Both goddesses are patrons of multiple things, and even have a patronage over household items, such as

Image 4.11a: Statue of Athena outside the Academy of Athens, Athens Greece, by Leonidas Drosis, 19th century, marble and bronze. Though this sculpture is a modern iteration of Athena, it is modeled on other known Athenian sculptures and descriptions of Athenian sculptures. © Shutterstock.com

Image 4.11b: Minerva as the Goddess Roma, the female personification of Rome, Piazza del Campidoglio, Rome, Italy. © Shutterstock.com

the hearth, but those elements are not highlighted here. Rather, it is their status as deity of war that is reiterated in every sculpture. By discovering why individuals belonging to this society chose to place emphasis on certain visual characteristics associated with each goddess, historians and art historians may use these types of visual cues to better understand the culture and people of this civilization.

Chapter 5

The Roman Empire

Soon after Octavian's triumph over Antony & Cleopatra, the Senate conferred on him the new title of Augustus ("Revered One"); the name he has since been called throughout the generations. Now that he was supreme ruler, Augustus Caesar intended to stay in power, reconstruct the failed government of the Roman city-state, keep its empire together, and launch it into an extended era of excellence. Interestingly, Augustus did his best to make it seem that little had changed. He set about consolidating his authority as much as possible within the traditional government of the Roman Republic. What followed was two centuries of imperial rule known as the Pax Romana ("Roman Peace"). This period of remarkable sustained growth and peace continued under leaders ranging from superb to completely incompetent. Indeed, this was a testament to Augustus' meticulous planning and the extraordinary fortitude of the Roman people. With the benefits of a more stable society during the Pax Romana, the Romans invented and built on a scale that was the envy of the world. It was also during this period that a new and eventually extraordinarily influential religion came onto the Western Civilization landscape: Christianity. It began as only one of many competing faiths, but its rapid spread threatened to shake the foundations of the Roman Empire.

The Pax Romana

Following his triumphal entry into Rome, in 27 BCE Augustus announced that he would "restore the Republic." However, he did so only outwardly by carefully blending republican institutions with his strong-willed personal leadership. One way in which he tackled governing was to disguise his power. Augustus accomplished this by referring to himself as a Princeps ("first citizen"), as this was a term usually reserved for prominent leaders considered indispensable to the Republic. At the same time, he gave himself the permanent role of tribune. Previously, this position had a one year term. As tribune, he was technically the defender of the people's rights.

Image 5.1: The Ara Pacis, also known as the Altar of Augustan Peace, was built c. 9 BCE to honor the conclusion of the wars in Gaul and Spain. Augustus allowed the altar to be built in lieu of parades, marking a new era, and new style of rule in Ancient Rome. © Shutterstock.com

Image 5.2: Statue of Augustus Caesar in the Via dei Fori Imperiali, Rome, Italy. © Shutterstock.com

Augustus could alter tradition and secure exalted titles because he showed respect for local institutions and encouraged provincial leaders to fulfill their responsibilities. He kept control over matters that affected the empire, but Augustus left local affairs to the individual provinces. Greek city-states, Roman colonies, Celtic tribes, and countless other communities all supervised their own day-to-day business. According to estimates, the entire empire needed no more than a few thousand Roman officials to run it. Through his active leadership, Augustus earned the admiration of many Romans.

For Augustus, the reorganization of the army was a practical and pressing issue. In the past, Roman generals commanded their armies during times of internal conflict. To give Rome the order it needed, Augustus believed he needed to gain permanent control of all military forces. Rome did not have, unlike modern Western nations, a constitution that separated civilian and military leadership. By arrangement with the Senate, Augustus received confirmation as commander-in-chief of all the soldiers within the provinces. In return, he permitted the Senate to supervise lands where soldiers were not stationed and the whole of Italy, as well. Augustus made the army an all-volunteer force that served in permanent units for fixed terms of twenty-five years. By offering soldiers a choice to serve, and giving them a definite term of enlistment, he hoped to make the army stable and reliable.

After consolidating the power of the army under his leadership, Augustus moved to prevent political power brokers from inflaming the people against the government. There must be no more power-hungry governors and dishonest officials arousing fury among the subject peoples. In addition, Augustus desired that ambitious commanders who wanted to become independent warlords could no longer sway discontented soldiers to join their efforts. Accordingly, Augustus brought the system of government appointments under his personal control. Politicians still hoped to work their way up the ladder and seek influential positions. However, under the new system, none got far unless they performed competently, honestly, and remained loyal to the emperor.

After Augustus died in 14 CE, the succeeding Roman Emperors ranged from horrible to great. In the more immediate time after his passing, several incompetent and even insane men held the position. His immediate successor was Tiberius (ruled: 14–37). Unfortunately, his time in power included periods of vengeful acts and he executed several alleged political enemies. After Tiberius died, Caligula (ruled: 37–41) came to power. From supposedly making his horse a consul to ordering Roman soldiers to bring home sea shells as wartime treasure, Caligula exhibited irrational behavior in a variety of ways. Tragically, members of his security force murdered him. Another controversial ruler, Nero (ruled: 54–68) left his mark as emperor. Nero's frivolous nature became one of his legacies. He loved dabbling in poetry and music. When a disastrous fire hit Rome, Nero panicked and looked for easy targets to blame the disaster on. He targeted Christians and ordered public executions of them via methods such as sacrifice to wild animals and burning at the stake. In the end, Nero succumbed to his own excesses and committed suicide.

On the other end of the spectrum, there were emperors that exhibited political competency and policy innovation. Emperor Hadrian (ruled: 117–138) left a legacy of effective military planning and promotion of the arts. Others such as Antoninus Pius (ruled: 138–161) exhibited sound financial leadership, engaged in forward thinking legal reforms, and promoted useful public works construction. Influenced by the Hellenistic philosophy of Stoicism, Emperor Marcus Aurelius (ruled: 161–180) found significant meaning in its celebration of a purposeful universe functioning in accordance with an overall divine plan. This philosophy of Stoicism coincided with many Romans' sense of mission and destiny. Marcus sought to embody Plato's dream of the philosopher-king. Day by day, while commanding his legions in fierce frontier wars, he set down his innermost thoughts in a book called *Meditations*. Marcus's landmark treatise established his legacy as a wise statesman.

Image 5.3: Map of the Roman Empire at its height by 117 CE, before the crisis of the 3rd century. © Shutterstock.com

The Impact of Roman Architecture

It can be argued that while the Romans did not eclipse the Greeks in philosophy, they did so in architecture. After centuries of erosion and vandalism, the ruins of Roman buildings still stand across the empire's former territories—all the way from the Euphrates River (modern day Iraq) to the Atlantic Ocean. The Romans did not invent large-scale architecture, but they remain unique in two key areas: their sheer amount of construction and the constant desire to make each project more grandiose and impressive. The Romans greatly expanded on the techniques of older builders. For truly remarkable structures, the Romans found the Greek style of columns and beams inadequate. Instead, they preferred the arch, vault, and dome. All these forms dated back to ancient Sumer, but the Romans exploited and developed them on an unprecedented scale.

The Romans engineered arches with materials designed to support a greater amount of weight.

These items of construction included concrete and brick. Due in large part to their superior design and development, Roman arches served as a robust and reliable component for a diverse array of infrastructure projects. Innovations in the construction and placement of domes allowed the Romans a new avenue to express their dominance. A large dome was built from a series of progressively smaller horizontal rings of brick, stone, or concrete. When completed, each part formed a single unit firmly set in place. One of the grander domes linked to the building prowess of the Roman Empire is the Pantheon. It was originally constructed around 27 BCE. After experiencing two destructive fires, the structure was completely rebuilt under the Emperor Hadrian. The Pantheon's purpose was to honor all the Roman gods, and it consists of a circular central hall capped by a vast concrete dome. For visitors, then and now, the Pantheon is a dramatic expression of Roman skill and fortitude. One Roman writer, commenting on this dome-wonder, stated "Thanks to its dome it resembles the vault of heaven itself."

Image 5.4: The exterior and dome interior of the Pantheon, Rome, Italy. The Pantheon was an engineering feat and the most famous example of domed architecture in Ancient Rome. © Shutterstock.com

Throughout the Roman Empire, all cities of consequence contained a forum. Within the city of Rome itself, the central forum evolved over time from an area of shopping and commerce to a meeting location for all range of public functions. Overlooking the central forum was the sacred Capitoline Hill, topped by the temple of Jupiter, Juno, and Minerva. Many Roman buildings were erected to satisfy the recreational needs of the people. Some of these included large swimming pools, gymnasiums, gardens, libraries, galleries, theaters, lounges, and taverns. Particularly popular were the public bathhouses equipped with steam rooms and small pools filled with water. The more elaborate of these structures could hold several thousand people at one time.

Overindulgence and entertainment were everyday features of life in the Roman Empire. Most enjoyed the chariot races of the circus or the violent gladiator fights in the arena. Every city of the empire had locations for mass entertainment, but the Colosseum was the most famous arena of Rome. Completed in the late 1st century, the awe-inspiring structure was the largest of its kind and originally coated in marble. The Colosseum covered about six acres and seated more than fifty thousand spectators. Underneath the arena floor resided a maze of corridors, chambers, and cells where animals and people (mainly slaves or criminals) awaited their turn at combat. The entertainment sessions were lengthy affairs, lasting from early morning until dark. Wealthy donors seeking

Image 5.5: Exterior and interior of the Roman Colosseum, Rome, Italy. © Shutterstock.com

popularity usually paid the bills, including the cost of refreshments.

The Romans were Western civilization's greatest builders of infrastructure surpassed only by the growth of modern cities. For example, to supply their cities with water, Romans built great aqueducts. Water flowed into the cities from the surrounding mountains through pipes that were atop well-constructed conduits. These structures had to be precisely engineered to allow water from as many as forty miles away to come into the cities via gravity alone. Due to its superior infrastructure, the Roman Empire became known as an urban culture where its citizens enjoyed the benefits of advanced technology.

Great cities were very impressive, but Roman culture could not spread throughout the empire without navigable roads. Like the Assyrians and Persians before them, they needed a swift and reliable means of overland movement to control, defend, and expand their vast territories. Over the centuries, they built or improved over fifty thousand miles of roads that reached out from Rome to the farthest corners of the empire. The typical roadbed was about fifteen feet wide and five feet deep. The surface was usually dirt, but in heavier traffic areas, thick blocks of hard stone were used. The roads were regularly patrolled, and on the major arteries there was a stable every ten miles and a hostel every thirty miles. Land travel under Rome's rule was easier than it had ever been before or than it would be again for nearly fifteen hundred years.

Image 5.6: Roman Aqueduct, Segovia, Spain. Roman architecture and engineering feats were not limited to Italy, but were transported to every corner of their empire. © Shutterstock.com

Image 5.7: Roman road in Jerash, Jordan. Roman roads were so well constructed and centrally located that they are the basis for the modern highway system throughout Europe, and in some cases the original roads still survive intact. © Shutterstock.com

The Concepts of Romanization

Improving ease of travel helped speed the process known as Romanization. The empire found it could spread its influence by the dispersion of people and ideas that would convince others of the superiority of Roman culture. This happened both directly and indirectly. In the days of the Roman Republic, Romans established colonies for military veterans in the provinces, and colonial expansion continued under the empire. After serving twenty-five years, veterans were awarded with citizenship and land. Over time, these auxiliary troops brought the tenets of the urban society they had known to colonized areas. In turn, colonies became the cities in Britain, North Africa, Germany, and the East. The cities boasted all the amenities that Romans had come to expect: theaters, baths, an amphitheater, roads, and townhouses. Town councils collected taxes and maintained public works such as water systems and markets. Officials maintained census figures on both the human population and agricultural produce and reported it all to Roman superiors. This combination of local rule, Romanization, and business-like accountability helped hold the huge empire together.

The army was the primary instrument of Romanization, and in turn, was itself changed by the incorporation of new citizens eligible to serve in the ranks. In the Republic era, soldiers tended to be drawn from the city of Rome and surrounding regions (Roman citizens). As citizenship increased and the Roman Empire expanded, the army took advantage of a vast new supply of soldiers. Military veterans introduced new recruits to the Roman language, religion, and values. Many towns arose full of former military personnel and their friends, families, and small businesses. After conquests, Roman armies remained in place as occupying forces. The Romans spoke a different language than their subjects, worshiped different gods, and enforced strange and unwelcome rules. However, as the occupying Romans settled in and raised families with local women, many defeated peoples chose to assimilate rather than resist.

To give common cause to disparate communities across the empire, Rome began granting special status and privileges to some colonized people. Under the Roman Republic, only a small number of people in the provinces earned Roman citizenship, but during the Roman Empire, leaders learned it was valuable to grant this rank to many more individuals. Those awarded this status included people that proved useful in local government, children of the marriages between male citizens and colonized women, and

Image 5.8: Rome transplanted elements of their culture wherever they went. Baths were a benefit to Roman citizens abroad. The ancient Roman Baths, Bath, England, remained a place of exclusivity and seen as a retreat for the elite in England for centuries after the Romans left the island. Though the original architecture dating to the Roman era was destroyed, the current structure is the result of centuries of building and improvements. © Shutterstock.com

veterans of auxiliary army units. Non-Romans who became citizens gained valuable advantages like the right of legal appeal, immunity from torture in some instances, and the possibility of lucrative careers in the government and army. Above all, new citizens gained identities as Romans while remaining leading members of their communities.

The rulers expected these "more cultured, noble, and powerful" people to be guided by their identity as Romans in governing "the rest." For the emperors and others who governed the empire, there was an important distinction between "the rest" and those who had been thoroughly Romanized. As a rule, Romans considered those outside of the empire as barbarians. For those living in Rome, even people who had become citizens were often viewed as less than civilized. Romans were inherently conquerors who looked suspiciously at any group who did not ascribe to their beliefs. Thus, those who were different were potentially hostile, and as Romans encountered an increasing number of people who fit this description, the drive to continue to invade and subdue distant lands became stronger.

In response, foreign people wavered between accepting the benefits of Roman society and rebelling in favor of self-rule and provincial religious and secular beliefs. Roman law helped erode the local loyalties and traditions of the diverse provincial peoples and furthered the process of creating one Roman, imperial culture. As did its army, Roman law made for a potent weapon that helped facilitate the process of Romanization. A Roman citizen possessed legally-protected rights that included the guarantee of freedom from enslavement. Male citizens had the right to compete for public magistrate positions, vote in public assemblies, serve in the legions, and make an appeal in a criminal trial. No matter where Roman citizens lived, they took pride in their centuries-old legal code and in their rights of citizenship.

The Romans were the first to distinguish between civil and criminal law. Civil law defined relations among different classes of Roman society. Criminal law addressed theft, homicide, sexual crimes, treason, and offenses against the government. Romans developed the idea that law codes, although the product of societies and circumstances, were based on universally applicable principles. It should not, however, be hastily concluded that true equality existed in the Roman Empire. There were different legal rights for the wealthy upper class and the poor. For example, the elites were spared the most gruesome punishments like crucifixion and being thrown to wild animals in the arena. Even after the year 212, when all freeborn inhabitants of the empire had been declared citizens, the government made a legal distinction between worthy and humble citizens. In this way, the population of the empire continued to be essentially divided into two parts: the wealthy, educated, arms-bearing, and mostly town-dwelling few, and the unprivileged, mostly country-dwelling majority who paid heavily for the splendor of the emperor, the upkeep of the army, and the beautification of the cities. Therefore, Romanization was never intended to create equality nor was it even a possibility given the precepts of the empire.

For some people, membership in a prosperous community was enough, while others were more critical of Rome. To those who wished it, citizenship in a large empire undoubtedly inspired a new sense of belonging to a family. There are many versions of Rome. What is most accurate depended on one's perspective. All visions of Rome reflected different realities of an empire that forced itself on many peoples, made them live together more or less peacefully, and brought great changes to both rulers and the ruled. This dynamic would continue for centuries even after Rome's peoples went their separate ways.

The Rise of Christianity

It was the rise and spread of a new monotheistic religion, Christianity, that eventually changed the nature of the Roman Empire's mission. Christianity is a faith based on the life, teachings, death, and resurrection of a Christ figure known as Jesus. He taught for about three years and was then executed by the Roman government on charges of sedition. There was not an empire-wide knowledge of Jesus at his death, but after it attempts were made to record his words and actions. Although he lived in relative obscurity, since the 6th century CE the birth of Jesus has been used as the primary date from which the world measures time. The religion that grew after his death has more followers than any other religion in the world.

Christianity entered a Roman-dominated world where people were aware of and practiced a diversity of religious practices. In addition, emperors were careful to link religious worship with respect for Roman authority. In Palestine, in the eastern part of the empire, the monotheistic religion of Judaism still

thrived, and its temple hierarchy was integrated into the Roman administrative structure. In the capital city of Jerusalem, the aristocracy cooperated with the Romans who protected their power and allowed them to practice their faith. Several interpretations of Judaism co-existed, however. Some adhered to established Jewish law, while others were more open to foreign cultural traditions. Certain Jewish groups like the Zealots (originally a Greek term that indicates a zealous follower) wanted to overthrow Roman rule, and some were even willing to assassinate Roman sympathizers. Thus, in Palestine, the process of Romanization was contested, as some Jews adopted Roman ways, while others felt imperial colonization was totally incompatible with the survival of an authentic Jewish identity.

It was in this context of competing Jewish sects that the teachings of one preacher, Jesus of Nazareth, became popular. Jesus was an itinerant charismatic preacher and, according to some, a miracle worker. After attracting a small, dedicated band of followers around Galilee, Jesus came to Jerusalem in his early thirties. Upon arriving there, he was met by excited crowds who had gathered to see him. His teachings urged compassion, forgiveness, love of the poor, and support of the weak. When Jesus was crucified, the Roman governor, the client king of Judea, and many of the leaders of the Jewish faith were relieved to be rid of a potential troublemaker.

The Romans thought Jesus advocated independence from the Roman Empire and executed him as a common subversive and rebel. Jesus' followers insisted that he had risen from the dead and ascended into heaven. Eventually called "Christians" (from the Greek word Christ, meaning "messiah" or "anointed one"), these men and women expected that Jesus would soon return and launch a new age of righteousness. The resurrection became the central act of the Christian faith. After the execution of Jesus, his small band of disciples dedicated themselves to spread his teachings among the Jewish people. Many ordinary Jews regarded the disciples' message as a grave insult to their beliefs, so Christians were driven out of towns, beaten, and killed. One of the most ardent defenders of traditional Judaism was Saul. He witnessed the martyrdom of the first disciple, Stephen, to be stoned to death for blasphemy, and Saul organized the investigation of many accused of Christian sympathies. Saul's family was devout adherents of Judaism and citizens of the Roman Empire. They were fluent in Hebrew, Aramaic, and Greek. Thus, Saul was a man capable of understanding provincial Judaism while living immersed in contemporary Roman culture.

Saul (thereafter known as Paul) became a Christian after he claimed to hear Christ's voice on the road to Damascus. Paul traveled throughout the Eastern Mediterranean region, preaching and writing letters of admonition and encouragement to the faithful. When Nero blamed Christians for the infamous catastrophic fire in Rome, Christian tradition holds that both Paul and the Apostle Peter were murdered in the persecutions that followed. The presence of a noticeable Christian community in Nero's Rome was remarkable. In the space of just thirty years, Christianity shed its Jewish roots and established churches in cities across the empire. Apart from the work of Paul, there were several reasons why so many people took up a religion that sprang from a small, seemingly insignificant, part of the Roman Empire. Why did people with no connection to Judaism come to believe that Jesus was the messiah sent by God? Why did they see him as a savior for all people and not simply as a figure related to the Jewish religion?

The appeal of Christianity had much to do with the evolution of religious thought and practice. Historically, world religions envisaged gods that controlled all aspects of the natural world. People viewed the gods as fickle, and to ensure success, communities emphasized pleasing the deities in various ways. One's relationship with the divine could mean life and death, because people depended on the seasons, the weather, bodies of water, and finally the soil itself to produce essential crops. A bad growing season, poor soil, or flooding could mean starvation. Over time, people still believed in the gods, took part in feast days, and made sacrifices, but society was rapidly changing. As the Greco-Roman world became more urbanized, the connection to the natural world diminished, and the link between spiritual awareness and religious worship was further disrupted. Most believed in supernatural forces, but the nature of those forces began to change. The time was ripe for a different conception of religious belief.

Christianity offered the Roman-dominated world a unique kind of spiritualism. Early Christians considered their church a body of people who were equal. They called each other brother and sister and talked often about the importance of helping one another.

Image 5.9: Bowl base with Saints Peter and Paul flanking a column with the Christogram of Christ, late 4th century, gold leafing on glass. The Roman Catholic tradition was built on the significance of the teachings of both St. Peter and St. Paul, as well as their burial in Rome.

Source: *The Metropolitan Museum of Art, New York.*

It was an inclusive religion that seemed especially aimed toward the have-nots of society. Jesus taught his followers to give to the poor, honor the downtrodden, and pray for their enemies. In a class-based world, where most people had little access to the channels of power, Christians offered any believers automatic membership to a community composed almost entirely of the poor and middling classes. Furthermore, the founder of this religion was the suffering Jesus instead of the typical Roman-like god who imposed his or her will on humankind. Thus, the masses could easily feel attracted to a group who promised fellowship with like-minded people, all of whom were duty-bound to provide material aid to other members, and salvation through a Christ figure dedicated to loving all people.

Roman authorities did not at first regard the Christians as anything other than one of the many small religious cults that existed within their borders. The Roman Empire tolerated local worship only when it was no threat to their absolutist rule. For about a century, Romans did not take much notice of Christianity due to their small numbers, and because they viewed Christians as largely indistinguishable from Jews.

In fact, one of the early disputes dividing Christians was whether to continue along the path of observant Judaism or to break from it. Historians and students of early Christianity are divided over whether Jesus even meant to found a new religion. Over time, however, the movement Jesus founded came to regard itself as a distinct one, and followers became known as Christians.

Paul never met Jesus in life, but he played a significant role in developing a doctrine that defined Christianity as distinct from Judaism. Paul, the great architect of the Christian church, argued successfully that the Jewish law should be set aside for non-Jews (Gentiles). He said that Christ should be regarded as fulfilling the promise of Jewish law, thereby making the law no longer relevant to non-Jews. Jesus never denied the validity of the old laws. In fact, in the famous Sermon on the Mount, Jesus pronounced that "I have come not to abolish the law, but to give it full meaning." Paul had an overriding conviction in the importance of a universal church based on his interpretation of the teachings of Jesus. This meant the admission of non-Jews into the faith, and that was something that many early members of the Christian movement did not support. The collection of books that became known as the *New Testament* helped to unify the early generations of Christians. There were many writings concerning Jesus, so Christian communities were charged with deciphering authentic works from a range of options. Over time, Christians tended to highlight certain works as inspired while devaluing others. Eventually, most Christian communities shared a common belief in the validity of the books deemed to accurately represent their faith. Much of this process, the motivations of Christians to believe this instead of that, has been lost to history. In other words, historians cannot explain the development of the *New Testament* canon with absolute accuracy. It would not be until the year 367 that all twenty-seven books that compose the *New Testament* were officially accepted. Then Christianity, like Judaism, had a written testament of the laws and wisdom that governed their faith.

Transitions, Reforms, and Tragedies

The 3rd century was a difficult period for the Roman Empire. During this time, apolitical succession crisis developed that saw more than twenty men claim, then lose with the lives, the title of emperor between the years 235 and 284. Most of these men were creatures of the army, chosen to rule by their troops. In fact, Emperor Severus Alexander (ruled: 222–235) was said to have advised his two sons: "Treat the soldiers well, and damn everybody else." The 3rd century produced thirty-seven emperors; considering that there were thirteen during the 1st century and nine emperors during the 2nd century, it is obvious this was a tumultuous time. In addition, nearly half of the 3rd century emperors endured violent deaths. Most rulers held power for only a few months. Preoccupied with merely staying alive and on the throne, they neglected the empire's borders, leaving them vulnerable to attack. Some generals from the provinces appointed themselves emperor and entered Rome, and in doing so, left large tracts of territory open to invasion. For example, in 249 the general Decius marched his army from Dacia (Romania) to Rome and became emperor (249–251). With the legions taken from the border, the barbarian Goths invaded Dacia with relative ease.

Often there were competing emperors who often wielded authority in different regions at the same time. They had little in the city of Rome, which, in any case, was too far from any of the fields of war to serve as military headquarters. For this reason, Emperor Maximian (ruled: 286–305) turned Milan into a new capital city, complete with an imperial palace, baths, walls, etc. Soon other favored cities—Trier, Sardica, Nicomedia, and eventually Constantinople—joined Milan in overshadowing Rome. The new army and the new imperial seats belonged to the provinces. They now served as imperial capitals whenever the emperor resided there. Since many were no longer stationed in Rome, they held court in these cities

Near the end of the 3rd century, Emperor Diocletian (ruled: 284–305) rescued the empire from its chaotic condition. Drawing on his brilliant organizational talents, he launched a succession of military, administrative, and economic reforms that had far-reaching consequences. Not since the reign of Augustus three centuries earlier had the Empire been so transformed.

He soon recognized that the enormous responsibilities of imperial government overburdened a single emperor. Therefore, he tried to stabilize the situation with a tetrarchy ("four-man rule") of two senior generals, one based in the east and one in the west, with two junior generals in training to take over from them. He knew that the empire's survival depended on a reliable succession strategy. This worked for a while, and Diocletian retired to his hometown on the east coast of the Adriatic Sea, instead of dying on the job.

To restore Roman military power, Diocletian reorganized the army, raising its total size to about four hundred thousand men, a significant size for the time. To protect the empire from invaders, he stationed most of these troops along the borders and built new military roads. Forces of heavily armed cavalry could race to trouble spots if enemies broke through the frontiers. He also attempted to reduce the army's involvement in politics. Although he was a soldier himself, he recognized that the army had played a disruptive role in earlier decades by renewed civil wars. He created many new legions led by commanders who were loyal to him, but he reduced the size of each legion to limit its leader's power and to increase its maneuverability. With these reforms in place, Diocletian could secure the empire's borders and suppress revolts.

But, Diocletian still faced enormous problems. One problem that was particularly troubling was a wrecked economy. By the time Diocletian came to power, Rome's known gold and silver mines had largely been tapped out. However, the empire's demand for money was just as heavy as before. To

Image 5.10: Porphyry relief sculpture of the Tetrarchs, c. 300 CE, Piazzo di San Marco, Venice, Italy. © Shutterstock.com

meet its demand, the Roman government debased the currency, increasing the proportion of inferior metals to silver. While helping it to pay its bills in the short term, this ill-devised policy produced severe inflation. Diocletian attempted to halt rapidly rising prices by with a price edict which fixed the maximum price for a broad range of goods, from basic foodstuffs to half-silk underwear with purple stripes to lions for public entertainment. It also set charges for transportation over specific routes and determined the standard wage for jobs ranging from sewer cleaner to teacher. Death was the penalty for taking goods off the market or otherwise breaking the law. The edict was displayed throughout the empire, and fragments of it have been found in over forty locations. He also increased taxes and endeavored to make tax collection more efficient by instituting a regular—and deeply resented—census to register all taxpayers. Although senators, army officers, and other influential citizens continued to be undertaxed or not taxed at all, the new tax system generated enough revenues to fund the large machinery of government.

The greatest tax burden fell on the peasants, those who were the least able to pay it. The law required these agricultural workers to remain where the census registered them. Sons were supposed to follow their fathers. This attempt to maintain the agricultural tax base was successful, but it lessened social mobility, and the gap between wealthy and poor continued to grow. Many poor peasants turned to a few rich and powerful men for protection against the ruthless imperial tax collectors. In return, these farmers granted ownership of their farms to these wealthy patrons. While they continued to work the land, they gave up their freedom for security.

The Roman government tolerated any religion that did not threaten the safety or tranquility of the empire. Christianity, however, was perceived as a subversive danger to society and the state. There were reports of strange activities among the Christians. They refused to offer sacrifices to the state cults on behalf of the emperor. This was considered an essential patriotic rite uniting all Roman subjects in common loyalty to the imperial government. For Christians, however, there was only one God, and they could not offer a sacrifice to another deity. In the eyes of many Roman officials, this attitude branded them as traitors.

To the Romans, the Christians were a secret antisocial group forming a state within a state—"walling

Image 5.11: Map of the Roman Empire c. 395, denoting the division between the Eastern and Western Empire. Though the Roman Empire would reunite briefly at various points throughout the next few centuries, it proved impossible to fully administrate and protect the Empire under one ruler. The East and Western empires began to become culturally distinct from one another as the East became the Byzantine Empire and the West fell to Germanic invasions. *Courtesy of the University of Texas Libraries, University of Texas Austin.*

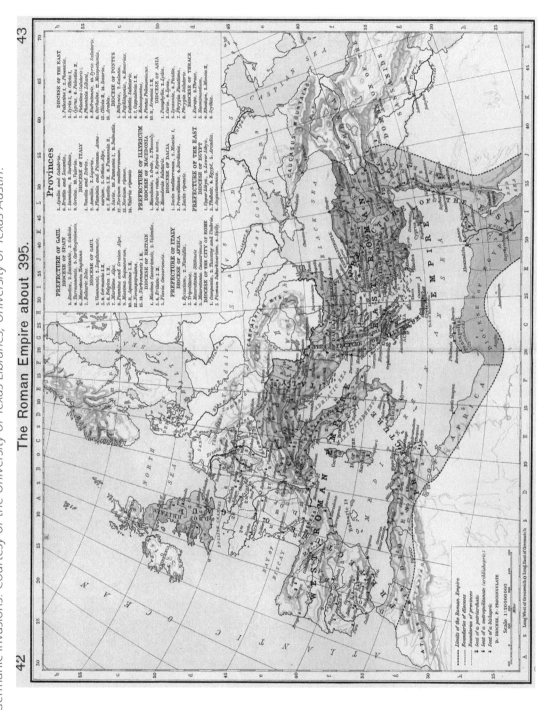

themselves off from the rest of mankind," as a pagan writer observed. Many were pacifists who refused to serve in the army, and all were intolerant of other religious sects in social functions that they considered sinful or degrading. During the first two centuries after Jesus' crucifixion, persecution of Christians was sporadic and local, such as that at Rome under Nero. But during the late 3rd and 4th centuries, when the empire was in danger of collapse, more organized efforts were launched to suppress Christianity throughout the empire. By far the longer and most systematic campaign against Christians, who now comprised perhaps one-tenth of the population, was instigated by Diocletian from 303 to 311. He stringently imposed the death penalty on anyone who refused to sacrifice to Roman gods. However, Christian martyrs seemed to welcome death, could not be silenced. "The blood of the martyrs is the seed of the church" became a Christian rallying cry.

Constantine and Church Growth

More than language or perhaps any other aspect of the Roman Empire, it was Christianity that bridged the gap between Rome and the Western world built atop its ashes. It was during a civil war in the year 312 that the Roman emperor Constantine pondered, which god could bring him victory. On the eve of the

Battle of the Milvian Bridge, Constantine saw in the sky a sign of the Christian cross with the Greek writing: "In this sign, conquer." That evening he had a dream explaining that his soldiers would triumph if they fought only under a Christian symbol. Constantine followed these instructions, and his army was victorious. Constantine became known as the first Christian emperor, and it was a marriage that would alter the future of multiple continents.

Historians do not agree on why Constantine suddenly became a Christian convert. Constantine might have realized that the old Roman gods did not inspire the people as in the past. Whatever the case, Constantine remained careful not to offend the traditions of the people. When he erected a triumphal arch in Rome that commemorated a significant military victory, he inscribed the words "to the will of the divinity" without reference to a deity. Constantine waited until his deathbed to be baptized a Christian, as well.

Part of the success of Christianity was due to the sophistication of its internal organization. There grew a distinction between the laity, the average Christians, and the priests. The priests led the worship, administered the sacraments (baptism, communion, confirmation), and acted as pastors for the laity. Christians developed their administrative hierarchy based on Roman administration. An imperial official directed each city's political affairs with a staff of assistants. Following this pattern, a bishop, who led a team of priests and deacons, organized each city's Christian

Image 5.12: Remains of the Colossus of Constantine, built c. 315 CE, marble, Rome, Italy. The Colossus is thought to have originally reached around 40 feet. © Shutterstock.com

community. There were bishops called a metropolitan (because he resided in the chief city, the metropolis, of the province) in the East and an arch bishop in the West. The hierarchy of metropolitan/archbishops, bishops, priests, and deacons linked the scattered communities of believers together into what emerged as the Christian Church.

With the administration in place, the Church grew quickly, and bishops became foremost authorities in their cities. A bishop supervised the city, and its surrounding villages in units called diocese. Many people learned to depend on bishops, as they soon became far more than religious teachers. As the Church grew wealthy due to donations, bishops became the primary instruments of charity to the poor. In the Roman world, benefactors provided some public services for the masses, but Christians taught others to follow a different principle. While the benefactor used his wealth in exchange for honor in the city, bishops offered the resources of his congregation based on fidelity to the Christian faith. Many bishops encouraged gifting endowments to churches and monasteries which could continue to support the poor by growing food or renting land to tenants.

Although early Christians agreed on the importance of giving, church communities did not always express the same religious doctrines. While the faith provided a shared belief system and new opportunities for participation in a religious culture, Christianity also opened new divisions and gave rise to new hostilities over conflicting interpretations of the beliefs of the faithful. There was a vast array of literature that circulated among many different Christian communities, and it is hard to create a unified set of religious ideas. Bishops took the lead in defining Christian belief. Still, given that there were many cities each with a bishop, it is not surprising that the clergy often argued among themselves. Christianity, therefore, produced what earlier religions had not: heresy. Unlike most every faith that preceded them, Christians were preoccupied with demarking true from false religious teaching.

Early Christians disputed if Jesus was the real son of God or something else. For a monotheistic religion, there was a potential problem making Jesus a divine figure. The rationale resulted in the new doctrine of the Trinity: God, Jesus, and something called the "holy spirit" were all divine, all different, and yet

all one. There were many debates about the Trinity. For example, the Egyptian priest Arius (256–336) argued that it was impossible to interpret Christianity as monotheistic if Jesus and his father were both godlike. He said the "Son of God" of the *New Testament* must have only been a human being while also being the instrument of human salvation. Indeed, it was difficult for some like Arius to consider Jesus as more than human because he endured a tortuous death on the cross.

The task of the first generation of Christian philosophers was to reconcile competing beliefs into a more unified church. The Christian community in each Roman city was in many ways an independent enclave under the authority of its bishop. They did not even agree to which books belonged in the Bible. Therefore, Constantine believed it was his responsibility to help unite the empire by finding solutions to doctrinal disputes. In 325, Constantine summoned bishops to a council at Nicaea in northern Asia Minor. The council decided to denounce the philosophy of Arius known as Arianism: the belief that Jesus was distinct from, and not equal to, God. The bishops issued the *Nicene Creed* that became the official statement of faith of the Roman Empire. In addition, the council officially adopted the administrative style that had already emerged in much of the Roman Empire. Each city had its bishop, and those of Alexandria, Antioch, and Rome were given the higher rank of patriarch. The Bishop of Rome, in the original capital city, became the most important Christian clergyman, because this office claimed apostolic succession from the Apostle Peter.

The achievements of the Roman Empire were crucial to the development of Western Civilization. Their advancements were both impressive and vital to later generations; from the Romance languages of today rooted in Roman Latin (French, Italian, Spanish, etc.) to the legacy of construction projects such as roads, aqueducts, baths, and public buildings. In addition, this extraordinary historical period developed countless other cultural, social, and economic legacies. Indeed, the Roman Empire's many accomplishments continue to enthrall historical scholars to the present day. Moreover, it was during the Pax Romana period of the Roman Empire that Christianity began and spread throughout the Mediterranean world. This unique religious faith developed to the point it became a permanent fixture on the Roman

Image 5.13: *Constantine speaks at the Council of Nicaea*, 17th Century, fresco, Seville, Spain.
© Shutterstock.com

scene. In time, it became the dominant religion of the Western world. By the 3rd century, the Roman world entered an age of decline. This was neither a sudden nor a complete fall. As a new religion, Christianity, helped redefine Western civilization, and as new centers of power developed in Europe and the Near East, the glory of Rome was not extinguished but rather redirected and transformed.

Chapter 6

The Middle Ages: Act One

In the 15th century, those in the cities of Italy thought they were living in a new time when cultural achievements of Greece and Rome were re-born. Consequently, they named the period between the collapse of the Roman Empire and their own time the Middle Ages. They believed the age was less civilized than either the ancient world or that of their own era. While it is true that some of the cultural achievements of the classical world were abandoned, not all was lost.

When it comes to medieval Europe, one still must confront the traditional idea of the "Dark Ages." Darkness has meant ignorance, superstition, cruelty, wilderness, and a host of other things. However, people who lived during this era did not necessarily consider their time a dark one. In fact, they made decisions hoping to improve their lives and better the lot of their children. Many medieval Europeans thought creatively and voiced displeasure at the policies of the church or government. Thus, the Middle Ages were not completely lifeless, unchanging, or dark.

Most medieval people worked small plots of land as subsistence farmers, and that made them like countless individuals from earlier times. But, without a great city like Rome and all it offered, there appeared nothing to inspire medieval farmers apart from toilsome work in the soil. In the Middle Ages, everyone maintained strong ties to the Catholic Church, and in turn, the clergy demanded people think about strict religious instruction instead of seeking personal fulfillment. These two factors, rural life and church commitment, did not crush every medieval existence, but the overwhelming burdens of the two could and did stifle intellectual progress.

The End of Rome

The appearance of the Huns set in motion events that would eventually result in the collapse of the western sections of the Roman Empire. In 376, in what is now Russia, an army of Huns forced a group of Visigoths from their farmlands. Subsequently, the refugee Visigoths secured an agreement with Roman leadership. The deal arranged allowed the Visigoths to establish a Balkan community in exchange for a manpower commitment to the Roman military. In the past, Roman rulers had frequently made this sort of arrangement. Roman officials in charge of the resettlement of the Visigoths exploited the refugees by charging them exorbitant fees for food and supplies. In 378, the Visigoths revolted. At the Battle of Adrianople, near the city of Constantinople, they killed the Roman Emperor Valens (ruled: 364–378) and defeated Roman troops. Valens' successor, Theodosius (ruled: 379–395), had little choice but to recognize the Visigoths as independent Roman allies, but in 395, they rebelled against the empire. The Visigoths moved into Italy and, in 410, took the city of Rome. This event shook Rome to its core.

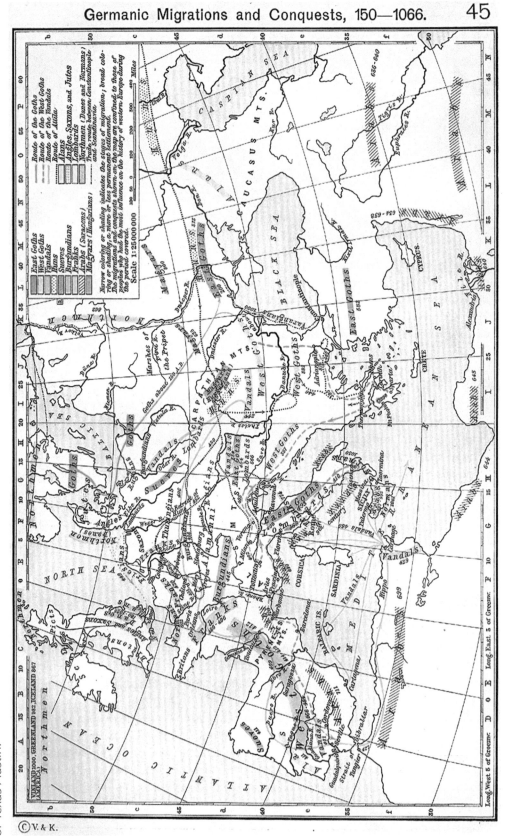

Image 6.1: Map of Germanic migrations and conquests between 150 and 1066 CE. *Courtesy of the University of Texas Libraries, University of Texas Austin.*

After they had conquered an area, Germanic tribes established states ruled by kings. The kingdoms typically did not have clearly defined geographical borders, and as tribes migrated their locations shifted. The Visigoths, after looting Rome in 410, eventually made their way into Gaul (France) and Spain where they established a kingdom. The king left in place what remained of cities and their tax-gathering administration.

In 476, Emperor Romulus Augustus (ruled: 460–476) became the last ruler to reside in Rome. In turn, the year 476 also marked the fall of the western territories of the Roman Empire. However, the eastern holdings of the Roman Empire survived for many more centuries. The influence of Roman civilization remained vital in most regions, but it took different forms in the lands now ruled by Germanic leaders. In Britain, Roman culture perhaps fared the worst and little of it survived. Here, the Germanic language of the Saxon invaders and their Anglo-allies developed into modern English. In Gaul, Italy, and Spain the Latin-based "Romance" languages grew into the early versions of French, Italian, Spanish, and Portuguese. Latin continued as the primary written language, and the settlers borrowed heavily from Roman literary forms. They produced histories of their tribal kingdoms modeled after those of Rome. The Germanic groups also composed Latin legal codes influenced by Roman sources.

As the Roman Empire headed toward the abyss, Augustine of Hippo (354–430), made tremendous contributions to the field of Christian philosophy. He believed society could attain a great deal of necessary knowledge and wisdom from the *Bible*. But, because such information is not always easy to interpret, Augustine felt individuals needed a proper education to assist in this endeavor. In his view, classical academic training allowed people to properly understand biblical lessons, and as such, appropriately seek Christian salvation.

Augustine's most noted work is *The City of God* (426). In this treatise, he argued against the theory that Christianity's rise led to the decline of the Roman Empire by eroding traditional Roman values. Augustine wrote that the Roman Empire was but one notable example of how all human institutions or civilizations rise and fall. People tend to try to dominate their surroundings, he argued, and this leads to conflict and distrust at every level of society. Augustine felt Rome could never have brought permanent peace and order to the world. It was this city of man, Augustine's term for the man-made world, which was

Image 6.2: Fresco of St. Augustine of Hippo and his mother St. Monica in the Basilica di Sant'Agostino, Rome, Italy. © Shutterstock.com

doomed to collapse. Conversely, the *City of God* was permanent and was the opposite of man's sinful nature. It represented truth, humility, compassion, love, and all things that a secular city could not sustain. Compared with the realm of God, Rome and its decline were unimportant.

The Birth and Rise of Islam

As the early Middle Ages came upon the scene, Christianity was not the only monotheistic religion to change the world. The new religion of Islam (which means "submission" in Arabic) was devoted to the same God worshiped by the Jews and Christians. It originated in Arabia, an arid peninsula that had largely remained outside the political domination of major civilizations. The founder of Islam, Muhammad (570–632), claimed to be the most recent, and final, prophet of the God of the *Old Testament*. Muslims believed that Muhammad received Islam's holy text, the *Quran*, directly from God.

In the years before Muhammad's conversion, the nomadic Bedouin tribes of Arabia worshiped several different deities. They regularly came to the city of Mecca to honor the multiple gods represented at the Kaaba shrine. Mecca thus served as a sanctuary where different tribes could gather to peacefully worship the traditional deities. The religious harmony that prevailed at Mecca also offered opportunities to

Image 6.3: The Kaaba, Masjid al-Haram, Mecca, Saudi Arabia. The Kaaba is located in Islam's most holy mosque and is at the center of the Islamic faith. According to Islamic tradition, the Kaaba was originally built by the prophet Abraham (Ibrahim) and his son Ismail, after which it was taken over by pagans, until Muhammad rededicated the structure to Allah. © Shutterstock.com

settle disputes and conduct trade. The Meccan fairs gave birth to a common culture, language, and social identity among the leading clans of Arabia. It was here that Muhammad was born.

Historians believe that Muhammad's revelations, infused with a deep sense of sin, gained inspiration from Christianity. From Judaism, Muhammad incorporated a sense of mission as a prophet sent to warn the world against impiety. The conflicts of his day and the long religious history of the region shaped Muhammad's message. At the age of forty, Muhammad reported that while meditating in solitude an angel appeared before him and said, "Muhammad, I am Gabriel and you are the Messenger of God. Recite!" Muhammad believed he was called to convey the message of God to all Arabs. He continued to reveal his revelations, and eventually, they were written down as the *Quran*. The book lays out five essential Muslim beliefs called the *Five Pillars of Islam*. These rules stated followers must recognize no God but "Allah" and Muhammad as his prophet, pray five times a day facing the city of Mecca, support the

poor, endure fasting during the holy month of Ramadan, and make a pilgrimage to Mecca at least once in a lifetime.

Muhammad's egalitarian vision, in which all believers were equal before God, directly challenged tribal loyalties and clan leaders. Like the message of Jesus, his teachings won favor among the lower classes while making enemies among the affluent and influential. Muhammad did not denounce Judaism and Christianity. However, he said that the Hebrew prophets and Jesus were God's spokesmen, but their messages had been confused and misinterpreted. He considered Jesus a major prophet but insisted he was only a man. Muhammad claimed no miraculous powers or divine lineage. He called himself "The Prophet"—God's final and definitive human messenger. Place, time, and culture shaped the tactics of Muhammad's religious mission. The tribes of Arabia lived by honor and retaliation. Tribesmen were expected to defend their lives and property in addition to that of other members. To cast one's lot with Muhammad and Islam was, in a sense, to give

Image 6.4: Map of the Growth of the Caliphate by 750 CE.

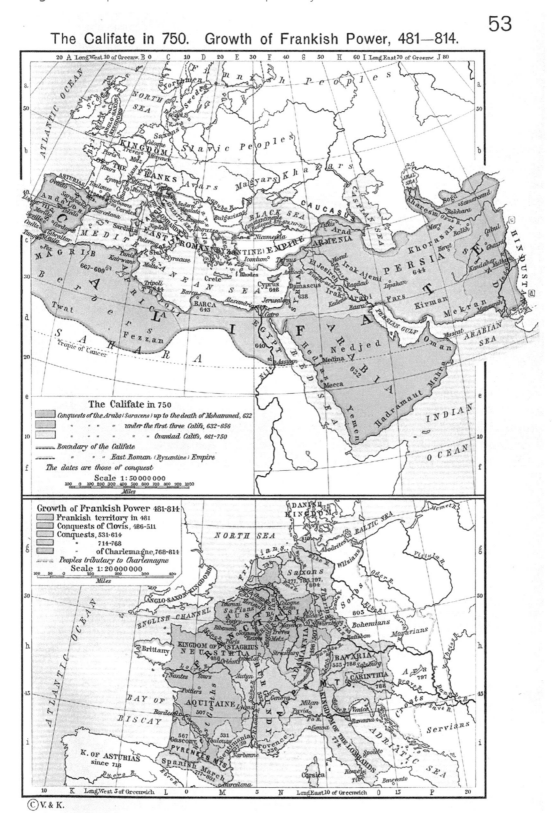

allegiance to a new type of tribe. Thus, Muhammad bore the responsibilities of a sheik to lead, defend, and avenge the members of his community. To fail in that responsibility would have made him unworthy of respect, and it would have potentially meant the end of his religious movement.

Muhammad's role was like Jewish leaders of the *Old Testament* who combined administrative, military, and spiritual authority. Muhammad forbade his people to fight each other but decreed instead that they devote their energies to waging jihad (holy struggle). Jihad asserts the umma (community) should defend itself, but it also implies a duty to campaign for justice and morality. Jihad can mean violence, but it also entails a spiritual struggle that all believers must wage against human temptation. In 630, Mohammad and his followers marched to Mecca and seized control of the city. When Mohammad died in 632, most of Arabia was under Muslim dominion. By 750, his successors had conquered an enormous part of the known world: from the Iberian Peninsula, across North Africa, over to Palestine, and into Mesopotamia.

Between the 8th and 10th centuries, the major Islamic city Cordoba, Spain was a model multi-cultural metropolis, and Arabs, Berbers from North Africa, Christian converts to Islam, and Jews all resided within it. Cordoba served as a supply line for the finest Arabian tableware, leather, silks, dyes, ointments, and perfumes.

In several vital ways, Muslims contributed to the evolution of Western Europe. They did so by inspiring people to create distinct cultures based on their inherited Judeo-Christian, Greco-Roman, and Byzantine roots. Also, by diverting the attention and energies of the Byzantine Empire, Muslims prevented it from expanding into and re-conquering Western Europe. That allowed Germanic peoples such as the Franks and the Lombards to establish independent civilizations.

The Grand Emperor Justinian

As we have seen, Germanic invaders in the late 5th century destroyed the Roman Empire's Mediterranean unity and ruled large portions of Rome's former domain. However, most of Rome's former eastern territories survived intact as the Byzantine Empire ("Byzantine" referred to an old Greek town Byzantium, incorporated in the imperial capital, Constantinople.) Containing the richer and more populated half of the old Roman Empire, the Byzantine state retained Rome's political and social structures and preserved its cultural heritage for a thousand years (476–1453). Justinian I (ruled: 527–565), perhaps the greatest Byzantine Emperor, combined the cultural heritage and political order of classical Greece and Rome with the vitality of the Christian religion. In so doing, he preserved and inspired many Byzantine contributions to civilization.

Image 6.5: Mosaic of Emperor Justinian in Basilica San Vitale, Ravenna, Italy, completed c. 547 CE. © Shutterstock.com

Justinian was a man of extraordinary talent and determined to strengthen and expand his empire. One act of enduring value was his codification of Roman law, known as the *Corpus Juris Civilis* (*Collection of Civil Law*). It made Orthodox Christianity the law of the land. Although inherently conservative, *Corpus Juris Civilis* improved the lot of freemen, slaves, and women. Moreover, it encouraged charitable gifts to the church and later became the basis for the civil law regulations of many European and Latin American nations. Justinian also took firm command of the Greek Church. Therefore, he appointed its presiding bishop (patriarch), decided theological disputes, and enforced clerical discipline. The Greek and Latin branches of Christianity were drifting apart in their relations to the state as well as to each other. While the popes, in response to the decline of civil authority in Italy, became more independent of the state, the patriarchs at Constantinople fell under the domination of the Byzantine Emperors. Both the emperors and the patriarchs rejected the claim of the popes to supremacy in religious matters.

Justinian also had a driving desire to reconquer the imperial territories in the west. At a severe cost in men and resources, he succeeded in wresting Italy and northwest sections of Africa from their Germanic masters. Justinian's military also won the Western Mediterranean islands, including Sicily, and gained a foothold in Spain. The Mediterranean world became once more the province of the "Romans." The popes, though threatened by Justinian's claim as protector of Italy, managed to preserve their independence, and after Justinian's death in 565, the peninsula slipped from Byzantine control.

Justinian managed to strengthen the internal administration of his empire. His successors, although harassed on every side, succeeded in keeping the machinery of government running. This was fortunate for Europe since Byzantine guarded the continent against attack from the east. Another key to imperial strength was the superb defensive position of the capital Constantinople itself, which was surrounded by water on three sides.

Byzantine also played a significant cultural role in the development of Western civilization. It was inherited from the Hellenistic past, the internationally dominant Greek culture of the Mediterranean and Middle East. Even when the Greeks lost their dominance to Islam, Byzantine continued to serve as the principal custodian of classical Greek culture. The rich literature of ancient Greece got conserved in archives and libraries, and Byzantine scholars enriched their heritage by adding their own commentaries and summations. Classical Greek education provided an

Image 6.6: Hagia Sophia, Istanbul, Turkey. Today the Hagia Sophia no longer serves as a church or a mosque, but rather as a museum unveiling the old Byzantine mosaics that had been covered up with white plaster while serving as a mosque. © Shutterstock.com

intellectual foundation for the Byzantine Empire. Although Justinian, in his role as Christian ruler, closed the philosophical schools of Athens, a great Christian university grew up in Constantinople.

In addition to conserving the culture that they had inherited, the Byzantines had impressive accomplishments of their own. Byzantine craftsmen produced superb objects in gold, silver, and enamel of lovely color and design. Western visitors were dazzled by what they saw. Justinian launched an ambitious building program for the capital. The principal monument became the mighty church of Hagia Sophia (Holy Wisdom). An elaborately planned structure, the Hagia Sophia employed domes and half-domes to create a vast interior space. The main dome measures over one hundred feet in diameter and one hundred eighty feet in height. Built in only six years, the Hagia Sophia combines the building principles of the Romans with the decorative splendor of the Persians. The temple inspires, in its fashion, the sense of marvel and holy mystery that the cathedrals of Europe achieved centuries later, and the structure served as a model for thousands of churches and mosques in the Middle East.

The Frankish Kingdom and Charlemagne

The Franks created their kingdom in Gaul, a place that eventually came to be called "Francia." Historians know more about Gaul than other barbarian kingdoms chiefly because of the survival of a vital primary source: Gregory of Tours' *History of the Franks* (594). As a bishop, Gregory became involved in the politics of the kingdom. His treatise recounted how King Clovis (ruled: 481–511) established the Frankish Kingdom and founded the House of Merovingian. The name Merovingian comes from a legendary sea monster, "Merovetch," from which Clovis and his family were said to have descended. Gregory's work evidenced continuity with Roman policies. The Byzantine Emperor named Clovis as his representative in Gaul and gave him the title "Consul."

While they held some similarities with Rome, the Frankish society that Gregory recorded was a unique place. Frankish customs tended to be communal and not legally encoded. They viewed taxes as personal gifts more than the state mandated fees. As a

wedding present, the Frankish King Chilperic (ruled: 561–584) gave his Queen Fredegund the right to the revenues of some of his towns. After two of her sons became gravely ill, however, she interpreted the episode as God's punishment for her greed. In response, she and Chilperic destroyed the documents that recorded what people owed to them. The queen supposedly said, "We may still lose our children, but we shall at least escape eternal damnation!" Also, much of Germanic law depended on something called wergild that equaled the sum measure of each worth. When a person suffered an injustice, the wergild determined the amount of compensation that the wrongdoer had to pay to the victim.

In 732, an Arab army, after conquering most of Spain, fought a Frankish force at the Battle of Tours. Led by the brilliant general and political leader Charles Martel, the Franks turned back the enemy in what Europeans would remember as a legendary battle. The Muslims (who soon came to be called the Moors or the Saracens to Western Europeans) retreated into the Iberian Peninsula (Spain) and held it under their control for several centuries. With their success, the Franks seemed close to establishing their empire. That would have to wait, however, for the rise of Martel's grandson, Charlemagne.

The momentum that led to the reorganization of Western civilization started with ambitious leaders who sought to establish their own enduring kingdoms. One of these men was the son of noted Frankish leader Charles Martel, Pepin. To earn his claim as King of the Franks, Pepin needed the official approval of the Catholic Church. For the Pope, the transition from one ruling family to another was a grave matter of great concern. Still, a grateful new Frankish King would be a valuable ally in this rough and tumble post-Roman world. With the Pope's approval, nobles came together and chose King Pepin (ruled: 752–768) as their new ruler. The Carolingian dynasty had formally begun.

The coronation of Pepin was a first in the history of Western Europe. It was like the *Old Testament* consecration of Israelite kings. Soon, it became standard practice for the pope to anoint kings via elaborate ceremonies. In this way, monarchs now claimed their power came from God as his representative on earth. Pepin, in return, did not disappoint the new king-maker of Europe, as his army engaged and subdued the rival Arian Lombards. Through the "Donation of Pepin," the pope received his own

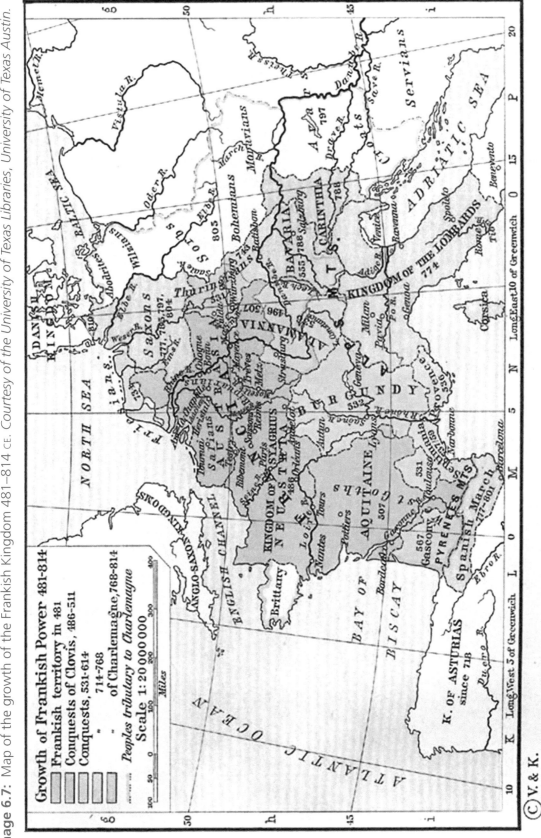

Image 6.7: Map of the growth of the Frankish Kingdom 481–814 CE. *Courtesy of the University of Texas Libraries, University of Texas Austin.*

land in the central part of Italy. This became known as the Papal States and remained the property of the Catholic Church for over one thousand years. It effectively made the pope an independent sovereign of a vast territory.

The close association between the papacy and the Carolingians reached its zenith under Pepin's son, Charles. History is more likely to know him as Charlemagne (ruled: 768–814), which in French corresponds to "Charles the Great." Charlemagne successfully combined several attributes that made him a very successful ruler. He was a talented military commander, a competent administrator, and a close ally of the head of the Catholic Church. By the end of his long reign, Charlemagne had made the Franks into the most prosperous kingdom in Western Europe. In fact, Charlemagne ruled an empire that today comprises most of France, Germany, and half of Italy.

Charlemagne came closer to uniting the peoples of the old Roman Empire than anyone. On Christmas Day in the year 800, Pope Leo III placed the imperial crown on Charlemagne's head and proclaimed him the "Emperor of the Romans." In addition, Charlemagne became the first Holy Roman Emperor, and the entity called the Holy Roman Empire existed until 1806. For the first time in over three hundred years, there was a Roman Empire in the west. Eastern rulers held that the Pope had no right to christen someone with such an exalted position. To them, Charlemagne was a barbarian upstart. So, instead of reuniting the two halves of the Roman Empire, Charlemagne's coronation drove them further apart.

Charlemagne was to be the new Constantine. He was a Catholic-sanctioned ruler of the Christian world, but a crucial question of authority threatened the unity of the secular and the spiritual. The church viewed the coronation as guaranteeing the primacy of the papacy over Charlemagne and all other monarchs. For his part, Charlemagne did not see his position as subordinate to any individual or organization, and that included the pope. Still, the coronation was a momentous event, even though its implications were not clear to all participants.

Image 6.8: Raphael, *The Crowning of Charlemagne*, c. 1508–1524, fresco in the Raphael Rooms in the Vatican, Rome, Italy. © Shutterstock.com

Life in the British Isles

Long before the Carolingians, the islands of Britannia suffered unrest and violence. As Roman armies withdrew from the British Isles to aid their countrymen further east, an opportunity arose for both the Germanic Angles and Saxons. The withdrawal of the imperial armies enabled barbarian tribes to establish settlements in the lands once-loyal to Rome. As Roman culture became a thing of the past, the islands fell on hard times. By around 450, cities either shrank to very small villages or lay abandoned. A century later, fortified villas in the countryside,

the last vestige of Roman life, had disappeared. The Latin language declined and many place-names were forgotten. Thus, the land became known as England ("Angle-land").

The fate of Ireland was tied to England, but its early history made it a place apart from the rest of Western civilization. Ireland had never been part of the Rome Empire or had much contact with its culture. It was rural and tribal, with little acquaintance with urban civilization. A change came in the 5th century when Irish raiders captured a young Briton, by the name of Patrick (Saint Patrick), and took him to Ireland as a slave. After an escape to his homeland,

Image 6.9: England after 886, when the East was controlled by Danish Vikings from Jutland, and the South controlled by Anglo-Saxons and the Kingdom of Wessex. Eventually all of England would come under control of Wessex before falling to the Norman Conquest in 1066. *Courtesy of the University of Texas Libraries, University of Texas Austin.*

something compelled Patrick to return to Ireland on a religious mission. Due to his work and that of others, Christianity flourished in pagan Ireland. Christian monasteries, along with interest in the literary legacy of the Greco-Roman world, soon spread to the Irish countryside. Irish monks earned acclaim for their scholarship at a time when learning was declining on the continent.

Few contributed to learning in the Middle Ages like the British monk the Venerable Bede. Although Bede never wandered far from home, his intellect was wide-ranging. He read Latin, Greek, and Hebrew. He was interested in literature, theology, history, and many of the sciences. Also, Bede popularized the custom of dating events from the birth of Christ, and his remarkable *Ecclesiastical History of the English People* (731) still engages readers. His respect for sources and incredible writing skill made Bede superior to other authors of the early Middle Ages.

English kings were more interested in establishing workable kingdoms than extending the reach of education. Monarchs divided their domains and appointed royal representatives to govern in their name. These aristocratic earls had many responsibilities including mustering the local men into armies and leading them into battle. Earls also served as judges presiding over courts and executing royal commands. Kings also appointed sheriffs to help the earls fulfill their duties. These officials helped the monarchy ensure that earls did not acquire too much power.

Most tasks, however, were handled at the local level. Community elders enforced village laws that formed the core level of administrative order, and parish priests and tax collectors joined sheriffs and earls in the bureaucratic structure. Most Anglo-Saxon kings were considered selfish and inadequate rulers. In contrast, Alfred the Great (ruled: 871–899) became a tremendous monarch. He implemented an efficient administration, supported the arts, and England flourished under his reign. Despite his natural curiosity and intelligence, Alfred did not learn to read until he was twelve years old. In adulthood, however, he would make up for lost time. Alfred made education a priority in England, and this meant translating Latin works into the native language. Also, he studied Latin, collected books, and invited scholars to teach within the kingdom. Alfred the Great encouraged singers to fill his court with sacred music and traditional folk songs, as well. A relentless threat from the North, led by the Vikings,

forced Alfred the Great to give up much of his territory. The Anglo-Saxon king kept an area in the South known as Wessex, but he signed a treaty that gave the Viking Norsemen the northeastern part of the island.

The last Anglo-Saxon ruler of England was Edward the Confessor (ruled: 1034–1066). Upon Edward's death, the Anglo-Saxon nobles crowned one of their own, Harold Godwinson, as king. However, Duke William of Normandy claimed that Edward wanted him to become the next king. William sailed a fleet across the English Channel and engineered the last successful large-scale invasion of England. He and his French nobles defeated Harold and his Anglo-Saxon army at the Battle of Hastings in 1066. Shortly afterward, William, known by the title "William the Conqueror" (ruled: 1066–1087), became King of England. His reign symbolized the triumph of the Normans and their Viking predecessors.

The Feudal System

The Viking invasions of Western Europe influenced the emergence of a new political and social arrangement that would eventually be called feudalism. Without a central government, people needed a way to defend themselves. Leaders, or lords as they were known, built military fortresses aimed at protecting against attacks from groups such as the Vikings. These defensive structures were called castles, but most of them were simply private homes strategically built atop hills. In addition to being homes, castles became centers of authority that allowed lords to rule over small regions.

Castles could not safeguard their inhabitants unless lords employed small armies to protect them. To solve this problem, lords offered grants of land to men classified as vassals who in turn agreed to be a soldier for the landowner. Thus, the feudal system changed the way European warfare was conducted. For example, the Frankish army initially consisted of sword-bearing foot soldiers with little protection from enemy weapons. Now, they wore armored coats of mail (larger horses could carry the weight) and wielded long lances that enabled them to act as battering rams. For almost 500 years, heavily armored cavalry, more famously known as knights, defined the European way of warfare. Both lords and knights needed each other because wealth was based primarily on land. In fact, the importance of land must be put into context to grasp the economic and social relationships of medieval Europe. Land was not only a commodity but the link between different classes of people.

By the 9th century, a vassal's land grant became known as a fief. The practice of fief-holding carried with it rules and rituals that characterized the relationship between a lord and his vassal. To the lord, a vassal owed military protection from outside invaders. A vassal was required to appear at his lord's court and offer him advice. He also might be asked to sit in judgment in a legal case as one of the peers of another vassal. Also, lords depended on vassals for financial considerations in special circumstances, or in case they were captured and held for ransom.

The logic of the economic relationships between classes of people in the medieval period depended on manorialism. Under it, peasants (serfs) gave up their freedom to a lord, provided him with the fruits of their labor, and from him derived protection and use of the land. Most serfs had little choice but to work the land. They were required to offer their labor to the lord while living subject to his authority in most matters. Labor services consisted of working the lord's demesne (land retained by the lord), and peasants utilized the remaining land. Building barns and digging ditches were also part of the duties.

Inequality, a lack of opportunity for advancement, and poor working conditions characterized the lives of most Europeans. But, serfs suffered the most. Peasants were legally bound to the land and could not leave without permission. Although free to marry, they could not wed anyone outside their manor without the lord's approval. At the same time, lords held certain legal rights on their lands that gave them the authority to try peasants in their own courts. In fact, most serfs only knew the law as interpreted in the manorial courts. Thus, a lord's far-reaching power gave him virtual control over both the lives and property of his peasants.

Despite the clear injustices of the early medieval period, European civilization slowly evolved and changed. Monarchs strove to increase their authority over the growing feudal nobility. In fact, tension between the landed earls and the kings and queens of Europe was commonplace. The mutual obligations between individuals in a feudalistic system made it difficult for one class to assume control of social and economic interactions. In other words, even kings relied on others to guarantee and protect their privileges. For these reasons, and because so many people at the bottom of the social ladder suffered, class conflict inevitably threatened to upset the ordered rules of feudalism. Cracks in the system began to cause unrest and brought new demands from various classes of society.

The Crusades

To the south and east of the European mainland, Muslim lands clearly represented a rival to the Christian world. From as early as the 4th century, Christians often visited holy places of their religion's origins. Crowds of thousands sometimes traveled to these locations, and in doing so, they passed through Byzantine and Muslim controlled territories. For centuries, these trips, albeit hazardous, were possible. The Turks occupied Jerusalem and were somewhat friendly to pilgrims, but they did impose taxes on foreign travelers. Many Christians resented the policy and believed travel to sacred areas should not have restrictions.

It was simmering discontent that stirred many in Christendom to take up the crusading spirit. The series of events that led to the crusades had their beginning in the central part of Asia. The Byzantine Empire reached the height of its expansion and power in 1056, but soon after it endured a considerable decline. The Byzantine army lost its effectiveness as a fighting force, and the emperors started recruiting expensive mercenary soldiers to fill the ranks. When the empire became vulnerable on several fronts in the late 11th century, neither the army nor the treasury was prepared. The Normans threatened Byzantine provinces in Italy, and Muslims slowly encroached onto the empire's eastern holdings. A fierce Central Asian tribe known as the Seljuk Turks converted to Islam and reinforced the Muslim armies threatening the Byzantine Empire. In the 11th century, the Seljuks conquered Baghdad and won the title of sultan (ruler) from its caliph (successor to Muhammad). Members of this family pushed westward from Baghdad into Syria, Palestine, and Anatolia. They established themselves as rulers of several small states in those areas and were less tolerant of Christian minorities than previous Arab leaders.

While resentment mounted in Western Europe against the Islamic groups who controlled the holy land, to Byzantine Christians the expansion of the Seljuk Turks was a formidable new danger. Over the centuries, differences of belief and practice divided the two fronts of Christianity. In essence, the popes' insistence on absolute rule over all of Christendom created a clash of cultures in European Christianity.

Eastern rulers had their own ideas about the faith and a long history of acting independently of Rome. However, the potential for Muslim domination tended to mend old wounds. In 1071, the Turks defeated a Byzantine army at Manzikert in Eastern Anatolia and then moved westward toward the imperial capital. Byzantine Emperor Alexius I (ruled: 1081–1118) appealed for help to Pope Urban II.

Urban viewed his situation as a golden opportunity to rally Christendom's warriors to liberate Jerusalem and the other sacred lands. At the Council of Clermont in France near the end of 1095, Urban challenged Christians to take up their weapons and join in a holy war. In return, the pope promised to absolve participants of their sins. The series of military engagements between Muslims and Christians that continued for roughly two hundred years are called the Crusades.

Europeans took up arms on a crusade for several reasons. Many of them had a sincere belief in the cause. Other crusaders wanted land and wealth. In general, Europeans answered Urban's mandate with tremendous support. The first to respond included scores of peasants who followed two self-appointed leaders, Peter the Hermit and Walter the Penniless, in the crusade to conquer the holy land. It was soon apparent that their passionate commitment would translate to unforeseen cycles of violence.

The first crusading army consisted of roughly a few thousand cavalry members and about ten thousand infantrymen. After the capture of Antioch in 1098, crusaders proceeded toward Palestine and reached their primary target of Jerusalem in 1099. After a five-week siege, they took Jerusalem, and in the process, massacred many men, women, and children. After an invasion of Palestinian lands, the Christian armies organized four crusader states: Edessa, Antioch, Tripoli, and Jerusalem. Muslims surrounded the new, Christian sponsored colonies, and thus they grew increasingly dependent on Italian cities for European supplies. Some Italian cities, such as Genoa, Pisa, and especially Venice, became rich and powerful in the process.

Over time, the Muslims counterattacked, and they recaptured Edessa in 1144. Christians in the west assembled new armies to support those already in the holy land, but the subsequent crusades were not as

Image 6.10: Peter the Hermit rallies supporters and followers for the first wave of the First Crusade, also known as the People's Crusade, engraving by Wattier, 1844, Paris. © Shutterstock.com

Image 6.11: Map of Asia Minor and the Crusader states c. 1140 CE. *Courtesy of the University of Texas Libraries, University of Texas Austin.*

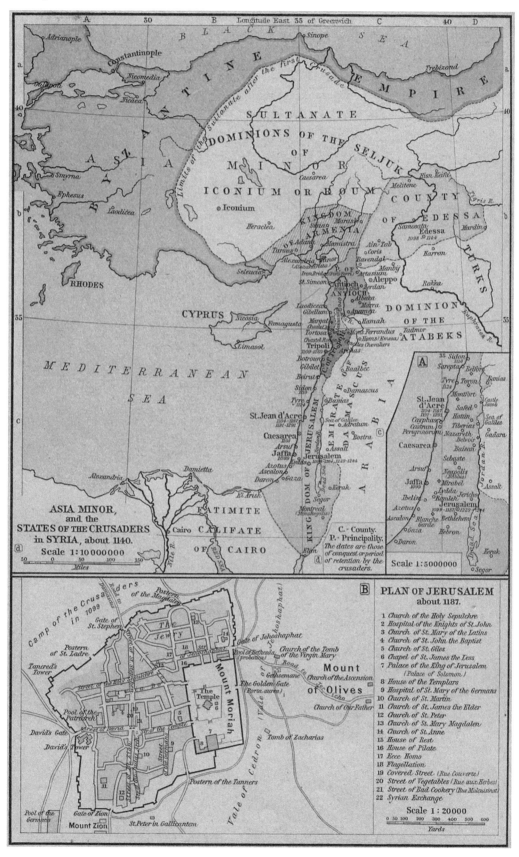

successful as the initial effort. Defeats only tended to make church leaders more loudly proclaim the need to regroup and reinvest in the crusading ideal. The European crusaders met their match with the rise to prominence of a new Muslim general. From Syria came a talented leader named Saladin. Using the newly invigorated spirit of jihad, in 1187 Saladin coordinated a force that retook Jerusalem. Saladin proved more tolerant to his defeated opponents, and the practice of Christianity, than many expected. Saladin fought his opponents to a standstill. Even the most famous Christian warrior of the time, King Richard I of England (ruled: 1189–1199) could not secure the sacred areas. However, he reached a settlement with Saladin to allow Christian pilgrims free access to Jerusalem. There would be other crusades, but none very successful. For more than 200 years, Christian soldiers found it impossible to hold places deep within the heart of the Muslim world.

The Impact of a Building: Norman Architecture

By Christina McClellan

Architecture and art play a key role in conveying messages that can resonate louder than words.

The Norman Conquest of England supplanted Anglo-Saxon rule with that of the Norman, William the Conqueror. In order to consolidate control of this new country, William traveled throughout England displacing Anglo-Saxon Thegns with Norman nobility, building strongholds in each major area from which they were to control and manage in the name of the king.

While changing leadership was instrumental in establishing control, a person is not visible to the populace all the time. In order to emphasize the change in authority, and create a stronghold from which the new nobility was to work from, Normans built motte and bailey castles out of wood for an immediate effect, and later out of stone. The motte is an earthen mound, usually artificially made, that is flattened at the top upon which the castle stood. The bailey was an enclosed courtyard at the base of the motte and would contain various structures, including residences, workshops, and stables. The castle was often round, with few windows. The structures were an impressive and imposing sight to remind the locals of who was in charge and protect the newly acquired Norman interest.

As Normans consolidated their control, they started to build other more subtle architecture with distinctively Norman features. The center of everyday life in medieval Europe revolved around the

Image 6.12a: Church of St. John the Baptist, Leeds, United Kingdom, built c. 1150–1170 CE. © Shutterstock.com

Image 6.12b: Detail of door, Church of St. John the Baptist, Leeds, United Kingdom, built c. 1150–1170 CE. © Shutterstock.com

church. Changing of the seasons and tides in the harvest were heralded by religious festivals marking changes in each occasion. Priests conveyed news and current events to their parishes, which were largely illiterate. Thereby, Norman control was reinforced by the construction of new churches in the Norman style. Norman architecture elaborates on the Romanesque style with arches, prominent masonry, and few windows. It is distinguished from the Romanesque, however, by the inclusion of chevron patterns adorning the doors and some windows. Though the structure appears minimalists, it provides a key function in its community, and is an imposing sight that was a distinctive departure from the Viking-esque style of the Anglo-Saxon rule.

Image 6.12c: Cornwall, United Kingdom, built c. 1068, rebuilt in stone in the 12th century. © Shutterstock.com

Chapter 7

The Middle Ages: Act Two

The end of the Crusades marked a vital turning point in the Middle Ages. One of the most significant consequences of the Crusades was the expansion of trade and economic networking. The Italian cities that provided transportation and supplies to the crusading armies profited more than most. These cities served as the heartland of new trading ventures that included luxury goods such as silk, Persian carpets, medicine, and spices. These were all expensive and exotic consumer goods found in the bazaars of the Middle East. Profits from this trade helped stimulate the economy of Western Europe and led to an era of substantial economic growth during the 12th and 13th centuries.

The Crusades also forced Europeans to reconsider the practices of the Catholic Church. It might not be a surprise that support for crusading activities waned as victory appeared impossible. If anything, the Crusades proved that religious officials were not infallible and should be held accountable for their actions. During this period, economic, social, political, cultural, and religious changes were part of a great transition. Before a new Europe could emerge, however, one crisis after another occurred. Compounding this series of crises were dynastic struggles between English and French monarchs which led to the disastrous One Hundred Years War. However, these crises did not stop the continued evolution of society, and in fact, may have encouraged it.

Developments in the Church

Despite disunion in some regions, most Europeans found common ground under the banner of the Catholic Church. Ironically, because the church had decentralized, their influence grew increasingly prominent. Local lords saw the churches on their manors as their own property and priests as their vassals. Nobles sometimes treated bishop dioceses as rewards for loyal subjects rather than as religious positions. Critics of these practices began to voice demands for reform, and some sought a leader who could preside over a universal Christendom. As a result, the Roman Catholic Church experienced a period of tremendous expansion. The pope reigned over the territories in Italy that came to be known as the Papal States, and this often meant the head of the Catholic Church was more involved in political than spiritual matters.

The monastic ideal that had been instrumental in building the Christian community also suffered during the early Middle Ages. Benedictine (St. Benedict) monasteries had sometimes been exemplary centers of Christian living and learning, but the invasions of Vikings, Magyars, and Muslims destroyed or weakened many of them. Discipline declined and with it the monastic reputation for learning and holiness. In addition, local lords gained control over some monasteries. It must have seemed that the Church was losing its autonomy while becoming just enough of a secular instrument of government.

In the early 10th century, a spirit of reform for the Catholic Church began in Burgundy, France with the founding of the Cluny Abbey. The monastery dedicated itself to becoming the ideal representation of the Benedictine philosophy. The clergy purposefully kept Cluny out of the affairs of lords and the usual machinations of feudalism. As was stipulated in its original charter: "It has pleased us also to insert in this document that, from this day, those same monks there congregated shall be subject neither to the yoke of lords and dukes, nor to that of our relatives, nor to the sway of the royal might, nor to that of any earthly power." The Cluniac reform movement sparked an enthusiastic response in France and eventually in much of the western and central parts of Europe. New and existing monasteries adopted the Cluniac program. From their founding, Cluniacs supported a strong papacy, and their influence increased even further when Gregory VII, a cardinal highly sympathetic to their ideals, became pope in 1073. Gregory decided that the papacy should rule Christendom instead of any king or emperor. This outlook did not make for a good relationship with the Holy Roman Emperor Henry IV (ruled: 1084–1105).

The question of who should appoint or invest bishops in Germany ignited the trouble between the pope and the emperor. Since the time of Constantine, monarchs assumed a prominent place as religious as well as secular leaders. In a break from the past, Gregory argued that his dominion was not limited by any king while claiming to be the overlord of the

Image 7.1: Cluny Abbey, in Cluny, France. Though parts of the abbey were deconstructed after the structure was sold, some of it still survives today as a representation of Romanesque Architecture. © Shutterstock.com

rulers of Western Europe. He surmised that Henry IV was his vassal because Charlemagne originally owed his title to Pope Leo III. In other words, popes choose emperors and therefore outrank them. Gregory also objected to the fact Henry selected German bishops. Gregory felt that bishops were spiritual officers and could be invested with ring and staff, the symbols of their religious authority, only by the pope. What he sought, of course, was papal control over important elections. In 1075, Gregory issued a decree that clarified his position on papal power. He stated, "We decree that no one of the clergy shall receive the investiture with a bishopric or abbey or church from the hand of an emperor or king or of any lay person."

The struggle between Henry IV and Gregory VII is known as the Investiture Controversy. It continued until 1122 when Pope Calixtus II and Holy Roman Emperor Henry V (ruled: 1111–1125) achieved an agreement called the *Concordat of Worms*. This compromise made it official policy that clergymen of the church would select German bishops. At the same time, officers of the church paid homage to the king. In turn, the king symbolically gave the bishop the authority of his title. The process was created to promise that neither king nor pope was forced to admit dominion over the other. These types of arrangements were common during a period when society had not yet defined the line between church and state. Still, further disagreements were on the horizon.

Some Christians, called heretics by the orthodox, disagreed with established doctrine and criticized the leadership of Rome. Some of these people questioned the church's wealth and power. Inspired by the biblical text, "If you wish to be perfect, then go and sell everything you have, and give to the poor" (*Matthew* 9:21), many Christians valued a simpler, value-driven life. Unlike monasteries, the new lay communities did not withdraw from, but worked in the world and they lived according to self-defined rules. The Catholic Church welcomed these initiatives but worried that untrained preachers might misrepresent them. With this in mind, Catholic officials forbade preachers who the church did not officially sanction.

In the late 12th century, the French city of Lyons became the place where a merchant named Peter Waldo created the exact scenario that worried the Catholic Church. The Archbishop of Lyons forbade Waldo from preaching to the masses. Waldo questioned many of the Church's positions and even

Image 7.2: During the Investiture Controversy, in 1078, Pope Gregory excommunicated Emperor Henry IV. Excommunication meant that his people no longer had to obey his commands, and he would be cut off from supplies and housing since he was dependent upon the loyalty of the bishops he had invested. In order to reverse the excommunication, Henry's forces surrounded Canossa Castle where Pope Gregory had sought refuge. Henry circled the castle, barefoot, calling for Gregory. In the end, they reached a compromise and Gregory lifted the excommunication. However, neither side would keep the agreement and conflict continued shortly thereafter. © Shutterstock.com

debated if the sacraments were essential to salvation. When he ignored them and continued to spread his beliefs, the Church made it known that Waldo's sect was in the wrong. His followers (The Waldensians) were declared heretics, imprisoned, excommunicated, and finally, in the early 13th century, expelled from the region.

The Cathars, more than other religious dissenters, defied and angered the Christian establishment. The Cathars were especially strong in Northern Italy and Southern France, and they were also known as Albigensians. The fundamental disagreement concerned the role and origin of earthly evil. For the Cathars, the world was the product of dark, impure forces. As a perfect deity, God created only the world of the spirit, which was eternal, and the corruptible, material realm was the offspring of a satanic entity: Jehovah, God of the Jews. Consequently, they rejected the *Old Testament* and denied Christ's Incarnation (Jesus could not be both purely good and wholly evil). They declared sacraments like baptism and the Eucharist inherently blasphemous.

Unfortunately for the Cathars, they would not relent without a fight. Pope Innocent III declared war on them and persuaded church and government leaders to participate in his cause. From 1209 to 1229, the Catholics waged a brutal and unmerciful campaign to rid the world of the Cathars. In one of the more well-known episodes, several thousand

men, women, and children of the town of Beziers died after barricading themselves inside a cathedral. When soldiers asked the papal representative how they could distinguish between the heretics and the faithful, he reportedly replied, "Kill them all; God will know his own."

In some cases, the Church listened to its critics without the need to suppress views deemed heretical. In the 13th century, popes approved two movements, the Franciscans and Dominicans, that promised to address public concerns. In previous monastic movements, men and women isolated themselves to come closer to God. By contrast, the new religious impulse called for clergymen to mingle among the people in the growing towns of Europe. The idea was to help alleviate the new problems of urban poverty and suffering. Franciscans and Dominicans served God by helping the needy in their villages and towns.

Francis of Assisi became one of the most prominent religious thinkers of the medieval world, and he founded his namesake order: the Franciscans. He was born in 1182 to wealthy parents and served for a time in the military. His life would never be the same, however, after Francis gave up his material possessions and vowed to spend life helping others. He attracted a following of like-minded people who dressed as beggars, preached in the streets, and aided the poor and suffering. Although Franciscans in some ways resembled the Waldensians, they differed in one significant aspect: obedience to the pope. Francis impressed the church establishment with his humility, and in 1209, he received papal approval to establish a new order of "friars."

Unlike the Franciscans, the Dominicans were a league of intellectual teachers. Spanish priest Dominic de Guzman founded the Dominican Order. He believed the best way to combat heresy was through learning and preaching to the masses. In 1217, Pope Honorius approved the Order of Preachers, or the Dominicans, who, like the Franciscans, did not live in secluded monasteries. Alarmed by the heretical doctrines of the day, Dominic believed he could best serve the Lord by instructing his believers. Therefore, while Francis appealed to people's hearts, Dominic appealed more to their minds.

Some creative thinkers combined religious meditation with scientific inquiry. The importance of Christianity in medieval society led to a school of thought called Scholasticism. Ever since the early days of Christianity, there had been those who insisted that God transcended reason, and any attempt to understand and explain him was futile if not blasphemous. However, there was a contrary view. Scholastics hoped to approach human rationality as a means to better understand God. The scholastic who bests represents the medieval attempt to merge faith and reason was Thomas Aquinas. His famous work *Summa Theologica* (written from 1265 to 1274) was the ultimate manifestation of Scholastic

ideas. He believed humans could prove the existence of God by systematic and logical questioning of the world. Aquinas argued that anything moving must have first been acted upon by some other object. He stated the world had to have originated with a "first mover," and he called that force God. For Aquinas, faith and reason were two sides of the same coin, and they both originated from God.

In the late 13th century, French King Philip IV (ruled: 1284–1314) and Pope Boniface VIII engaged in a dispute about money matters. The king decided to impose a tax on the church without consulting the pope. Law and tradition made this a difficult undertaking for Philip, because it was illegal to demand a tax from the church without the permission of the papacy. In 1296, Boniface issued a decree called the *Clericis Laicos*, and in it threatened to excommunicate any individual involved with tax collecting-both those who paid and those who collected. It seemed that yet another stalemate between church and state was on the horizon. Boniface found a way out of the dilemma and declared that the French king could indeed tax the clergy in times of crisis. As one might expect, there were more confrontations soon to follow.

Taxes were one thing, but Boniface faced a much more daunting concern. Philip ignored the papacy's stricture against bringing a bishop before a civil court. For the Catholic leadership, the law was clear without any gray areas. Philip rallied his people including the representative assembly, the Estates General, to offer him their support against Boniface. The pope responded with talk of excommunicating the king, but it was too late for Boniface. In late 1303, the outraged monarch raided the papal summer place located

Image 7.3: Neri di Bicci, *St. Francis of Assisi*, painting, Croatian Academy of Sciences. © Shutterstock.com

Image 7.4: Avignon Cathedral and Papal Palace, Avignon, France. © Shutterstock.com

in France and captured Boniface. He was ultimately released from custody but died a month later. Many people wondered if, during his captivity, Boniface had been abused and pondered if Philip played a role in his death. Regardless, Philip won this round of conflict between the Pope and the European monarchs.

A few years after the death of Boniface, Catholics chose a Frenchman, Pope Clement V, and he did not go to Rome. Instead, the new pope moved the church headquarters to Avignon, France, and it remained there, under French influence, from 1309 to 1377. During this period, papal prestige suffered enormously. Most Europeans believed that Rome was the only suitable capital for the Catholic Church. Moreover, representatives from several of the major European states accused the popes and the cardinals, most of whom were now also French, of being instruments of the French king. The Avignon Papacy strengthened the resolve of those who already held grievances against the corruption that some perceived as rampant within the Catholic Church. It did not help that the Avignon Popes called for new and increasingly higher payments from England, Germany, and Italy. At the same time, they built more lavish and extensive palaces and expanded the size of the Catholic bureaucracy. These actions provoked denunciation of the wealth of the church and increased demands for reform.

It is difficult to overestimate the problem, for the Catholic Church, of being centered away from its traditional home, Rome. The popes served in the role of Bishop of Rome, and that position was based on being the successor to the Apostle Peter, the first to hold this role. To many people, it was unseemly for the head of the Catholic Church to reside outside of Rome. There was also the view that by staying in Avignon, the papacy had become too cozy with the French leadership. In 1377, Pope Gregory XI heeded the call to return to Rome. It seemed that the fortunes of the church had improved. The next year Gregory died, and a papal election was held to replace him. During the period of the papacy's residence in Avignon, all the men who served as pope were French, and in addition, the same applied to the great majority of the cardinals selected by the French popes. The Catholics were so afraid of another French papacy that the College of Cardinals refused to leave Rome until a Roman or Italian was elected pope. Bowing to public pressure, the cardinals chose an Italian, Pope

Urban VI, as the church's new leader. A few months later, the French cardinals rebelled and announced one of their own as the rightful head of the Catholic Church.

Turmoil worsened the prestige of the Catholic Church, and it must have seemed to be under fire from all directions. During the Papal Schism (1378–1417), as the split of the church into two allegiances was called, there were two popes. Each one had their own College of Cardinals and claimed universal sovereignty. Moreover, both popes excommunicated one another. The nations of Europe aligned themselves with whomever promised to serve their best interests. As one can imagine, these developments caused Europeans to doubt and question the legitimacy of the church leadership. The Papal Schism finally ended with the calling of a church council. While it ended the period of division, church prestige suffered severe damage.

Disagreements within the Catholic Church, and battles between popes and kings, did not diminish the reality that medieval Europeans were increasingly defined by their Christian faith. Locally, bishops, priests, and other clergyman offered the rites and rituals of everyday life. Popes made the decisions that directed the future of individuals and nations. Christendom was an idea equally as much as a geographic location. The idea relied on the loose agreement that a group of Christian communities existed and were characterized by a set of morals and beliefs.

The Developments of a Modernizing Society

By the 11th century, towns and accompanying trade reemerged in Europe after all but disappearing in the years following the fall of the Roman Empire. From about 1200 onward, further economic changes occurred in Europe. Medieval guilds and their associated merchants, while having served an important function in the early years of the Middle Ages, were not as well-equipped to handle the burgeoning economic activity of the new age of capitalism. In the old guild system, prices typically remained fixed and business activity remained relatively small. Profits were limited, and usually only large enough to support a master craftsman, his family, and the upkeep of his shop. Simply put, there was not enough money to create a surplus, which in turn, could be used to expand operations.

By the 13th century, Italian merchants dominated the lucrative trade of the Mediterranean Sea region. Thus, they began reinvesting their profits in more ambitious business ventures. What the Italians achieved as middlemen between the Europe and the Far East, the merchants of the port cities of Germany accomplished in the Baltic Sea. They pooled their resources, built fleets of ships, and won joint trading privileges. By the 14th century, the leading towns of the northern territories of Germany had formed an effective commercial alliance, the Hanseatic League, which dominated the trade of Northern Europe from England to Russia. The cities of the Hanseatic League set up outlets in the trading centers of Russia, Poland, Norway, and England. From these distant outposts, rich profits flowed freely. Ultimately, a truly international commerce developed, and this new reality proved extensive enough to provide for the accumulation of profit surpluses and the growth of a capitalist class.

The old business arrangements of the guild system, with its limited markets and controlled prices, gave way to new business ventures that focused on how best to pool and invest capital. One new business idea to emerge was the concept of division of labor. In the old guild system, cloth merchants did the buying of material and then all else needed to make a raw product into a finished, usable one. By the 14th century, more cloth merchants were parceling out much of the work to individuals who focused on one aspect of the process. Each type of worker got paid by the piece or weighted amount. This included positions such as: cutters, dyers, spinners, and weavers. The cloth merchant, who maintained ownership of the cloth through the manufacturing process, sold the final product on the international market at a price dictated by supply and demand.

The wool merchants reaped the profits of both industry and commerce. They paid the laborers as low a rate as possible and permitted them no input in the operation of the business. Moreover, the workers were forbidden by law to organize or strike. This "putting-out" or "domestic" system became the principal mode of production in early modern Europe. It destroyed the close relationships between masters and journeymen that had existed in the medieval guilds, and it made profit motive the chief objective of business. While the division of labor introduced the possibility of tremendous profits for many businessmen, the new enterprise threatened

the social status and personal identity of others. Thus, class antagonisms developed between these new capitalists and workers which foreshadowed the fierce conflicts that would erupt during the Industrial Revolution. As Europe's economy became more closely tied to the activities of capitalists, the old techniques of exchange and finance proved inadequate. In the past, loaning of money was limited due to the Catholic Church's stance against lending money at an excessive interest rate. In addition, the limited economy did not create a need for a great deal of lending activity. As businessmen sought to increase their economic enterprises, they needed more ambitious means of financing. Investors who desired diverse methods of putting their money to work filled this role. Because of these occurrences, commerce expanded, and many people realized that lending was a useful and acceptable activity. Large-scale money lending became normal. Wealthy bankers of the period opened branch offices in the major commercial centers of Europe. They ventured into buying, selling, and speculating in all kinds of goods, and in addition, bankers provided financial services to merchants, high clergy, and rulers.

Capitalism unleashed forces that undermined the guilds, weakened the manorial system, and undermined the values that the Catholic Church applied to most economic transactions. The most far-reaching change, which impacted all relationships between nobles and peasants, was the substitution of money for payments in goods or services. Traditionally, serfs were required to cultivate the lord's estate. By the 14th century, however, nobles often found it more advantageous to rent out their land to free tenants who were now able to sell their crops at nearby markets and pay their leases in cash.

Once nobles began renting out much of their land, the days of serfdom became numbered and emancipation soon followed. Most freed peasants chose to remain on the lord's property and pay rent to use the land. By around 1500, serfdom had all but disappeared in England and become a rarity in Western Europe. The medieval lord, with his rights to the crops and services of the peasantry, transformed into a capitalist landowner living off his rents. Although many of the great estates remained intact, the traditional relationship of lord and serf changed. The nobility experienced disruption, and the rigid line separating aristocrats and commoners became blurred.

Closely connected to the new economy and growth in advanced technologies were noticeable changes in the patterns of government. Rulers looked to enhance their power and influence both at home and abroad. Traditionally, like other landowners, they collected rents from peasants who lived on their lands. Soon, rulers began finding other means of financial resources. With the growth in trade, tariffs could be levied. Rulers also entertained new forms of taxation. If money from all these sources was insufficient, wealthy bankers could provide necessary loans. With greater financial resources available, rulers were no longer beholden to the services of independent-minded vassals. They began to develop their own bureaucracies, composed of paid professionals who staffed the various branches of government. This was a significant development, for it put control of the government and the military directly in the hands of the major rulers. While governments took advantage of the new financial situation, developments in war making more than anything else did the most to shape the breadth and scope of modern governments. To pay for a modern military consisting of cannons, muskets, warships, and professional standing armies, governments needed a great deal of money. To access these potential resources, however, rulers had to develop a larger governing bureaucracy; hence, the modern state was born.

Europeans were unique in that they changed the world with innovations based on older and more well-known technologies. Up to around 1400, cannons were too small, inaccurate, and dangerous to their users to make much difference in warfare, but in the 15th century, improvements came quickly. Makers of church bells used their knowledge of large-scale bronze casting methods to manufacture guns that were solid and safe to use. Ironworks started turning out cannonballs that were heavier in proportion to their size, more accurately spherical, and far quicker to make than stone ones. Carpenters devised wheeled gun carriages that made the weapons mobile and absorbed the recoil when fired. Mathematicians tackled the problems of weight and motion involved in accurate aiming. Ultimately, cannons could be relied on to smash any castle or ship. Scaled-down versions of cannons began to appear in the form of muskets, which were small and handy enough for a soldier to load, aim, and fire.

The late Middle Ages also saw the introduction of history's first widely used automated operating machine: the mechanical clock. The basic idea of the clock seems to have come from astrolabes, which used dials with revolving pointers as sighting devices to

Image 7.5: Illustration of the use of cannons alongside a trebuchet at the Siege of Constantinople in 1453. As gunpowder weapons were used more frequently throughout the 15th century, the design of machinery varied vastly. To ensure accuracy or effectiveness, older, non-gunpowder weapons, such as a trebuchet, were still used. © Shutterstock.com

measure the motion of the sun, moon, and stars. Late in the 13th century, inventors in various countries began experimenting with ways to make the pointer imitate these heavenly bodies, in particular the sun, by moving around a dial. Since the movement of the sun determined hours and days, the motion of the pointer would measure the passage of time. The pointer, however, could not turn by itself so a falling weight, attached to a cord wound around a spindle, provided the necessary turning power. Monks created the first clocks around 1300 out of a desire to improve their communities' daily routines of work and prayer. High in a tower of the town hall or cathedral, clocks were visible to all as its coordinated hands moved precisely with the sun's movements. Before long, everyone could hear the tones of bells as they sounded to call attention to the progression of hours.

Developments in England and France

During this period, the nations of England and France grew in stature. However, they both also experienced some rough and transformative events. In England, the controversial rule of King John (ruled: 1199–1216) opened the door for those dissatisfied with their lot in life. The French King Philip Augustus (ruled: 1180–1223) attempted to reassert control over Normand, and this was a place John considered the property of England. To accomplish this, Philip alleged that these lands had been rightfully forfeited to the French. On this pretext, he invaded Normandy in 1203 and soon seized almost all of John's French holdings. During the next ten years, John waged a personal war of revenge against Phillip. To do this, he dramatically raised the tax burden on his English subjects. The English elite resented John both for his military failures and for his monetary demands; and so, on the field of Runnymede in 1215, barons forced him to sign the *Magna Carta* (Great Charter). The king pledged that he would consider increasing taxes only after evaluating the opinions of a council composed of the vassals. John also promised that he would not deprive any free man of life, liberty, property, or protection of the law, "unless by lawful judgment of his peers or by the law of the land."

Image 7.6: *King John Granting Magna Carta.* King John's constant disrespect for the rights of his nobility led to the drafting of the Magna Carta. In reality, King John never intended to abide by the document. He died a year later in 1216 from dysentery while on campaign against a rebellion of over two-thirds of his nobility supported by the King of France and the King of Scotland.

Source: Cassell's History of England-Book 1.

King John consented to these measures mostly because the armed barons pressured him at the risk of his life. It was not long before he and the barons were at war again, and conflicts of this kind continued during the 13th century. Some war-weary Englishmen believed only a powerful king could shape peace, justice, and prosperity in the kingdom. Still, law and custom dictated that kings must respect the claims of vassals, and this included the right to share the responsibility for governance. The king, technically, was under the same law as his subjects. From the collision between the desires of the state and the traditions of feudalism, England took its first steps toward constitutional and parliamentary government. In other words, the *Magna Carta* encoded the principle that the law is above the king. During the reign of Edward I (ruled: 1272–1307), another significant political development occurred: the beginning of representative government. In 1295, financial issues forced Edward to invite two knights from every county and two residents (burgesses) from each town to meet in what became the first meeting of the English Parliament. Eventually, barons and churchmen formed the House of Lords, while knights and burgesses served in the House of Commons.

France developed separately from England with major consequences for the future of Europe. In the early medieval era, England suffered setbacks and defeats to France due, in part, to the dynastic rule of Capetians. The major accomplishment of France's first four Capetian rulers was keeping the crown within their own family while slowly expanding their influence. However, many consider the Capetian Louis IX (ruled: 1226–1270) one of the greatest kings in the history of medieval Europe. Louis was a pious churchgoer who cared for the poor and sick, and he achieved an unusual distinction for a head of state: he was proclaimed a saint (St. Louis) by the Catholic Church. For all his piety, Louis did not neglect matters of the realm. Although he did not try to extend his landholdings, he nevertheless expected his nobles to be good vassals. He also took an interest in law and justice and wanted it dispensed equally to all his subjects. Under the leadership of Louis, officials began to codify the laws of France. Louis confirmed the Parliament of Paris, a judicial body and not a representative assembly, as the highest court in France. Saint Louis died while on a crusade, but his successors continued to centralize state power.

The reign of Philip IV, also known as "the Fair" (ruled: 1284–1314), capped three centuries of Capetian rule. The opposite of his saintly grandfather Louis, Philip was a man of violence and cunning. The ambitious king capitalized on anti-Semitism in Europe and expelled Jews from France while confiscating their possessions. While wanting to "purify" his kingdom of Jews, Philip also desired to expunge

Image 7.7: Parliament Building, London, United Kingdom. The system for an advisory council that grew into a representative body directly involved with governing was conceived during the regency of King John's son Henry III, who was nine years old when King John died. The British Parliament system was born out of the need to prevent another absolutist king like King John, while the Estates General was built out of a need for the French king to justify actions by receiving the support of his people through their representatives in the Estates General. © Shutterstock.com

his lands of the English. Philip engaged in intermittent wars against English King Edward I from 1294 to 1302. All these wars were expensive and drove Philip to look for additional funds.

The king's conflicts led to the establishment of a new French legislative body. In 1302, Philip needed money. With little choice, the king called leaders from the religious and secular elite to assemble in what was the first meeting of the Estates General. As these men gathered, those who prayed, fought, and worked took their separate places in the meeting. In England, Parliament usually deprived the king of achieving complete supremacy. In contrast, the Estates General functioned to curtail the strength of each class, lessen their potential for cooperation, while guaranteeing that kings would alone make most of the important decisions. By the end of the 13th century, France was the largest, wealthiest, and best-governed monarchical state in Europe. England and France were not only emerging as rivals, but their distinct styles of government set each on a different course.

The Hundred Years War and Beyond

In France, the most powerful stimulant to national feeling was the Hundred Years' War (1337–1453). This lengthy off and on again struggle with the English arose out of conflicting feudal claims. Since 1066, when William the Duke of Normandy sailed to England to claim the royal throne of which he thought he was the rightful heir, English kings had ruled parts of France. Since that time, English and French kings continued their territorial struggles, but a major eruption occurred when the French king Charles IV (ruled: 1322–1328) of the Capetian dynasty died with no heir. The French throne then passed to a cousin, Philip of Valois, who became King Philip VI (ruled: 1328–1350). King Edward III (ruled: 1327–1377) of England, however, was the grandson of a former Capetian king and believed he had a greater claim to the French throne. Edward, however, hardly expected France to turn itself over to him. Moreover, he was unlikely to conquer it with the resources of a kingdom that was only about one-quarter the size of France. His claim, however, did give Edward the excuse to loot, pillage, and harass the French as much as possible. Gradually, England found success on the battlefield.

With the 1420 *Treaty of Troyes*, the British appeared to have essentially triumphed, and most of France north of the Loire River was in the hands of the English. Under the agreement, the French also accepted English King Henry V (ruled: 1413–1422) as their king, and this development would have been unthinkable to their ancestors. There was a French king Charles VI (ruled: 1380–1422), but he was very weak and incapable of altering the reality of England's rule. In fact, when the English took Paris, Charles was dethroned and imprisoned.

While the French situation looked very bleak, the dethroned Charles had a son, Charles VII (ruled: 1422–1461), who technically was the rightful heir to the French throne. Known as "the Dauphin" (short title of heir to the French throne), Charles VII fled to safety in a region that was still controlled by loyal Frenchmen yet too disorganized to offer much resistance. Their prospects became renewed when both Henry V and Charles VI died the same year leaving the infant son of Henry V as heir. Since the rightful successor was only a baby, two uncles ruled in his place. It was soon apparent that there was plenty of friction between the two regents, and this development presented an opportunity to the French.

The French renewed their resistance given the fragile nature of England's new leadership. All the French needed now was inspiration. Few would have predicted it would come in the form of a peasant girl named Joan of Arc. On her own initiative, she made her way to Charles VII's court to inform him that God had sent her to save France. Charles was skeptical, but he had little to lose by backing her. His soldiers responded enthusiastically to Joan's encouragement, and they began to roll back the poorly led English. Charles VII would go on to lead his armies to a final victory over the English. However, the real hero, Joan of Arc, did not live to see that day. She fell into the hands of the English, and they put her on trial as a heretic and witch in 1431. Ultimately, Joan was convicted and burned at the stake. The martyred Joan of Arc has been revered for centuries as a glorious symbol of French patriotism. The French built on this unity and came out of the conflict victoriously in 1453.

The Hundred Years War devastated the French countryside, but the monarchy emerged stronger than ever. The war was fought almost entirely on French soil, and it left a lasting mark on the culture and opinions of those who experienced it. For many, the war

Image 7.8: Map of France in 1328 before the outbreak of the Hundred Years War. Note the small yet significant dominions held by the English versus those under direct control of the French crown. *Courtesy of the University of Texas Libraries, University of Texas Austin.*

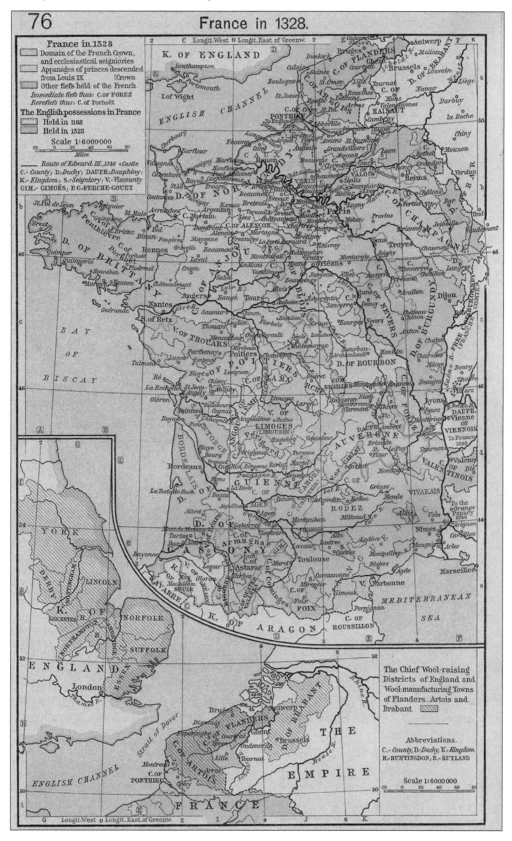

Image 7.9: France in 1428. English controlled areas marked in red, French controlled areas are marked in blue. *Courtesy of the University of Texas Libraries, The University of Texas Austin.*

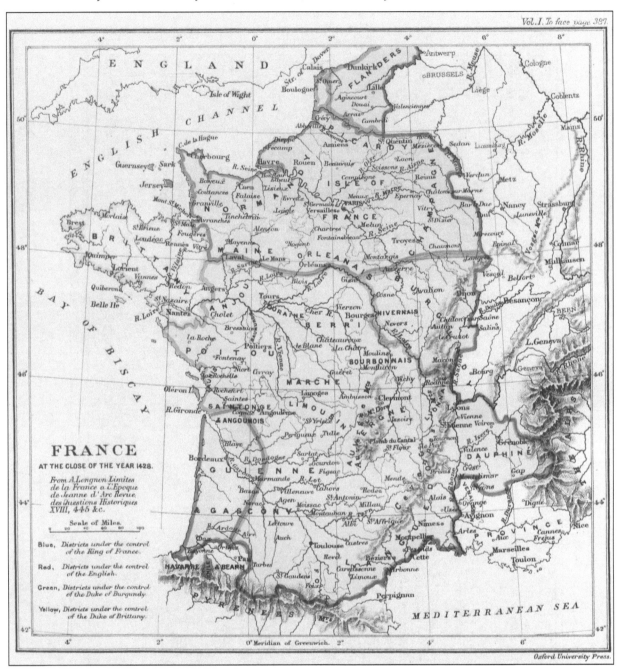

convinced them that any trace of feudalism should be expelled, as France needed a strong, royal defender. The king needed to have the power to act quickly and decisively, which helps to explain why the people were not more resistant to the king's taxation efforts, and his decision not to consult with them very often. In a burst of patriotic fervor, France's Estates General approved Charles VII's request for a national army and voted a permanent tax for its support. The Estates

General passed a land tax aimed mostly at the poorest citizens. With this substantial new revenue, supplemented by income from his own lands, Charles VII could now afford to act independently of his nobles. He was also able to gain the support of French nobles by largely exempting them from the tax.

While the Hundred Years War stimulated the growth of the French monarchy, the legitimacy of the English monarchy was challenged. There is nothing

Image 7.10: Emmanuel Fremiet, *Saint Joan of Arc*, c. 1874, gilded bronze, Rue de Rivoli, Paris, France. © Shutterstock.com

Image 7.11: The War of the Roses denotes a war between the direct descendents of Edward III's third and fourth oldest sons, John of Gaunt the Duke of Lancaster and Edmund Duke of York, over which family had the right to rule. Their houses' symbolic flowers were the red and white roses respectively. Henry Tudor, descended from the Lancastrian family via the female line, eventually won the war and married Elizabeth of York, merging the two house roses to form the Tudor Rose as their house flower. © Shutterstock.com

Lancaster Rose   *York Rose*   *Tudor Rose*

like a military defeat to cause people to raise doubts about its country's leadership. Thus, in England, a civil war broke out over which family would control the monarchy. This destructive conflict, known as the War of the Roses (1455–1485), pitted the House of York against the House of Lancaster. The nobles of the competing factions experienced heavy casualties and thus were both weakened to the benefit of the monarchy. When the smoke cleared, Henry Tudor, the founder of what became one of England's foremost dynasties, became King Henry VII (ruled: 1485–1509), the new ruler of England. A reinvigorated English monarchy notwithstanding, future British monarchs would rely more heavily on Parliament. They used it both as a safety value for grievances and a way in which to give legitimacy to their actions. Parliament became more important and deeply involved in government than ever before, and in the generations to follow, England would replace royal absolutism with a parliamentary system.

In the years chronicled in this chapter, Europe began a period of modernization and transition. There were great wars, economic upheaval, religious transitions, and governmental evolution. In addition, there were advancements in the ways people worked and thought that allowed for society to function in a more efficient manner. This age of transition from the Middle Ages to a more modern time shows Europe on the verge of cultural, religious, and imperial revolutions. Seen and unforeseen forces would develop and lead people into the light of an inquisitive age where, it seemed, human achievement had no limitations.

Chapter 8

The Age of Cultural Rebirth: The Renaissance

Human beings have an innate drive to express themselves whether through the invention of new technologies, building monuments, or capturing dreams or reality by way of paintings and drawings. As far back as seventeen thousand years ago, we see the paintings on the cave walls of Lascaux, France and Altamira, Spain. In Central America, we see the pyramids of the ancient Mayans. In England stands the mysterious Stonehenge. Throughout the world, we find statuary and cult symbols of various tribal religions. Creativity is inherent in the human species. At various times during human history, we can find periods of explosive creative energy. The European Renaissance is a quintessential example of an era where creative human beings expressed themselves through art, architecture, technology, and innovative thought.

Renaissance Defined

The word Renaissance is French and means rebirth. French historian Jules Michelet coined the term in the mid-19th century in his study on the period. The Renaissance era lasted roughly from the late 1300s to the early 1600s. While the Renaissance impacted all of Europe, it took place at different times in different areas. This rebirth fell along many lines of learning and disciplines including art, language, architecture, science, history, politics, and technology. The heart of the Renaissance involved Europeans rediscovering a vast treasure of lost antiquity; namely, the art, literature, and thinking of ancient Greece, Rome, and the early Christian fathers. Renaissance thinkers thought they could create a more vibrant future by learning from the past. This storehouse of knowledge had disappeared with the fall of Rome and stayed lost throughout the medieval period.

While this was a period of immense innovation, this was also a time of great internal strife and war, religious division (Protestant versus Catholic), and emerging nationalism as kingdoms strove to acquire prominence and empire with overseas exploration. Historians have noted that much of the medieval world still existed during a large part of the Renaissance, but it was indeed a period of creative upheaval and a transition leading to the modern world.

At its core, the Renaissance saw the revival of humanism which placed man at the center of the universe. This was a throwback to the spirit of ancient Greece. This humanistic focus led to the development of a more critical spirit. Tradition, whether artistic, religious, architectural, or political, was not to be meekly accepted but to be challenged and hopefully improved. While many Renaissance thinkers and artists remained devoted to the Christian faith, they paved the way for many to question or even move beyond it. The Renaissance has given us some of the greatest art and architecture the world has ever seen. It has given us modern political theory. This era provided the basis for modern science and set the standard for historical and critical scholarship. Out of the Renaissance came the technology that made the spread of knowledge even possible. Even a brief study of this era unleashes such a vast catalog of achievements that it leaves the reader in awe of the intellectual capacity of human beings!

Italy and the Beginning

Located in the center of the Mediterranean, Italy reigned as the hub for trade flowing from the East which included the Muslim world, but also China and India. Ideas, spices, and new technologies like the compass came from the East into the ports of the Italian city states before being diffused further throughout western Europe. The city states of Venice, Pisa, and Genoa controlled much of the trade with the eastern Mediterranean. The city of Florence sold manufactured goods. Italian banks grew powerful. Kings and popes came to these banks for the funding of their ventures. The vast amount of commerce and the money it generated allowed the financial leaders and church officials the means to express themselves through artistic projects.

From the earliest era of human civilization, it seems to be a natural conclusion that when a culture encounters economic prosperity, then great works of art and architecture flourish. That is evident with the Sumerians and their ziggurats, ancient Egypt and their pyramids, Greece with its art and buildings like the Acropolis, Rome and their basilicas, and Muslims with their beautiful mosques. In Renaissance Italy, it was no different. With the wealth flowing in from the east, learning and art were luxuries that thrived.

Florence set the standard. With its banking and trade, it burst with resources and men who were determined create an atmosphere of intellectual and creative output. The Medici were key tradesmen and supporter of the arts. A family of wool merchants, and later bankers, the Medici came to control the city during the fifteenth century. Cosimo de' Medici, also known as Cosimo the Elder (ruled: 1434–1464), supported a variety of artists and architects such as Donatello and Brunelleschi. Medici's grandson, Lorenzo (ruled: 1469–1492), went even further in his support of the arts. Called Lorenzo the Magnificent, de' Medici supported artists like Botticelli and the ultimate Renaissance man, Leonardo da Vinci.

Lorenzo not only supported artists but also the influx of ancient scholarship. With the interchange between Italy and the east, knowledge found in

Image 8.1: Statue of Cosimo de' Medici. A banker and politician, Cosimo de' Medici was one of the major perpetuators of the Italian Renaissance. He and his family created a political dynasty in Florence, Italy, and demonstrated their wealth, power, and prestige through commissioning great works of art.
© Shutterstock.com

ancient Greek, Roman manuscripts, lost to Europe for centuries, began to trickle back in. Lorenzo worked to bring these valuable treasures into Florence. He employed agents to bring him ancient manuscripts from the east. One delivered from Constantinople two hundred ancient Greek manuscripts. Forty percent had never been seen in Europe.

Patronage paved the way for scholars and thinkers to do what they did best: study, write, paint, build, and think. Thus, a new birth in architecture (studying Roman and Greek ruins), a new birth in critical studies (studying classic and new-found manuscripts), and new birth in art and architecture (rediscovering classical Greek and Roman forms), all began to develop across the Italian city-states. Patronage came from churches for artists to create paintings or architects to create new cathedrals. Over time, patronage came from rich individuals who wanted their villas adorned with beautiful paintings and architecture. During the 15th century, wealthy Florentines built almost 100 palaces and had them decorated with impressive works of art, architecture, and sculpture. The Italian city-states developed a reputation as the place to be for innovators and free-thinkers.

Early Renaissance Writers and Scholars

Dante Alighieri (1265–1321), or Dante, as he is commonly known, was an Italian poet, writer, and moral philosopher. He is credited with helping bridge the medieval period to the Renaissance. He is most famous for his poetical trilogy known as the *Divine Comedy*. It is considered a classic treatise and had a monumental influence on European literature and church theology. The poem is an imagined tour of the afterlife. The narrator is the Roman poet Virgil. The afterlife consisted of three tiers, purgatory (Purgatorio), heaven (Paradiso), and hell (Inferno). While traveling through purgatory and hell, Virgil interviews its inhabitants. Dante's long-lost love, Beatrice, guides the reader through heaven. Dante served in politics in Florence and was banished in 1302. Humorously, many of political enemies end up in hell in the poem. The poem serves as a commentary on the human condition and strives to warn the reader of the worldly evils to be avoided such as greed, cruelty, and self-righteousness, but it is also a call for the reader to seek that which pleases God such as humility, love, and kindness. This work was also important because it was written in the Tuscan dialect which eventually became the basis for modern Italian. For the most part, important works were written in Latin during this period, but Dante wrote it in the language of the people. This, like so much of the Renaissance, is a challenge concerning tradition.

Born in Tuscany, Giovanni Boccaccio (1313–1375) started out in business but later studied law. Like many Renaissance scholars in Italy, he also earned a living as a government official. While writing prose and poetry, he served as a diplomat for Florence beginning in 1350. He traveled on diplomatic missions to Rome and its replacement city Avignon, France. In 1348, the Black Death hit the Italian city-states and spread throughout Western Europe over the next four years. Scholars estimate that the plague wiped out over half of Europe. Boccaccio began writing his account of the Black Death in 1348. He named it the *Decameron* and completed it by 1358. In the story, seven ladies and three gentlemen flee to the country to avoid the illness. They tell ten tales a day for ten days. *Decameron* is Greek for "ten days." The stories give insight into people's reaction to the plague. Some became more religious, others gave themselves over to drunkenness and sexual debauchery thinking

Image 8.2: Statue of Dante Alighieri in Verona, Italy. Dante's most famous work *The Divine Comedy*, was written while he was on political exile from Florence in Verona, Italy. An early Renaissance writer, Dante set the style for later Renaissance writers by writing in the vernacular, rather than high-Latin, the language of the church that had hitherto been preferred. © Shutterstock.com

they did not have long to live. Boccaccio gives insight into human responses to immense and horrific tragedy. In these stories, he shows how the Black Death eradicated normal traditions, and he dealt with themes like sexuality not normally discussed in this religion dominated age. The work is also important because it criticized the church and its response during this trying period. Like Dante, Boccaccio also wrote in the Italian vernacular and not Latin. His observations into human nature later influenced literary giants such as William Shakespeare.

A good friend of Boccaccio, Francisco Petrarch (1304–1374) is considered to be the father of humanism, and helped spark the rebirth of knowledge in Italy. As a young man, he was supposed to study law but instead left it to study the classics. He became a diplomatic envoy for the church, and his travels gave him the opportunity to dig out ancient texts. In his career, he wrote three hundred sixty-six poems and popularized the sonnet form of poetry. Sonnets have fourteen lines and use a variety of rhyming schemes. He was also a prolific letter writer, essayist, and historian. Fascinated with the knowledge of Greece and Rome, he collected a vast array of ancient works. At

Image 8.3: Statue of Giovanni Boccaccio in Florence, Italy. © Shutterstock.com

Image 8.4: Statue of Francisco Petrarch. Influenced by the vernacular writings of Dante Alighieri, Francisco Petrarch was one of the early literary humanist writers. Writing in the vernacular, Petrarch invented the Petrarchan Sonnet, influenced by his research into ancient Greek and Roman texts. © Shutterstock.com

one time, he possessed one of the largest libraries in Europe. He believed that studying and applying the classic lessons from Greece and Rome could improve the lives of his contemporaries. The ancient Greeks believed in the concept of *arête* which meant virtue or excellence. For the Greeks, one sought to achieve *arête* by living up to one's potential. Petrarch wanted his contemporaries to recapture that spirit. It became known as humanism. The writings of Dante, Boccaccio, and Petrarch laid the foundations for modern Italian and served as the bridge between the Middle Ages and this new age of critical thought.

Manuel Chrysoloras (1350–1415) was a scholar from Constantinople and considered one of the first humanists. A teacher of Roman and Greek classics, he first came to Venice in 1390 to urge the leaders of Venice to help the Christians of Constantinople fight the growing threat of the Muslim Ottoman Turks. In 1397, the city of Florence invited Chrysoloras to come and teach. There he created a Greek grammar later used by Italian humanists. Chrysoloras shared his knowledge of the classics in cities such as Rome, Bologna, and Florence.

Leonardo Bruni (1370–1444) is considered to be the first modern historian. He wrote a twelve-volume history of the Florentine people using the archives of the city. He is credited with introducing a more realistic form of history writing. During his career, he served as secretary for four Popes and a Chancellor in Florence. His writings influenced later history writers for over two centuries. He translated many Greek

works like Plato and Aristotle into Latin. Bruni was responsible for getting Chrysoloras to come to Florence in 1397. He wrote biographies of Dante, Petrarch, and Boccaccio. Borrowing from the ancient Roman scholar Cicero, Bruni used the phrase "*studia humanitatis*" or study of the humanities to teach his philosophy of life. A person, to be a good citizen, should be educated in the humanities including rhetoric (how to speak), grammar (how to write), history, law, poetry, and moral philosophy. These subjects would help the denizens of a city become better citizens. What makes this groundbreaking is that Bruni promotes this goal disengaged from the church. Thus, this is the origin of the idea of humanism. Bruni and the aforementioned writers and scholars shared several characteristics. They brought realism to their work. They sought to inspire their readers to better conduct and moral excellence through the study of the past. They were also critical of the institutions of their day and called for improvements. These attributes stood as common components of Renaissance humanism.

Lorenzo Valla (1407–1457) is considered one of the most important textual scholars of the Renaissance. A humanist, a rhetorician, literary critic, and Catholic priest, he is best known for exposing the

Donation of Constantine as a forgery. The document was supposedly written during the time of Emperor Constantine and claimed that he had given control of the western territories of Roman Empire to the pope. Doing careful critical analysis, Valla demonstrated the document contained anachronisms that pointed to an 8th-century composition. Thus, Valla undermined the authority of the pope. He later found textual errors in the Latin translation of the *Catholic Bible* called the *Vulgate*. He translated the ancient Greek historian Herodotus into Latin. Valla's work later influenced Erasmus of Rotterdam to revise the Latin *Vulgate*. Valla's last book, which was a textual analysis of the New Testament, was later put on the Catholic Church's condemned list because he dared to question the origin and context of the New Testament text. While a Catholic, he paved the way for later Protestant Reformers to question the veracity of several aspects of Catholic orthodoxy.

Niccolò Machiavelli (1469–1527) is one of the most famous names to come out of the Renaissance. He is considered the father of modern political theory. Born in Florence, he lived in chaotic times. He served as a diplomat for Florence, and he wrote dispatches

Image 8.5: Stamp depicting portrait of Niccolò Machiavelli. Machiavelli concludes in *The Prince* that if a ruler cannot be both feared and loved simultaneously, than it is better to be feared as human nature does not allow a Prince to follow idealized morals. Machiavelli's ideology gave rise to the modern term Machiavellian, denoting unscrupulous cunning, particularly when advancing one's political career. © Shutterstock.com

concerning what he saw and experienced. He saw the French invade Italy and come to the gates of Florence in 1494. He saw the Medicis retake power in 1512, and he was subsequently tortured and forced into retirement. Machiavelli wrote several historical works concerning Florence, and a tome of the Roman historian, Titus Livius. His most famous work was *The Prince*, later condemned by the Catholic Church. *The Prince* can be seen as practical but also diabolical as he advises that a Prince does (changed from do) whatever was needed to rule. Out of the work came famous lines like "it is safer to be feared than loved." From him comes the term Machiavellian which refers to an unscrupulous, manipulative person.

The Italian Masters

When one thinks of the Renaissance, art immediately comes to mind. The Renaissance Era saw an explosion of some of the greatest art ever created, whether in paintings, sculpture, or architecture. The Renaissance served as a quantum leap forward from the styles of the Middle Ages or Medieval period. Medieval paintings centered on religious themes and were for the most part, crude, flat, formulaic, and lifeless. Renaissance art demonstrated rationality. It had symmetry. It demonstrated the full range of human emotions whether the theme was religious or not. Regardless of whether the painting was of Jesus, Venus, or a country peasant, one could appreciate the beauty, the form, the depth and the feeling of the subject matter but also value the skill of the artist as well.

Giotto Di Bondone (1266–1336), or Giotti, as he was commonly known, is considered the father of Renaissance painting. He revolutionized the concept of producing art. His paintings went back to the classical ideals of expressing art but also the glory of man. He painted religious scenes, but humans stood at the center of his art. He painted a more natural and realistic world. His paintings consisted of frescoes which were works created on plaster walls, usually in churches. Some of his famous works include Jesus being betrayed by Judas in the *Kiss of Judas*. Another one of his well-known works was the *Adoration of the Magi* where the wise men or Magi pay homage to the Christ child. His authorship is disputed (depending on the exact time of his death), but most scholars believe that he painted the famous work of St. Francis of Assisi receiving his stigmata (wounds like Jesus received during his crucifixion). Many previous artists

Image 8.6: Giotto di Bondone, *La Cattura di Cristo (The Arrest of Christ)* also known as *The Kiss of Judas,* 1306, fresco painting, Scrovegni (Arena) Chapel, Padua, Italy. © Shutterstock.com

portrayed these scenes with lifeless two-dimensional characters, but Giotto's characters stand out for their realism. His style influenced later artists to emphasize realism in their work.

As in ancient Greece, Renaissance art manifested itself in a variety of ways. Both eras saw architectural innovation. Filippo Brunelleschi (1377–1446) was the most influential architects of the Renaissance. He is considered to be the father of modern architecture. As a young man, he trained mostly to be a sculptor, but he found his greatest talent in architecture. When he was in his mid-twenties between 1402 and 1404, Brunelleschi spent time in Rome studying ancient ruins. In sketching these ancient buildings, Brunelleschi discovered, or to be more accurate rediscovered, something that was groundbreaking. The ancient Romans and Greeks had used linear perspective when building, but this method had been lost for almost a millennium. Linear perspective is an art technique where the

Image 8.7: Completed in 1436, the Duomo Santa Maria del Fiore of the Florence Cathedral, was an engineering marvel by Filippo Brunelleschi. To this day, the cathedral remains one of the largest in Italy, and a UNESCO World Heritage Site. © Shutterstock.com

artist creates the illusion of depth on a flat surface. All parallel lines meet at a single vanishing point on the horizon of the composition. As objects recede into the distance, they appear smaller. Using this technique, artists could create three-dimensional objects in two-dimensional space. Brunelleschi used his skills to build a dome for the Cathedral in Florence. This is the largest dome ever built. Later cathedrals like St. Peter's Basilica would follow Brunelleschi's pattern.

A friend of Brunelleschi, Donato di Niccolò di Betto Bardi (1386–1446), or Donatello as he was known, revolutionized sculpture in Italy. A forerunner of the style later employed by Michelangelo, Donatello is considered the greatest sculptor of the fifteenth century. During his career in Florence, Donatello received patronage from the ruler of the city, Cosimo de' Medici. Donatello was known for creating very realistic and lifelike sculptures. He supposedly would utter, "speak damn you, speak" as he worked. His most famous sculpture was that of a young *David*, created in 1430. This is considered the first free standing life size nude bronze sculpture in Europe for over a millennium. In the work, *David* is wearing a laurel topped hat and boots holding a sword with his foot on Goliath's head. This blatant realism and frank sexuality were controversial in its day. It would set the stage for other masters in the 16th century.

Sandro Botticelli (1445–1510) won fame as an early Renaissance painter. Like many talented artists, he received patronage from the Florentine leader, Cosimo de' Medici. He also helped Michelangelo with the painting of the Sistine Chapel. What stands out about Botticelli is his painting of non-religious themes or pagan themes. His most famous work is the *Birth of Venus*. It is noteworthy because it was painted on canvas instead of wood panels. Canvas painting eventually became the primary medium for Renaissance painting. In addition, the painting does not have a Christian theme, and Venus is painted nude. It is apropos since Venus is the Roman goddess of love, sex, beauty, and fertility. The nudity offended the sensibilities of many of the age, and thus it was hung in Lorenzo de Medici's private villa. Historians have noted that most Renaissance paintings hung for the public display used Christian themes, but those in private usually contained classical pagan ideas. One

Image 8.8: Sandro Botticelli, *Birth of Venus* (c. 1486), tempera on canvas, as recreated for postage stamp in France.

can see in the work of artists such as Botticelli, the glorification of the human body but also the glorification of the artist. Botticelli and others were keen on stretching the norms of their day.

The name that stands out among Renaissance artists and thinkers is, of course, Leonardo da Vinci (1452–1519). He is considered by most to be the true Renaissance man. What does this mean? It refers to the fact that da Vinci excelled at many artistic and intellectual pursuits. During his career, he worked as an architect, a painter, an inventor, an anatomist, and a scientist. da Vinci filled notebooks with drawings and observations on a variety of subjects. He was born near the city of Vinci, not far from Florence. As a young man, he studied with masters but mostly taught himself many subjects. From his teen years to his mid-twenties, da Vinci studied under artist and painter Andrea del Verrocchio of Florence. da Vinci earned his living as a commissioned artist, but that only captured a portion of his interest. He studied mechanics, weaponry, anatomy, architecture and other subjects. da Vinci did not see these subjects as separate spheres but as a part of the whole. His painting output was not as prolific as others because of his varied interests. In regards to his painting, he is credited with developing and mastering the technique of chiaroscuro. Using this technique, the artist uses light and shade to define three-dimensional works. The shading gives the work a more natural look.

Image 8.9: Page from a notebook of Leonardo da Vinci depicting a gear device disassembled, c. 1500. © Shutterstock.com

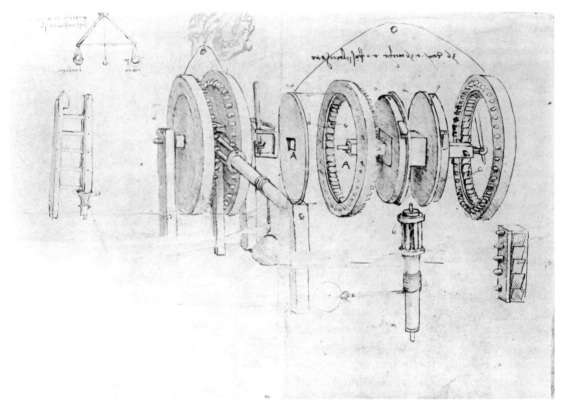

da Vinci created works of art that are known the world over. The *Mona Lisa* is his most famous work. It is believed that his model was the wife of a Florentine citizen, Francesco Del Giocondo. Her enigmatic smile has spawned debate for five centuries. Another well-known work is da Vinci's *The Last Supper* which portrays Jesus with his twelve disciples on the night he was betrayed. da Vinci painted more personal works such as the *Lady with an Ermine*, a painting with a young, beautiful Italian woman holding a weasel. He painted his self-portrait at age sixty in *Self Portrait in Red Chalk*.

da Vinci was more than a painter. He dissected more than thirty corpses and took copious notes and created over two hundred drawings of the human body. He is known for creating the first accurate sketch of the human spine. Through his researches, da Vinci provided minute descriptions of human musculature as well as discovering that the heart has four chambers. One of his most famous sketches was the *Vitruvian Man*. It is named after an architect named Vitruvius. In this drawing, da Vinci placed a man with various positions of his legs and arms inside

Image 8.10: Reproduction of Leonardo da Vinci, *Mona Lisa*, 1503, oil on wood. © Shutterstock.com

a circle and a square. da Vinci was trying to capture man and nature in proportion.

da Vinci was also an unparalleled inventor. In his lifetime, he drew a model of a workable parachute. da

Image 8.11: Completed c. 1515, the portrait of an elderly man mad with red chalk on paper, is widely accepted to be a self-portrait of Leonardo da Vinci around the age of sixty. © Shutterstock. com

Vinci sketched an aerial screw which many today think it is the forerunner of the aerodynamic principles that led to the helicopter. He drew a theoretical flying machine, a tank, and a crude kind of machine gun to name a few of his ideas. da Vinci embodied the Renaissance, the idea that human beings could achieve greatness by maximizing their potential.

Andrea Mantegna (1431–1506) studied to be an artist as a young boy, and as an adult earned his living as a commissioned painter. He studied the ancient ruins of Rome and helped recapture linear perspective much like Brunelleschi. Art critics note that his painting style mirrored classic architecture. His paintings have a depth of realism and perspective seen by few that preceded him. His *St. James Being Led to Execution* got destroyed in a World War II bombing, but photographs remain. In the painting, the observer can see how linear perspective works. It is almost like a photograph with the crowd and James in the forefront and a large arch in the background. In his *The Dead Christ*, the observer can see the muscled body of the dead Jesus lying on a crumpled sheet as his mother cries at the bedside. But there is even more than the religious theme. Jesus is a real man. One can appreciate the artist's capturing the glory of the human body. One can also appreciate the artist's skill in capturing a scene in time. Mantegna's *The Oculus* is one of the most interesting of his paintings. Mantegna was the court painter for the Gonzaga family who ruled the city of

Mantua. One of his most important commissions concerned his painting of the *Camera degli Sposi* (*Bridal Chamber*) also known as the *Camera Picta* (*Painted Room*). On the ceiling, he created a painting known as *The Oculus*. It appeared to be a circular opening giving the observer a view of the blue, cloudy sky. Using linear perspective, one can see party goers and cherubic angels peering down from the circle. Humorously, Mantegna has a potted plant peeking slightly over the edge of the circle. It looks like it is ready to fall on the viewer's head! In many of Mantegna's works, his characters seem like they are ready to step out of the canvas or fresco. Realism infuses in his work.

If da Vinci is the most famous Renaissance artist, then surely Michelangelo Buonarroti (1475–1564) is right on his heels as the second. Michelangelo excelled at both painting and sculpture. His works stun the viewer with their beauty but also realistic detail. During his career, both popes and wealthy Italians such as Lorenzo de' Medici gave the artist commissions. His most famous painting is, of course, the biblical scenes on the ceiling of the Sistine Chapel. Commissioned by Pope Julius II in 1508, it took Michelangelo and assistants four years to complete the work. What started out as a painting of the twelve disciples, expanded into an iconic panorama of biblical scenes on the ceiling and walls ranging from Adam and Eve to the Second Coming of Christ. The most iconic is the center of the ceiling where God, displayed as a majestic white-haired man, reaches his finger to touch Adam and instill his divine image into the frail man. Once again, the painting can stir religious sentiments but also take the observer into an appreciation for the human form.

Michelangelo is equally known for his amazing sculptures. Commissioned by a French Cardinal to create a sculpture for the Cardinal's future tomb, Michelangelo created the masterpiece, the *Pieta*. In this work, Mary holds the dead body of her son Jesus. Today it resides in St. Peter's Basilica in Rome. The details are amazing, from Mary's utterly devastated face to the folds of her garment. A two-figure sculpture was very rare for the period, but Michelangelo was able to create a piece that has great feeling, not to mention skill. In regards to sculpture, Michelangelo's pièce de résistance was his statue of the young *David*. Over seventeen feet high, the sculpture arises from one block of marble and weighs almost six tons. While Michelangelo captures a biblical hero, *David* is totally in the nude. In the Greco-Roman classical

Image 8.12: Leonardo da Vinci's sketch, now titled the Vitruvian Man, demonstrates da Vinci's understanding of how each element of the human body was in proportion to the rest of the body. The sketch is called the Vitruvian man because it was taken from the ideology of Roman architect Vitruvius. Leonardo da Vinci then tried to apply the same principles to understand patterns in nature. © Shutterstock.com

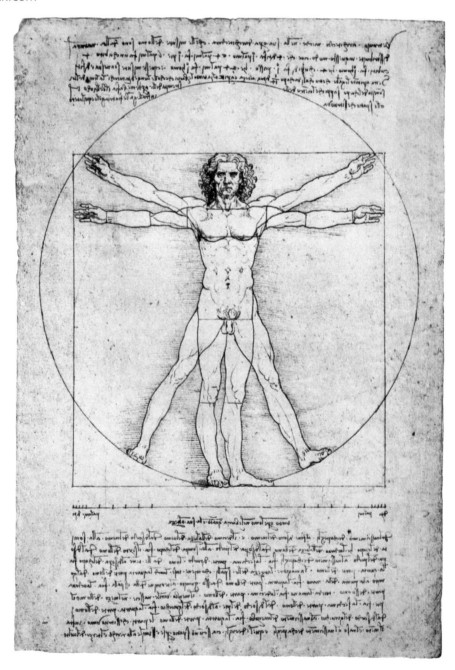

style, Michelangelo sought to display the innocence of the young *David* as he was about to take on the giant Goliath. But the artist also exhibits the greatness and glory of the human body with *David's* majestic head and hair and the supple features. This is the ideal man, strong and beautiful at the same time. If there is one piece of art that defines the Renaissance, then Michelangelo's *David* is it!

Raphael Sanzio da Urbino (1483–1520) lived a very short life, only thirty-seven years, but earned lasting fame as a Renaissance painter. His paintings, full of Madonna images (paintings of Mary) and

Image 8.13: The fresco paintings on the ceiling of the Sistine Chapel, completed by Michelangelo in 1512, were commissioned by Pope Julius II in 1508. Arguably the most famous of the frescos, *The Creation of Adam*, figures prominently at its center; and on its concluding wall is the fresco *The Last Judgment* by Michelangelo, completed at the same time. © Shutterstock.com

cherubic angels express religious themes, but they also sought to recreate the classic realistic ideal. Raphael's most famous work is the *School of Athens*. It is located on the wall in the Signature Room in the Vatican, the residence of the Pope. The work sought to create a synthesis of Greek (worldly) and spiritual (Christian) thinking. In the work, Raphael tries to capture the pantheon of classical thinkers and philosophers. One can see Plato discussing with others in a corner. In another corner, one can see the Persian religious teacher Zoroaster. Sprawled on the front steps is the Greek Cynic Diogenes. In one corner, the mathematician Pythagoras writes down his computations. The center of the painting shows Plato and Aristotle walking and carrying on a debate. Plato has his right hand and index finger pointing up. He is directing Aristotle to look to the spiritual world beyond, the world of forms and ultimately God. Aristotle has his right hand extended and facing palm down. He is pointing to the world of reality, science, and reason. It is ironic that Raphael's vision of human wisdom, namely secular, is painted on the wall of the Pope's apartment. Here we can see the essence of the Renaissance. There are religious themes that are displayed, but many times the greater theme is the greatness of humanity.

Michelangelo Merisi da Caravaggio (1571–1610) excelled in the classic Renaissance style. Born in Milan, he came to fame in Rome between 1592 and 1610. His paintings are known for his lifelike realism. For example, in his painting, *Boy with a Basket of Fruit*, Caravaggio captures the beauty of a teenage boy but displays details right down to a fungus lesion on the fruit. Caravaggio painted multiple works with religious themes, but also gave glimpses into everyday street scenes and celebratory scenes like the *Lute Boy*. Some of his most stunning realistic works are religious paintings. In the *Entombment of Christ*, Caravaggio gives us the moment Jesus is taken down from the cross. The artist shows the observer various details from the majesty of the body of Christ and the grief-stricken faces of the family of Jesus, down to the grain of the wood of the cross. In a painting based on a story from the book of *Judith*, a book that contains biblical history but is not accepted as part of the official biblical canon, Caravaggio displays the heroine Judith cutting off the head of the hated Assyrian general Holofernes. The painting overflows with color and realism. It is also shocking as the viewer can see the blade sink into Holofernes neck and bring forth a shower of blood. Even in a scene of gore, Caravaggio

Image 8.14: Michelangelo, *Pietà*, c.1498–1499, marble. Michelangelo claimed that the marble used to create *Pietà* was the most perfect block of marble he had ever used. Though the natural proportions in *Pietà* are not perfect, sculpting a statue of two human figures together was a feat during the Renaissance. © Shutterstock.com

Image 8.15: Michelangelo, *David*, 1501–1504, marble. The sculpture *David* was originally proposed to sit atop the Florence Cathedral. Thus, the statue stands at nearly 17 feet tall, as it was intended to be seen from a distance. Instead, the sculpture resided in the Palazzo della Signoria outside of the cathedral until it was moved inside the Galleria dell'Accademia in 1873. © Shutterstock.com

can demonstrate idealistic beauty and appreciation for the artistic skill.

During the Renaissance, there were only a handful of female painters. It was considered common knowledge that women could not paint. In reality, the male dominated society discouraged women from stepping outside the traditional role of wife and mother. But there were some women who painted. Usually, they were encouraged by their families. Sofonisba Anguissola (1532–1625) stood out among the limited number of female painters. She was the oldest of seven children, six of whom were girls. The young woman displayed artistic ability. Through her father, she met Michelangelo Buonarroti. He sent her a drawing which she copied and sent back to the great artist. He was impressed and encouraged her to continue to hone her craft. Eventually, King Philip II of Spain commissioned her as the royal portrait painter. Facing a world of gender prejudice, many times her works were ascribed to be creations of male painters including da Vinci. Yet even some of her male peers gave honest assessments of her work and described her as one of the most skilled painters of her era.

Image 8.16: Raphael, *School of Athens*, 1509–1511, fresco. The Renaissance represents an era of renewed interest in the classics. No other work in the Renaissance captures this interest so literally as Raphael's *School of Athens*, which portrays some of the greatest scientists and philosophers of the ancient era. © Shutterstock.com

Image 8.17: Copy of Michelangelo Merisi da Caravaggio, *Entombment (Deposition) of Christ*, c. 1600–04, oil on canvas, by M. Koch (1797). Caravaggio's religious art employs the Baroque theme of movement in its subjects to incite emotion in its viewers. The Catholic Church used religious paintings in the wake of the Protestant Reformation to instruct the faithful in the life and sacrifice of Christ, and inspire passion in its following. © Shutterstock.com

Northern Renaissance

As we have seen in other chapters, a new idea, whether it is about economics, science, metallurgy, religion, art, or architecture, rarely remains the domain of one group. Through trade, war, or travel, human innovation spreads from group to another. This story repeated itself during the Renaissance. The new spirit of inquiry did not simply take root exclusively in Italy, it spread north throughout the rest of Europe. This can be seen in the art of Northern Europe.

A Flemish (modern day Belgium) artist, Jan van Eyck (1390–1441) created works with mostly religious themes. This was standard fare, but the realism of his oil paintings were an innovation and set van Eyck apart. van Eyck became known as the father of oil painting. Previous artists mostly painted wall frescoes using a style of paint known as tempera. This made the paintings remain static. Oil paintings could be changed by the artist. Some of van Eyck's most famous paintings are the *Ghent Altarpiece*, *Man in the Red Turbin*, and *The Arnolfini Marriage Portrait*.

The prime example of Italian influence in the north came in the hands of Albrecht Dürer (1471–1528). Art experts consider the German-born Dürer to be the greatest of the Northern Renaissance artists. While a young man, Dürer studied in Italy in 1494 and 1495. He also spent time there between 1505 and 1507. What he learned forever influenced his art. He took the Renaissance style of painting and other techniques back to Germany and produced a large catalog of drawings, watercolors, woodcuts, and engravings. His genius covered a variety of disciplines. He was not only renowned for his paintings but equally so for his printmaking which he elevated to an art form. He served as court artist to two successive Holy Roman Emperors, Maximilian I and Charles V. Some of his famous paintings are his own *Self-Portrait*, *Adam and Eve*, and *The Adoration of the Magi*. He is equally known for graphic woodcuts and engravings

Image 8.18: Black and white reproduction of Jan van Eyck, *Portrait of Giovanni Arnolfini and his wife*, 1434, oil on oak. Commonly known as "The Arnolfini Portrait," the painting by Jan van Eyck depicts a wealthy merchant and his wife in an iconographic rich portrait to convey their position in life. © Shutterstock.com

such as *Four Horsemen of the Apocalypse* and *Knight, Death, and the Devil.*

Like Dürer, Pieter Bruegel the Elder (1525–1569) studied in Italy as a young man. He challenged art traditions by painting everyday scenes of common people, scenes of everyday life, and landscapes. A very influential painter and draftsman, his focus on commoners earned him the nickname "Peasant Bruegel." While his compositions captured common themes, Bruegel was actually employed by the elite, and he associated with many of the humanist thinkers of the Netherlands. Artists such as van Eyck, Dürer, and Bruegel left a lasting impact on the artistic and intellectual world of Northern Europe.

Northern European writers and thinkers also left a legacy of free thought and of inquiry. Called the "Prince of the Humanists," Erasmus of Rotterdam (1466–1536) demonstrated skill in a variety of linguistic disciplines. His most famous treatise came out in 1509 entitled, *In Praise of Folly.* While a devout Catholic, Erasmus unleashed criticism on the Church for what he thought were superstitious practices and for its rampant corruption amongst the clergy. In his career, he traded barbs with the Protestant Reformer Martin Luther. But unlike Luther, Erasmus had no desire to leave the Church. He thought it needed improvement, not

Image 8.19: Albrecht Dürer, *Adam and Eve,* 1504, engraving. Dürer was preoccupied throughout his life with the proportionality of the body. His belief that an idealized body could be drawn using a system of measurements is conveyed in the engraving *Adam and Eve.* © Shutterstock.com

schism. Erasmus criticized Protestants and Catholics and denounced theological hair-splitting. He also criticized much of the clergy for focusing on wealth and luxury instead of charity, humility, and pious living.

A linguistic scholar, Erasmus collected over five thousand Latin and Greek sayings and proverbs. He titled the work, *Adages.* In 1516, he also edited and produced a complete Greek *New Testament.* This was the first Greek *New Testament* seen in the western part of Europe since the fall of Rome over a thousand years before. He used this volume to create a newer and more accurate Latin translation in 1519. His works were later used by both Catholic and Protestant Reformers. The *King James Version of the New Testament* (1611) is based on Erasmus's Greek edition.

Looking back to the ancient Romans and Greeks, Erasmus used the term *Ad fontes* which literally means "to the fountain or source." It became a rallying cry for Renaissance humanists and later reformers. They, like Erasmus, argued that scholars needed to return to original sources to better understand traditions. Thus, return to the ancient Latin and Greek masters for inspiration, but also return to the original Hebrew and Greek languages to better understand the *Bible.* Erasmus helped unleash a spirit of inquiry that would later aid Protestant and Catholic reformers and assist investigations in the scientific realm.

Thomas More (1478–1535) was an English humanist and writer, but he was also a staunch Catholic. He rejected the creation of the 1534 *Act of Supremacy* which severed the Church of England from the Catholic Church and the authority of the Pope. Instead, the Act made Henry VIII the head of this new Church. More's opposition to the *Act of Supremacy* resulted in his execution. Yet, his protest demonstrated the spirit of the Renaissance, that is, a man had the right to think for himself and challenge the king or tradition if the man thought either committed an error. His lasting intellectual contribution came through the 1516 publishing of his book *Utopia.* In this work, More created an ideal society which was based on reason. In this world, everyone worked but property and goods were owned communally. The word *Utopia* was a play on words since in Greek the term utopia means can mean either "good place" or "no place." More is considered the father of the literary genre where utopias place a central role.

The Renaissance artists' desire to capture the realism of the natural world has to be seen in a wider

Image 8.20: Nineteenth century engraving of Hans Holbein the Younger, *Portrait of Sir Thomas More*, 1527, oil on oak. © Shutterstock.com

Image 8.21: Artistic rendering of Nicholas Copernicus, the founder of the heliocentric theory. © Shutterstock.com

context of the movement toward a more in-depth scrutiny of the natural world. This led many to question the traditions handed down from the past. The ancient Greek physician Galen had been accepted as the medical authority for centuries. Normally, human dissections were performed to verify the teachings of Galen and other ancient teachers. Andreas Vesalius (1514–1564) went against the grain. He taught at the University of Padua, but also served as the personal physician to the Holy Roman Emperor, Charles V. He performed his own independent dissections of corpses and mapped out the human anatomy. His 1543 work, *De Humani Corporis Fabrica (The Structure of the Human Body),* proved to be a monumental work because it swept away many traditional misconceptions about the body and laid the foundation for modern anatomy. For his work, Vesalius is lauded as the father of modern anatomy.

While Vesalius studied the human body, Nicolaus Copernicus (1473–1543), a Polish-born Catholic priest, studied the heavens. Copernicus focused on the motions of the stars and planets. For over a millennium and a half, traditional science in Europe followed the conclusions of the Greek philosopher Ptolemy. Ptolemy theorized a geocentric, or earth-centered, universe. This "science" meshed with church orthodoxy based on biblical accounts where the Sun is mentioned as moving across the sky. Through his observation and calculations, Copernicus theorized that the sun is the center of our solar system. This came to be known as heliocentrism or

"sun-centered." His findings were published upon his death in 1543. He feared the backlash of the Church which considered geocentrism to be biblical. The Italian astronomer Galileo Galilei later verified Copernicus's findings and help spark the Scientific Revolution.

Today we take for granted the free and rapid flow of information. We read newspapers and journal articles online, we download books to devices, or carry a favorite paperback in our pocket. This access to information would not be possible without the contribution of a Northern Renaissance printer.

Johannes Gutenberg (1398–1468), a German printer from the city of Mainz, created a moveable type print press in 1440. Why was this revolutionary? Before Gutenberg, if you wanted a copy of a book, you had limited options. You could hire a scribe to copy the work on cured calfskin known as vellum, but this was very expensive and beyond the means of most. Printers also would use a woodblock as a page and carve out the words onto the block, dip it into the ink, and then place the block neatly on paper. Several printings would wear down the block, and no new edits could be made to the manuscript. Needless to say, books were not plentiful because of the time and expense. Gutenberg's genius lay in creating a moveable type press. Using wooden and then later metal characters, he could make infinite changes to words and fonts. By 1455, he had created the first of his elaborate *Bibles*. The Gutenberg Press allowed for

Image 8.22: Unlike earlier print methods that used wood, Johannes Gutenberg found that using metal for the type molds allowed for characters or letters to be used multiple times, rather than having to carve new letters after a few uses, revolutionizing printing. The first complete book that Gutenberg printed, the Bible, remains the most widely printed book to this day.
© Shutterstock.com

the creation and spread of all kinds of books and pamphlets: religious, agricultural, political, and scientific. Gutenberg's press drastically cut the cost of printing and publishing, thus both flourished. With books and pamphlets more available, it led to a democratization of information. The laity could question the clergy. Scholarship and science grew more reliable since everyone had access to it and could spot errors. By 1500, sixty German cities had printing presses, and two hundred more existed throughout Europe. Thirty-five thousand books were in press by 1500. A literate people could question Popes, kings, and all manner of authority.

The Renaissance ushered in a three-century era that promoted the questioning and challenging of tradition in art, architecture, religion, and textual analysis. In reality, it planted the seeds for its own end. An example came with the Protestant Reformation, started by the German monk, Martin Luther, in 1517. Building on the works of Valla and Erasmus, Luther challenged the authority of the Pope and Catholic Church itself. The Protestant Reformation led to a Catholic backlash. In 1545, the Council of Trent officially condemned those who opposed Catholic teaching. With the help of like-minded governments, this

resolution stifled critical introspection and revelry in humanism. Much of the 16th and 17th centuries saw Europe split in religious wars. In addition, the massive amount of income coming into the coffers of Italian merchants and the Church began to dry up as countries like Portugal, Spain, England, France, and Holland acquired wealth through overseas expansion in the Americas, Africa, and southeast Asia. As the wealth moved into Holland and England, the Renaissance moved in that direction somewhat, eventually being replaced by the Scientific Revolution and the Age of Enlightenment.

Although it has been over five hundred years since the high mark of the Renaissance, it still affects us to this day. The Western world is still a place that values inquiry, beauty, and the role of the human spirit. We still are asking the questions Renaissance thinkers asked. What does it mean to be a good person and a good citizen? Although some may dismiss it in this modern world of science, technology, and business, we still need the *studia humanitatis*. We need to write and speak clearly. We need to learn history and moral philosophy. We still need our hearts stirred with great poetry. If we do that, then the Renaissance will never die.

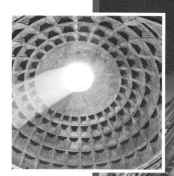

Chapter 9

Age of Exploration: Europe Meets the New World

In 1991, the world was allowed access to the Internet. This monumental event triggered a global revolution through the World Wide Web. Yet, this is not the first wave of globalism, but the second. The first came almost exactly five hundred years before. The first wave of globalism came when Europeans started leaving their home shores and sailing around the world in search of riches, expansion of the Christian faith, and empire. This chapter looks at the motivations for European exploration, how Western European countries attempted to explore, and the results of exploration for these countries as well as the disastrous effects on native populations.

Crusades, Contact, and Interchange

To understand European exploration which began in the 1400s, we must briefly go back over three hundred years to roughly 1100. In 1095, European Christian knights engaged in what became a two-hundred-year struggle to wrest control of the holy land (Israel) from Muslim armies. The attempt had success at first as Christian warriors took Levant cities like Odessa and Jerusalem. Ultimately, the Crusades proved to be a failure. Muslims retained control of the lands of the eastern part of the Mediterranean. But these Christian warriors encountered items that proved even more important than land. They encountered the riches of the Far East.

A vast trade network called the Silk Road connected China, India, and areas under Muslim control namely North Africa, the Levant, and Mesopotamia. Muslim and Indian ships also carried trade goods back and forth across the Indian Ocean from Africa to Southeast Asia. Trade flourished as spices, pepper, gold, silver, tea, and Chinese silks flowed back and forth. In addition, these areas bustled with scientific and technological advancements.

Although the Crusades failed, many Europeans took the opportunity to enrich themselves through the purchase and distribution of these products throughout Europe. Italian city-states, namely Venice, Pisa, and Genoa dominated this trade. They benefited from Italy having the geographic advantage of being in the middle of the Mediterranean and very close to the trading ports on the eastern shores of the Mediterranean. These Italian traders purchased these goods and then shipped them to French, Portuguese, Spanish, English ports.

What one person has, another person usually wants. By the 1400s, European kingdoms on the Atlantic seaboard lusted for their own routes to the Far East. New technologies helped make this possible. The Portuguese developed the caravel, a ship that was leaner but contained deeper hulls for carrying more cargo. The Portuguese also employed a new kind of sail known as the lateen. This large triangular sail could swivel back and forth and was better equipped to catch the wind. In addition, other technologies that originated in the East had filtered into Europe. Muslim geographers created maps that contained latitude lines, measurements that determine one's position north or south of the

Image 9.1: 3D rendering of a caravel. While square sails remained a fixture on the foremasts and mizzenmasts of larger ships to provide power and speed in open waters, lateen sails were included on the rear (aft) rigging for greater maneuverability. © Shutterstock.com

Image 9.2: Arabic astrolabe, c. late 11th century, housed at the National Archaeological Museum in Madrid, Spain. Astrolabes measure the angle of the sun and thereby a sailor's position. This type of astrolabe was used in early sea navigation, as well as to teach Spanish and Portuguese navigational techniques. © Shutterstock.com

Equator. The Chinese invented the compass, and it came to be used by European navigators. By the 15th century, navigators were using the Astrolabe. This instrument measured the position of the stars and allowed its user to determine longitude, how far a person was east or west of a fixed point. With these new technologies available, and a strong desire to make their mark in the world, Portugal became the first European country on the Atlantic seaboard to make an attempt to reach the Far East.

Portugal

Under Prince Henry the Navigator (1394–1460), Portugal began to send out sea captains and crews to find a route to India. The most natural route was to sail south down the coast of Africa. Prince Henry had two motives for this enterprise. The primary one was for his sailors to find gold and other riches. But he also had a religious motive as well. As a Christian ruler, he wanted to spread the Christian faith. Since the Crusades, a legend existed that said a Christian king named Prester John ruled his kingdom surrounded by Muslims and pagans. By Prince Henry's time, the legend had evolved and said Prester John was somewhere in Africa. Thus, Prince Henry hoped his sailors would find and aid this Christian king.

Throughout the 1400s, Portuguese captains slowly moved down the West African coast and brought gold, ivory, and other trade goods, including cargoes of African slaves, back to the Portuguese city of Lisbon. In 1487, Bartolomeu Dias rounded the southern tip of Africa. His men refused to go any further for fear of not being able to return home. Dias's King, John II, called this landmark the Cape of Good Hope. Though he did not go all the way, Dias had found a route to India.

A decade later in 1498, Portuguese captain Vasco da Gama sailed around the Cape of Good Hope. He landed in several cities on the east coast of Africa but had to flee from local resistance. He and his fleet sailed across the Indian Ocean and came to the Indian city of Calicut. He traded with the local rulers. His take of spices was stunning. He returned to Portugal with a cargo valued at over sixty times the cost of the journey. He and other Portuguese captains would return with heavily armed Armadas. By the early 16th century, the Portuguese established trading colonies on the west coast (Goa) and the northeast coast (Calcutta) of India. These Portuguese captains, along with Catholic priests, established trading colonies and churches in the Philippines, China, and Japan. By the mid-1500s, the Portuguese rivaled their Muslim and Italian counterparts as major players in the East.

Christopher Columbus

A few years after Dias rounded the Cape of Good Hope, and half a decade before Da Gama made it to India, an Italian sailor named Cristoforo Colombo (Christopher Columbus in English) hatched his own scheme for reaching the riches of the Far East. He presented his plan to the rulers of what eventually became Spain, Ferdinand of Aragon and Isabella of Castile. These two monarchs, while retaining control of their separate kingdoms, married in 1469 and worked together to complete the *Reconquista*, the ejection of the last Muslim stronghold in the southern part of Spain. They succeeded in 1492. That same year Columbus gained an audience with the monarchs. Ferdinand and Isabella wanted to access the economic gains acquired by their Portuguese neighbors. Columbus convinced Isabella of the worthiness of his plan. She not only desired to attain a route to India, but she also wanted to spread her Catholic faith to the heathen. Columbus appeared to be the perfect vehicle to both goals.

Columbus convinced Isabella that he could sail west and go around the globe and gain access to China and India. Europeans knew the world was round but remained divided over its circumference. As early as the 3rd century BCE, the Greek geographer Eratosthenes calculated that the world was over twenty-four thousand miles in circumference. He was off by only a few hundred miles. These findings were not universally accepted in Europe. Some rival calculations stated the world was only sixteen thousand miles in circumference. Columbus based his scheme on a German mapmaker's creation that went with the latter calculation. Thus, Columbus thought that he could sail three thousand miles west and reach Japan, the outskirts of the Far East, in less than a month. The distance was actually twelve thousand miles, and Columbus did not know that two continents stood in his way. Convinced that Columbus's scheme might work, Isabella financed his excursion.

Columbus sailed from Spain on August 3, 1492. He landed on an island off the coast of Florida which he named San Salvador (Holy Savior) on October 12, 1492. He met with the Taino people, but he was convinced he was near India. Thus, he called the indigenous natives Indians. Between 1492 and 1502, Columbus made four voyages to what is now the Caribbean Islands. He explored and settled the Island of Hispaniola (Haiti/Dominican Republic), explored Cuba, and reached the shores of the Isthmus of Panama. To his dying day, he never admitted that he had not found India. Columbus did not actually "discover" America, but he did pave the way for future European exploration.

Image 9.3: Christopher Columbus being received in Barcelona, Spain by King Ferdinand and Queen Isabella, 1492. © Shutterstock.com

Image 9.4: Martin Waldseemüller, *Universalis cosmographia secundum Ptholomaei traditionem et Americi Vespucii alioru[m]que lustrationes,* 1507. Map of the known world in 1507 based on the drawings of Amerigo Vespucci. *Library of Congress, Geography and Map Division.*

Image 9.5: Statue of John Cabot in Bonavista, Newfoundland. Bonavista, on Newfoundland's northeast coast, claims to be roughly the site of John Cabot's landing in America in 1497, in which he reportedly said "O boun vista!" (Oh happy sight!) upon seeing land. Since the early 16th century, French and English fished off the coast of Cape Bonavista. © Shutterstock.com

Ominously, Columbus' arrival marked the beginning of the end of countless Native American cultures. Columbus wrote in his diary that he was looking for "pearls, precious stones, gold, silver, spices, and other objects and merchandise whatsoever." These people had little gold or any other precious metal. Yet, Columbus did find that he could exploit these people, and the Italian captain took full advantage. He left forty men behind as he went and explored the island of Hispaniola. Upon returning to San Salvador, Columbus found that his men had abused the natives and that they had retaliated and killed some of his men. In revenge, he took over five hundred natives as slaves and shipped them off as compensation to Queen Isabella. The start of Spanish exploration and the exploitation of the native peoples had begun.

Isabella's sponsorship of Columbus' expeditions angered her neighbor Portugal. Portugal protested and said Spain had entered territory that belonged to them. Since both kingdoms were Christian, they agreed that Pope Alexander VI would arbitrate. The negotiation proved complex since Alexander was Spanish born. Despite the difficulties, the pope had the two kingdoms sign the *Treaty of Tordesillas* in 1494. The agreement basically divided up the world along a longitudinal line between the two kingdoms. The boundary line sheared off the eastern hump of South America. This is modern day Brazil. All new lands east of this line belonged to Portugal. All new lands west of the line, thus most of the Americas, belonged to Spain. The audacity of this treaty alarmed and angered Spain and Portugal's neighbors. Later remarking on the treaty, King Francis I of France quipped, "The sun shines for me as for others, and I should very much like to see the clause in Adam's will that excludes me from a share in the world." Spain and Portugal's successful efforts soon aroused other European countries to try their hand at exploration.

Columbus' moderate success spurred another Italian to launch out into uncharted waters. Sailing first for Spain, then later for Portugal, Amerigo Vespucci sailed west in search of a route to the Far East. Unlike Columbus, he let his findings determine his conclusions. In three voyages between 1499 and 1504, Vespucci explored the northern and eastern coasts of South America. He realized Columbus was wrong. This land was not the coast of India, but what he called the *Mundus Novum* or New World. Letters from Vespucci concerning his travels soon circulated among Europeans. A German mapmaker, Martin Waldseemüller, read the letters that included Vespucci's descriptions and created the first map of the new world. He named the new land America in honor of Vespucci. The name stuck and was eventually applied to North America as well.

England felt compelled to jump into the exploration game not long after the publication of the Treaty of Tordesillas. He, like the other European monarchs, wanted to find a Northwest Passage to India. An Italian, Giovanni Caboto, known as John Cabot in English, took the commission. Historians are not sure where Cabot exactly landed, but most think somewhere in Newfoundland which is part of Canada. Cabot was lost at sea during a second voyage and other concerns kept England from exploring for almost another century.

France came late to the game, but they made their mark just the same. In 1524, Giovanni da Verrazano received a commission from the French crown to find a Northwest Passage to India. He was not successful. A decade later, Jacques Cartier took the same commission. He explored St. Lawrence Bay in Canada and traveled southwest down the St. Lawrence River to the area that is modern-day Montreal. Sixty plus years passed before explorer Samuel de Champlain established Quebec in 1608.

The Conquistadors

While the English and French failed in their initial attempts at exploration, Spanish explorers experienced many stops and starts, but they eventually found treasures that transformed their country into a world power. Historians have noted that these Spanish explorers were driven by three passions. The three motivations were God, Gold, and Glory. Many explorers or conquistadors, as they were called, brought along Catholic priests. Thus, they explored new territories and encountered indigenous peoples for the purpose of converting them to Christianity. Of course, as noted before, the primary reason for exploration was the acquisition of riches. Finally, the explorers sought to bring not only glory to the mother country, but also notoriety for themselves. A successful explorer received a title of nobility, land in the new world, wealth, and laborers.

Vasco Núñez de Balboa went to the New World to discover wealth and make a name for himself. He was originally a part of a group that explored the coast of Colombia. He went to Hispaniola but was forced to sneak away because of debts. He landed in Colombia and met survivors of the fledgling colony of San Sebastian located near the modern Colombia/Panama border. Balboa and the survivors moved up the Isthmus of Panama and founded a settlement called Darién. In 1513, Balboa led a group looking for gold. While he failed to gain any riches, he is credited with

Image 9.6: Engraving of Ponce de Leon (on horseback) mortally wounded during battle with Native Americans in Florida in 1521.
© Shutterstock.com

being the first European to see the Pacific Ocean. He claimed the territory for Spain. Balboa later ran afoul of the new governor of Darién, was arrested, and then beheaded for treason in 1519.

Juan Ponce de León is believed to accompanied Christopher Columbus on his second journey to the new world in 1493. Ten years later he served as Governor of Hispaniola. He later led an expedition of Puerto Rico. On another exploration, he landed on the coast of Florida. Supposedly, he was looking for a famed fountain of youth, but he was actually looking for rivers of gold. He returned to Florida in 1521 to colonize the area, but he died from an arrow wound sustained in a battle with natives.

Ferdinand Magellan, like Balboa and Leon, died in his pursuit of riches. Yet, he is credited with being the first European to circumnavigate the world. Although he later sailed for Spain, Magellan was born in Portugal. Between 1505 and 1509, he sailed with a Portuguese fleet that traveled around Africa and made it to the Spice Islands in the South Pacific. By 1517, Magellan offered his services to the Spanish. He spent a lot of his career studying maps and astronomy. He thought he could succeed where Columbus had failed. Magellan convinced the Spanish crown that he could successfully sail west and find a sea route to the Far East. With five ships and a crew of two hundred seventy men, Magellan set out in 1519. He and his crew sailed south down the coast of South America and managed to make it into the Pacific Ocean. Magellan died while fighting with natives in the Philippines in 1521. Eighteen out of his original crew of two hundred seventy men managed to make it back to Spain in 1522. In less than a century after Prince Henry's initial efforts, Spain and Portugal had made it around the world.

Hernan Cortés was the Spanish conquistador who changed everything. He came to America as a soldier in the Spanish army and participated in the conquering of Cuba in 1511. Cortés heard native tales of golden cities to the west, and he longed to lead an expedition in search of gold and conquest. In 1519, he disregarded orders forbidding him from going on an excursion west. He took five hundred men, eleven ships, and sailed west to Mexico. He demonstrated his determination when he destroyed all his ships once he and his party were on land. The native inhabitants were stunned at the vision before them; men who wore glistening armor and riding massive horses. Cortés found allies among thousands of Indians who were

Image 9.7: O. Graeoff, *Hernando Cortés, Battle in Tlaxcalan Territory,* 1892. © Shutterstock.com

being abused by the dominant tribe, the Aztecs. Other tribes fought Cortés but were defeated. Cortés and his men made their way north to the capital city of the Aztec empire, Tenochtitlán. The Aztec ruler, Montezuma II, sent gold and even threats to dissuade Cortés, but he would not be deterred. Upon entering the capital city in November 1519 with his men and several hundred native allies, Cortés decided on a strategy of taking Montezuma hostage. He was going to use his hold on Montezuma to rule the country.

An event happened that forced Cortés to change his plan. He received word that a group of Spanish soldiers were coming to arrest him. Cortés left a quarter of his troops and some of his native allies in the city and marched to take on his Spanish rivals. He quickly defeated them and returned to the capital. He found his men in a pitched battle with the Aztecs. The heat of the fighting forced Cortés to abandon the city. His contingent suffered a great loss of life and treasure. Undeterred, Cortés regrouped his men and native allies, and using cannons, besieged the city in December, 1520. Cortés and his men fought a street to street battle with the Aztecs and totally subdued the city in August, 1521. Although politics and attacks from his enemies would plague him the rest of his life, he basically conquered Mexico for Spain. In

turn, Spain reaped the massive benefits. Agricultural products like potatoes, cocoa, and maize, along with tons of silver and gold, flowed out Central America into the coffers of Spain.

The son of a pig farmer, Francisco Pizarro went on to be as famous a conquistador as Cortés. He is credited with the conquering of the Inca Empire. He served with Balboa in 1513. With his three half-brothers and another Spaniard named Diego de Almagro, Pizarro got permission from the Spanish crown to take on the Incas in 1531. Using Cortés's playbook, they wormed their way into the capital city of Cajamarca and took the Inca leader Atahualpa hostage in 1532. Even after a large ransom was paid for the Inca king, Pizarro had him killed in 1533. Pizarro and his men also took the Inca city of Cuzco. They established Lima as the capital. This is the modern capital of Peru. Again, gold and silver and foodstuffs began to load down Spanish ships headed to Spain. Pizarro died at the hands of a political rival in 1541.

While Cortés and Pizarro found grand wealth, Hernando De Soto failed to find great riches. However, he was the first Spaniard to explore the southern part of what is now the United States and left behind a reputation of greed and brutality. De Soto's first claim to fame was his skill as a slave trader in Nicaragua. He

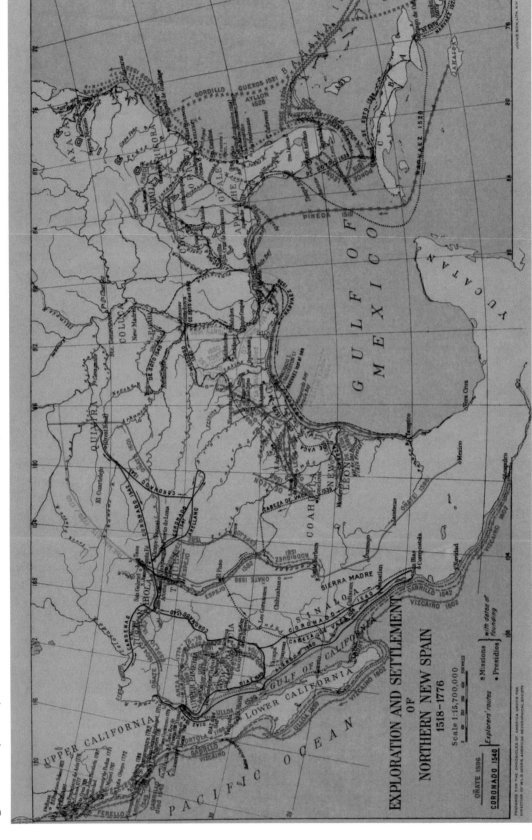

Image 9.8: Map of Exploration and Settlement of Northern New Spain 1519–1776.

accompanied Pizarro in the conquering of the Inca and acquired a lot of wealth. Yet, he longed to lead an expedition that would find even greater riches. He set his sights on conquering Florida for Spain. In 1538, he led ten ships and seven hundred men and landed near modern day Tampa Bay. Between 1538 and 1542, De Soto's party trekked through Florida, Georgia, the Carolinas, Tennessee, Alabama, Mississippi, Arkansas, and Louisiana. Much of the way he and his men fought angry tribes of Indians. He and his men were the first Europeans to see the Mississippi River. In Louisiana in 1542, De Soto succumbed to a fever. His men sank his body in the Mississippi River. With about half his party still alive, his men created rafts and sailed down the river. They eventually made it to Mexico in 1543.

Once the initial conquests took place, then what followed was the establishment of order and the organizing of the Native American peoples. The Spanish developed the *encomienda* system. This originated during the *Reconquista*, the long period when the Spanish sought to expel Muslims (and later Jews) from what was considered Spanish lands. The monarchy demanded tribute from the Muslims and Jews who remained in the land. This involved forced labor.

In America, the Spanish gave official permission or grants to conquistadors, soldiers, government officials, called *Encomenderos*, to exact tribute and labor from the Native Americans. In return, the *Encomenderos* were expected to feed, clothe, and shelter the natives while also ensuring they were being instructed in the Catholic faith. In reality, the *encomienda* became a vehicle of enslavement. It was first used in the Caribbean islands conquered by the Spanish. The natives were forced to work producing agricultural staples like sugar cane. Later it was used in Peru in the silver mines. The *encomienda* helped contribute to the massive decimation of native populations.

To be fair, many Catholic priests really did want to bring benefits to the natives of the America through the gospel of Jesus Christ. In reality, the insatiable drive for riches and empire subverted this effort. One man, Bartolomé de Las Casas, started out as a conquistador but turned away from that way of life and spent the rest of his career trying to mitigate the terrible effects of conquest concerning the native peoples.

He arrived in Hispaniola in 1502, was given an *encomienda*, and began to teach Catholicism. The Catholic Church ordained him as a priest in 1512. In 1513, he helped in the conquest of Cuba. Yet, his

Image 9.9: Engraving of Bartolomé de Las Casas greeting the natives. Las Casas, a Dominican friar, dedicated his life to championing the rights and fair treatment of natives in Spanish controlled Central America. © Shutterstock.com

faith soon conflicted with the human cost of conquest. He gave up his *encomienda*, and traveled back to Spain to serve as an advocate for the natives. He later returned to America and wrote several pamphlets and books concerning the Spanish ill-treatment of the natives. His most famous work was called *Historia de Las Indias*. For well over forty years, he called for his Spanish brethren to treat the indigenous people better. He denounced the Spanish lust for gold and how it drowned the biblical call for loving one's neighbor. He prophesied God's judgment on the Spanish for their perpetual abuse and exploitation of the native peoples of America. For the most part, De Las Casas' jeremiad fell on deaf ears. The amount of wealth pouring out of America into the coffers of Spain trumped any real concern for the humane treatment for the indigenous people. In addition, this economic boom propelled Spain into becoming the greatest European power throughout the 16th century.

Native Americans, African Slavery, and the Cost of Empire

Throughout the late 19th century and well into the 20th century, textbooks and monographs looked at the European exploration of the world from only one perspective, that of the Europeans. Explorers like Columbus got portrayed as bringers of progress, agents of capitalism, and spreaders of Christianity. Modern treatments see Columbus and the others as much less heroic and see them more in terms of greed and the striving for personal glory. Historians today not only try to understand the European perspective but also attempt to look at the Age of Exploration through the eyes of the conquered, namely, the indigenous peoples.

Two questions arise. Where did these people come from and why were they so easily conquered by the Europeans? First, the peoples that inhabited the Americas from Alaska to Tierra del Fuego (the southern tip of South America) descended from Asians who came to the American continents in waves during the thawing of the last major Ice Age some fifteen to twenty thousand years ago. These Asians followed herds of animals who themselves were looking for grazing lands as the ice melted and new vegetation grew. Eventually, these peoples scattered south, but also east and west throughout the two American continents and the Caribbean Islands. It is believed that inhabitants reached the southern end of South America by 10,000 BCE. Diverse groups with

various dialects and customs inhabited the Americas. Some in what is now Mexico domesticated maize or corn by 5000 BCE. The level of sophisticated agriculture led to the great city and pyramid building of the Mayas in the first millennium BCE. The Aztecs and Inca later followed this pattern. Smaller civilizations like the Mississippians built large grass-covered pyramid mounds from Missouri to Alabama. Many other tribes survived as hunter-gatherer groups with small levels of farming.

Historians and scientists believe that somewhere in the vicinity of forty million inhabitants dwelt in the Americas when Columbus arrived in 1492. Unlike erroneous beliefs in the past which portrayed Native Americans as crude and unsophisticated, these native civilizations proved themselves to be highly advanced. From Cahokia, the capital city of the Mississippians, to Tenochtitlan, the Aztec capital, Native Americans demonstrated a great ability to organize and create sprawling urban centers. The Inca Empire developed a runner system for getting messages spread thousands of miles throughout the kingdom. In North America, a vast trade network existed that spanned thousands of square miles. In their own way, and despite geographical limitations such as possessing no draft animals, these Native Americans proved themselves on par with any European.

So then, why did the Native Americans succumb so quickly to the Europeans? For the longest time, Europeans touted their racial superiority and the power of their religion, the Christian faith (whether Catholic or later Protestant). The belief in white supremacy became a cornerstone of European and later American thought. The idea basically stated that whites from Europe were intellectually, psychologically, and emotionally stronger than the native peoples. In addition, the Christian God had willed victory for Europeans as they spread the Christian faith and developed empires. Like the Israelites of the Hebrew Bible who annihilated the pagan Canaanites and took over the land that became Israel, white Europeans saw themselves as the people of God perfectly justified in taking from its backward inhabitants an unspoiled wilderness and turning it into a paradise for the glory of God.

Scholars and scientists in the last century have turned these notions on their head. Native Americans and Europeans did not differ in regards to intelligence, strength, or emotional makeup. While the Europeans possessed advantages in technologies like steel swords and firearms, this does not explain how men like Cortés or Pizarro, with a few hundred men, carved out empires in the face of resistance from thousands of thousands of angry natives. The answer came in the understanding of diseases.

Because Native Americans lived thousands and thousands of years separated from Eurasia, they did not come in contact with diseases that evolved from animals indigenous to Europe and Asia. Most diseases that have plagued mankind originated in horses, cows, pigs, and sheep. Europeans and Asians endured all kinds of diseases shared with these animals, and through natural selection, those that survived produced generations of offspring that developed greater immunities. Not so the Native Americans; their immune systems were not geared to handle these diseases.

Thus, when the Europeans began to arrive in the Caribbean, Central, and South America, it was not primarily the Christian faith that they were bringing. Instead, it was germ warfare. Unknowingly, the Europeans dropped the equivalent of a germ atomic bomb on native populations. For example, there is no way to know exactly how many Tainos lived in the islands that Columbus visited during his four voyages, but historians believe it could have been at least a million people or more on Hispaniola alone. What is known is that less than sixty years after Columbus arrived, there were less than one thousand. European disease is considered the number one factor in their disappearance.

Cortés noted in his accounts that natives soon began to drop and die from smallpox by the hundreds very soon after he and his men arrived in Mexico. These numbers continued to mushroom. Today, scholars believed that over ninety percent of all native inhabitants died in a little over a century after the first Europeans arrived in the late 15th century.

In 1972, environmental historian Alfred W. Crosby coined the term Columbian Exchange in his book by the same name. The term was used to describe this monumental meeting between Europe and the New World. This encounter had a transformative effect on both sections of the world. As explained earlier, the contact between Europeans and the indigenous peoples of America proved disastrous for the latter. Diseases like smallpox, influenza, whooping cough, typhus, and many others were introduced to the Americas. Entire groups of Native Americans disappeared. Others were later conquered and dispersed.

One question that many people ask concerns this; did Native Americans pass on any diseases to the Europeans? Scientists that study disease track syphilis back to the new world. They find its point of origin in Europe occurred in the late 15th century in the Spanish port of Cádiz. Here, sailors returning from the journeys of Columbus visited the city's brothels and passed on the disease which eventually spread throughout Europe.

The Columbian Exchange also refers to the animals and products that were transferred between areas. Cows, pigs, sheep, goats, and horses came to the Americas and transformed the landscape and the people. Horses escaped from Spaniards exploring the southwest part of what is now the United States in the 1540s. A century later over half a million horses roamed the North American plains. Plains Indians domesticated the horse and used it as a vehicle of conquest against other tribes. As De Soto roamed through the southeast part of what is now the United States, he was spreading disease but also lost some of his domesticated swine. These animals roamed free and eventually returned to their wild boar ancestry. Longhorn cattle in Texas were originally Spanish cows that escaped and roamed free. Even European grasses embedded in the hooves of these domesticated animals changed the ecology of the New World.

Native Americans developed foodstuffs that radically altered the European diet over time. Europeans fell in love with Indian corn, white and sweet potatoes, tomatoes, chocolate, beans, avocados, peppers, tobacco, and many other products. Tomatoes became over time the basis for most dishes in areas like Italy. Native American chili peppers found their way into the spicy dishes of India and China. From the other end of the spectrum, Europeans introduced crops such as wheat, coffee, bananas, sugarcane, and onions into the New World. The Columbian Exchange is almost a misnomer since it seems to imply that the exchange helps both sides. It's obvious that Europe and Asia benefited greatly from this encounter while the indigenous populations did not.

Across Central and South America and the Caribbean, the Spanish and the Portuguese in Brazil forced Native Americans to work on agricultural plantations as well as in gold and silver mines. The harsh work plus the ever-present plague of disease killed off scores of Indians and left their masters with a labor shortage by the mid-17th century. This forced

Image 9.10: British abolitionist broadside (poster) printed c. 1790 to demonstrate the crowded and in-humanitarian conditions of slave transport as exemplified on the slave ship the *Brooks,* built in 1781. © Shutterstock.com

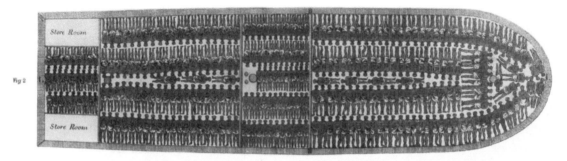

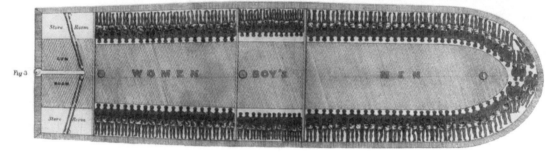

Spain and Portugal to find other sources of labor. They turned to Africa.

As early as the mid-1400s, the Portuguese had tapped into an already existing slave market and sent several thousand Africans to Portugal. These slaves worked the plantations on the Portuguese held islands off the northwest coast of Africa. By the early 17th century, the plantation economy had developed in the Caribbean, Mexico, Brazil, and the English colony of Virginia. Thus, Europeans purchased African slaves and sent them to the Americas. The slave trade became known as the Triangular Trade because it involved three continents, Europe, Africa, and South America. Later this included North America. Europeans took trade goods, including liquor and weapons, and sailed to West Africa. Eventually, Spain, England, France, Holland, and England built armed fortresses on the coast for slave transactions. African Kingdoms such as the Ashanti, the Mali, and the Yoruba already had long established slave trading networks to Muslim markets along the North African coast. They captured Africans living in the Central African interior. With the allure of European goods, these kingdoms began to capture and

ship more and more of their fellow Africans to the west coast European fortresses.

The third leg of the triangle came to be known as the Middle Passage. This was the terrible trip Africans had to endure as they traveled in the bottom of slave trips from Africa to New World. Between the early 1500s and the 1860s, historians calculate that up to thirteen million Africans endured all or part of the terrible trip across the Atlantic. About ten million actually made it. Most went to the Caribbean, Mexico, and Brazil. About six percent (six hundred thousand) came to the thirteen British colonies. As with the Native Americans, the European quest for riches and empire proved to be a catastrophe for millions of Africans, and slavery would come to define the economies of the United States, Brazil, and the Caribbean well into the 19th century.

European Rivals

As we briefly saw before, in the late 15th and early 16th century, other Atlantic based countries tried to compete with the Spanish and the Portuguese. As the

16th century progressed, England became a major thorn in Spain's side. England and Spain had been at odds since British King Henry VIII (ruled: 1509–1547) had his marriage to Catherine of Aragon annulled in 1533. Catherine was the daughter of Spanish King Ferdinand of Aragon (ruled: 1479–1516) and Queen Isabella of Castile. While Catherine bore Henry six children, none lived to adulthood except a daughter, Mary Tudor. Henry wanted to remarry and produce a male heir. Charles V, Catherine's nephew and the Holy Roman Emperor (ruled: 1519–1556), pressured Pope Clement VII to not heed Henry's demands. Henry did not wait for the Pope Clement VII's approval and divorced Catherine and married Anne Boleyn in 1533. The Archbishop of

Canterbury proclaimed that Henry was the head of the Church of England through the *Act of Supremacy* of 1534. Boleyn failed to give Henry healthy male heirs, but she did give birth to a daughter Elizabeth who would rule England for over forty-four years.

Henry's two daughters, each from a different mother, were estranged. Mary Tudor (ruled: 1553–1558) re-established Catholic rule and persecuted Protestants and executed dozens. She also angered her subjects by marrying Philip II of Spain. Her reign lasted only five years and her half-sister, Queen Elizabeth I (ruled: 1558–1603), ascended to the throne. Thus, England and Spain's enmity toward each other was two-pronged. One, they held to competing versions of Christianity, and two, they competed over empire.

Image 9.11: Artistic rendering of the first colony of Roanoke, and artistic interpretation of soldiers discovering the word "Croatan" written on a tree at the abandoned colony of Roanoke. The word carved on a tree by the abandoned settlement, was the only clue soldiers discovered when they returned to the now abandoned colony in 1589.

During her reign, Queen Elizabeth I indirectly attacked Spanish treasure ships coming out of the Americas. She gave sanction to privateers like Francis Drake. Drake and others had the crown's permission to attack and plunder Spanish ships and towns. If successful, they handed over most of the treasure to the monarchy and the "Sea Dogs" as they were known, would be allowed to keep some of the wealth and receive titles of nobility. Drake became Sir Francis Drake because of his exploits and became the first Englishman to circumnavigate the world. He and others used Caribbean islands as bases from which to attack the Spanish, but he did not think about developing permanent settlements.

Others, such as Walter Raleigh, thought settlement in America was the answer for thwarting the Spanish presence. He financed an expedition that landed on an island off the coast of modern-day North Carolina. This colony named Roanoke was founded in 1585. Spanish anger at continual English attacks resulted in the Spanish sending an armada of one hundred thirty ships to invade England in 1588. Many men from Roanoke returned home to fight for their mother country. Led by captains such as Drake, the English soundly defeated the Armada. This gave the English an even greater motivation to explore and settle in America. After the war, many who had left Roanoke for England returned home. They found the village deserted. Many scholars think that they settlers were probably captured and carried off by local Native American tribes.

England would first take root on American soil in 1607 in Jamestown, Virginia. Given a charter by James I who had succeeded Elizabeth upon her death in 1603, the Virginia Company sent an exploration team to America to find riches. The name Virginia was used in honor of Elizabeth, the Virgin Queen. The expedition traveled over thirty miles up what they christened the James River to escape Spanish detection. While they did not find gold, the settlers did eventually grow tobacco which became a lucrative venture and permanently established an English presence in North America.

While Jacques Cartier had sailed for France down the St. Lawrence River to what is now Montreal in 1534, the French did not try to settle Canada for almost another century. Samuel de Champlain founded Quebec in 1608. Unlike later Englishmen who came to America to settle and create a new future, New France consisted mostly of trading posts where French trappers established good relations with the natives and captured beavers for their pelts. By 1700, French missionaries and explorers established outposts in the Ohio Valley, and well down the Mississippi River.

Both countries also tried to follow Spain's example in carving out for themselves islands in the Caribbean. Between 1609 and 1640, England established colonies in Bermuda, Barbados, St. Kitts, Antigua, Nevis, and Montserrat. The French followed suit and colonized Dominica, Martinique, and Guadeloupe. In the mid-1600s, the English took Jamaica from the Spanish, and the French took half of the island of Hispaniola, namely Haiti. Both countries, by the mid-17th century, were importing slaves to grow sugarcane. The British East India Company received a charter in 1600 from Queen Elizabeth to conduct trade in what was once Portuguese domain, namely the Indian Ocean. By the mid-18th century, the British East India Company dominated much of India. While starting off behind the Spanish, the English and the French quickly caught up.

In the mid-16th century, the Netherlands, north of France and just across the North Sea from England, consisted of provinces and cities ruled by the Spanish. With the Union of Utrecht signed in 1579, these cities and provinces agreed to a union called the United Provinces of the Netherlands or the Dutch Republic. The Dutch Republic reached its zenith in the 17th century. After a long war, Spain recognized Dutch independence in 1648.

Even before that, the Dutch were walking in step with Spain, Portugal, England, and France and trying to set up a trade empire. In 1602, the Dutch East India Company was formed, mirroring its British counterpart. It sought to protect and develop trade in the Indian Ocean. By the early 1600s, Dutch ships drove the Portuguese out of modern-day islands of Jakarta and Java and gained a foothold in India. The Dutch carved out trade contacts and posts throughout Indonesia. In 1609, the Dutch East India Company hired Englishman Henry Hudson to sail west and attempt to find a Northwest Passage to India. He explored what is today Hudson Bay, the entrance into New York City. He went up the river that bears his name to modern-day Albany. He claimed this area for the Dutch. By 1624, the Dutch purchased Manhattan Island from local Native Americans and founded New Amsterdam. It would remain until the English drove them out in 1664 and renamed the area New York.

Image 9.12: Colonial Dominion, 1700–1763. *Courtesy University of Texas Libraries, University of Texas Austin.*

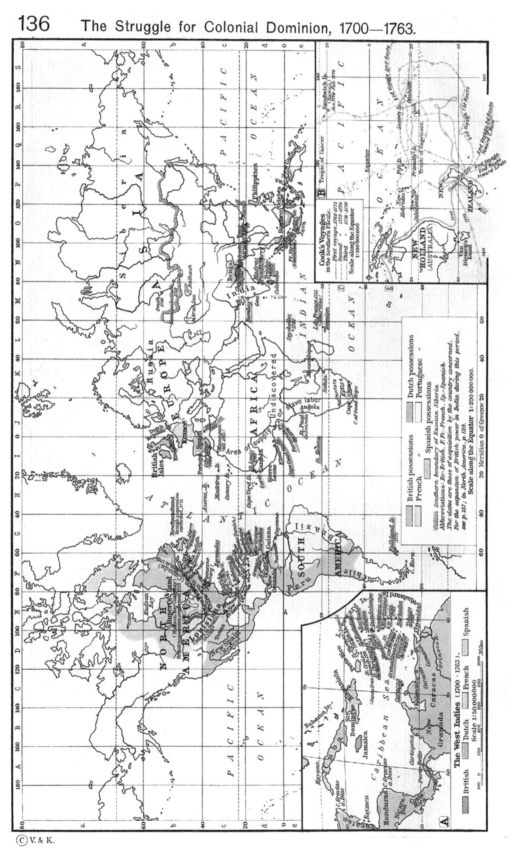

136   The Struggle for Colonial Dominion, 1700—1763.

Finally, we conclude with an understanding of how the Europeans saw their colonies. They all came to follow an economic policy known as mercantilism which basically means these countries practiced economic nationalism. Mercantilism dictated that a country keep as much gold and silver as possible. To be successful, a country had to have more exports than imports. Concerning their colonies, everything was geared toward benefiting the mother country. Official policy forbade manufacturing in the colonies. A colony shipped its raw resources (sugar, cotton, wood, fish, tobacco, etc.) to the mother country, and then the mother country sold finished products to the colony. The mercantilist policies of England eventually angered the thirteen colonies of America enough to start a revolution in the 1770s.

For us, a century seems like a long time, but in the greater scheme of things, it is a very short period. In the 1490s, the Portuguese reached India, and Columbus sailed to the Americas. Both events had worldwide consequences. In the following century, Western European countries on the Atlantic seaboard successfully circumnavigated the world, opened international trade routes, and developed trading colonies and settlements on every continent except Australia and Antarctica. This explosion of trade and conquest led to Spain, Portugal, France, England, and the Netherlands becoming super powers. Of course, one very negative downside of this Age of Exploration was the subjugation, and in the Americas, the annihilation of native peoples. This all-encompassing drive for riches and empire destroyed ninety percent of all Native Americans and led to the enslavement of over thirteen million Africans. We can appreciate how the Age of Exploration helped create the modern world, but we must never forget the human cost in this process.

Chapter 10

Christendom Shattered: The Reformation

The Reformation helped to create the framework for the modern age. The movement provided a Christian alternative to Catholicism that led to multiple, and often conflicting, interpretations of church rules and spiritual principles. Because of the Reformation, what could now be called Western civilization grew much larger, and the consequences shaped, for better and worse, the lives of tens of millions of people. The Reformation, at first glance an act of rebellion against the Catholic Church, was a complex series of events that appear to contradict the rules of historical cause and effect. While its followers wanted to return to the communal piety of the early church, the most profound legacy of the Reformation was the creation of the individual conscience. The magnificent drama of the medieval church was replaced by the devout Christian, standing alone before God.

For the medieval European, the Catholic Church was the center of a life in which the physical and spiritual were inextricably linked. The clergy were special people; literate and celibate men who were the intermediaries between God and the common people. Catholic Church authorities relied on the clergy to both regulate the faithful and direct the affairs of the secular world. Bishops ruled over scores of church parishes but were also great landowners, as they often held as much power as counts or dukes. The cathedral at the center of a diocese was an immensely powerful commercial, political, and spiritual institution. The pope was at the center and head of this vast network of priests, bishops, and holy orders. The pope was a holy figure, a law-giver, and God's representative on earth. Catholics believed that he was descended from St. Peter by a divinely granted, apostolic succession. However, by the late 15th century the papacy was viewed by many observers as an office that had strayed from its original role as the mouthpiece for the divine's message.

Martin Luther and John Calvin

In the several proceeding generations to the Reformation, the Catholic Church confronted multiple opposing entities. For example, one such group was mystics. These practitioners and their followers built a spiritual doctrine around an emotionally direct divine illumination that secured salvation. In addition, during this time there was a growing philosophical school of thought called nominalism. It emphasized that the tangible was of utmost importance, and in turn, this belief set pushed aside the abstract nature of faith. Moreover, the humanist movement spurned Christian doctrines, and as an alternative, these intellectual crusaders believed the classical universe held true prudence. During these transitional times, European monarchs began yearning for expanded empires. In turn, this developed a race among the nations of Europe to discover and claim new territories around the globe. This rising tide of voyages also spurred a push for spiritual growth to justify the conquering of divinely inspired new frontiers.

Image 10.1: Statue of Martin Luther outside of Wittenburg Church, Wittenburg, Germany. © Shutterstock.com

Amidst all these new movements and changes, a spiritual and intellectual pioneer came upon the scene. This man, Martin Luther, was the most vital figure of the Reformation. Without him there may not have been such a grand shift at all. As a young man, Luther gained a formal education in both theology and law. In addition, he became an avid reader of classical texts. Ultimately, Luther became a theological scholar. In part, he credited this professional choice with a grand conversion moment triggered by a lightning strike. To Luther, God determined this and all occurrences. In total, he grew into a man of great intellectualism and spirituality. Luther utilized these two strong characteristics to make history.

Martin Luther was an ordained priest and teacher of theology at the University of Wittenberg in the German state of Saxony. His father had encouraged him to study law, but he, like many others of the time, changed course and dedicated himself to God and the Catholic Church. He entered a monastery and earned a doctorate in theology. For whatever reason, however, Luther never felt assured about his relationship with God. He was a good Catholic who attended mass, confession, and other church functions. At the same time, Luther wondered if he had confessed all his sins and was penitent enough to earn God's forgiveness. Even the Catholic Church's promise of salvation through obedience to Catholic ritual and rite did not bring him comfort. He instead focused on the *Bible's* commandment that the "just

shall live by faith" (*Romans* 1:17). Luther reaffirmed his faith and developed a view of Christianity emphasizing that people were saved only through God's mercy and not through their own efforts. Political corruption and greed within the Catholic Church hierarchy coincided with Luther's struggle to define his spiritual beliefs. Luther was especially perplexed over the issue of indulgences. The Catholic Church taught that salvation came with the sacrament of baptism. Furthermore, humans committed sins that needed to be remitted before a person could enter heaven. Depending on the situation, priests sometimes offered a person an indulgence, which would reduce the time one spent in purgatory.

The idea was that the saints of old were so good, that they had more righteousness than they needed, and the Catholic Church could, under special circumstances, channel some of it to another soul. Historically, acts worthy of an indulgence focused on works of charity or a gift of money to the Catholic Church. In 1517, Pope Leo X decided to fund a plan for the rebuilding of St Peter's Basilica through the sale of indulgences. Monks and priests, acting with the special authority of the pope, promoted the sale of indulgences even more than before. From Luther's viewpoint, these acts were an abomination and heretical. He believed this was an abuse of church power and had nothing to do with his interpretation of Christ's teachings. In October 1517, Luther posted a copy of his *Ninety-Five Theses*, or arguments against indulgences, the uses of relics to aid one's search for salvation, and other criticisms of the Catholic Church, on the door of the church at the University of Wittenberg. Soon after, this work was printed and distributed to the public. In December 1517, Cardinal Albrecht von Brandenburg forwarded Luther's treatise to the authorities in Rome together with his own denunciation of its content.

The stage was set for conflict. Luther, by posting his *Ninety-Five Theses*, started a theological war that would soon engulf Europe. The Catholic Church did not take this significant threat to its authority, lightly. Luther could have been silenced by Prince Frederick the Wise of Saxony, who was a high-ranking and strident Catholic. However, he decided to protect Luther, because Frederick did not like Vatican leadership interfering with German affairs. Despite a papal request, Frederick declined to arrest Luther or banish him from Saxony. As such, Luther was secure so long as he stayed in Saxony.

Image 10.2: The church in Wittenburg, Germany, on which Martin Luther hammered his *Ninety-Five Theses*. Notices and announcements were often tacked to the doors of churches, but Luther tacking his *Theses* to the door of a church perhaps carried added emphasis to his message. The doors have since been replaced, but the church remains an iconic landmark symbolizing the start of the Protestant Reformation. © Shutterstock.com

Luther, now convinced that the papacy had become an instrument of evil, produced a stream of new pamphlets including *The Babylonian Captivity of the Church* and *To the Christian Nobility of the German Nation* (both in 1520). These new critiques directly attacked the pope and called on German princes to reform the Catholic Church. Luther found many that were agreeable to his message. It helped that he appealed to German nationalism to stir people against the Italian-dominated Catholic Church establishment. His freedom to do and to write what he pleased made the Catholic Church look impotent to stop either him or the ideas he promoted. In January 1521, Luther was excommunicated, and he was then free of all Roman authority.

The political culture of Germany, together with the development of printing, allowed Lutheranism to flourish. Luther became the focal point for millions of Christians who sympathized with his point of view. His need for a deep understanding of the Christian faith and hope of salvation echoed their hopes and fears. Luther provided a religious alternative which claimed to fulfill the needs of devout, dissenting

Christians. He wrote prayers and hymns for the reformed church, gave orders of service, and provided a new administrative and physical structure. Luther altered the role of priests and changed the meaning of the Catholic Mass. Church services went from the notion of a holy sacrifice, conducted by a special person (the priest), to a ceremony of communication between God and the faithful. The high marble altars were replaced by wooden tables in clear view, and ministers preached from the chancel steps or from pulpits in the body of the church. Luther's emphasis on the German language was a striking and important aspect of his new teaching. After Luther's translation of the *Bible* became widely available, thousands of literate Germans could read the sacred scriptures for themselves. Christians delighted in reading *Bible* stories for the first time, and this drew many of them to seriously consider Luther's doctrine. Church services were now conducted in German. This gave the people ownership of their church and forged an alliance between an emerging national identity and religious faith.

John Calvin developed the other great innovative wave of spiritual and intellectual changes at the core foundation of the Reformation. Indeed, his program of reform was a second windfall upon Europe of the Protestant Reformation. While Luther and Calvin came to prominence within similar time frames, they differed in personality and approach. As a young adult in Paris, Calvin studied theology and law. As a man, he was private, very intellectual, and always confident in his convictions. Like Luther, Calvin was very well versed in the vital works of classical authors, and he became an expert in multiple languages. In addition, he also read and gained insight from Luther's writings too. Calvin settled in Switzerland, and in 1536, Calvin published *Institutes of the Christian Religion*. This eighty-chapter tome was a truly grand literary effort. Indeed, Calvin dedicated a large portion of his life to finish it.

Institutes of the Christian Religion laid the theological foundation for a religion completely at odds with the centuries old Catholic interpretation of Christianity. One of his primary arguments was that a Christian could not earn salvation through good works. In addition, Calvin espoused that individual salvation was predestined. In other words, each person was entirely lost unless it was part of God's plan that they be saved. Calvin also stressed that Christians should have self-discipline and commit themselves to

a life of strict morality. This led to his followers committing themselves to focus on working hard, saving money, and laboring to ensure that the community upheld Christian standards. Much of what Calvin preached became the spirit of what became known as the "Protestant Work Ethic." This philosophy called upon followers to always demonstrate a sober-minded, morally sound, financially prudent, and hardworking approach to daily life.

A significant theme that runs through seemingly all aspects of Calvinist teachings is a strong commitment to rules. It is apparent that his training in the law developed a strict sense of order in Calvin. There are great considerations and historical ties connected to these types of concepts. The histories of global religions are filled with dedicated adherence to the creation of carefully laid out and very strongly worded laws, rules, and ordinances of all kinds. These vital spiritual edicts could be both simple and complex. While at times they inspired and offered positive enlightenment to believers, mostly these guidelines provided a firm mandate of what is not allowed within a religious community. In addition, people that strayed from these requirements often experienced severe repercussions. Options such as expulsion from the larger community, imprisonment, whippings, beatings, public branding, and even death were all fair game as punishments under these laws. Calvin influenced followers in Europe and the American colonies to develop and implement these concepts and

penalties, and in turn, they made them fit their own very legalistic societies.

As with any religion, Lutheranism and Calvinism had to attract followers to spread their religious belief sets. Lutheranism spread into Germany, Scandinavian areas such as Denmark, Sweden, Finland, and even Iceland. Calvinism developed dedicated followings in Switzerland, France, Scotland, Hungary, and several other European territories. In the next several generations after Luther and Calvin's time, their respective teachings also spread to the American colonies. To the present, both have a spiritual family tree of many millions of followers all over the globe.

The English Reformation

England was the only country to make a total break with the Catholic Church, and the cause had as much to do with politics as religion. King Henry VIII (ruled: 1509–1547) became king as a teenager and married his brother's widow, Catherine of Aragon. Henry was a devout Catholic and even defended the Catholic Church against Luther's accusations in a book published in 1521, *The Defence of the Seven Sacraments.* Because of his devotion, the pope awarded Henry the title, "Defender of the Faith." His devotion to the Catholic Church, however, was challenged by personal and political events.

As Henry's marriage to Catherine unfolded, it became evident that she was not going to produce a

Image 10.5: Michael Sittow, *Portrait of Catherine of Aragon*, c. 1500–1505, painting. © Shutterstock.com

Image 10.6: Engraving c.1831 of GerlachFlicke, *Portrait of Thomas Cranmer,* 1545, oil on canvas. © Shutterstock.com

male heir. Catherine had multiple miscarriages and pregnancies, however, only one child survived beyond infancy, Mary. Henry's desire for the Tudor dynasty to continue became the driving force of his life and he sought for ways to secure a son. He soon decided that the only measure that could be taken was to marry another woman, specifically Anne Boleyn. Therefore, the king asked the Catholic Church to annul the marriage. Henry argued that the marriage was cursed and blamed his wife, yet Pope Clement VII denied the request. He argued that since Henry's marriage to his brother's widow, Catherine, was allowed under special papal dispensation he could not intervene. The Pope also feared Catherine's nephew, the reigning Holy Roman Emperor Charles V (ruled: 1519–1556). However, Henry moved forward on his own.

In 1533, ignoring the Pope's answer, Henry had Archbishop Thomas Cranmer secretly wed him to Anne Boleyn. Within a short period, the British Parliament passed the *Act of Supremacy* (1534), and this measure formally cut ties with the Catholic Church and recognized Henry as the head of The Church of England. Although the newly formed Church of England separated from the Catholic Church, the organization and beliefs of the English (Anglican) Church were not that much different from the Catholic Church. Under the new church and state association, the king was the head of the church, but it retained its Catholic, now Anglican, form of governing structure. Between 1536 and 1539, the king ordered the

dissolution of all Catholic monasteries in England and confiscated the land. He also oversaw the translation of the *Bible* into the English language. Although there were some initial dramatic moves away from Catholic teachings, Henry settled his theological beliefs with the issuance of *An Act Abolishing Diversity in Opinions* in 1539. This edict became the official base of the Anglican beliefs. It reaffirmed the Catholic beliefs of transubstantiation, clerical celibacy, the practice of confession, and permission for private masses, but it also included an injunction against heresy to combat the more Protestant leanings of the people.

The personal life of Henry continued to direct the course of his nation's religious life. Anne Boleyn bore Henry a daughter named Elizabeth, but when her second pregnancy was a miscarriage, he accused her of adultery and had her executed. Henry's third wife, Jane Seymour, died not long after giving birth to the long-sought male heir, the future Edward VI (ruled: 1547–1553). Upon Henry's death in 1547, nine-year-old Edward ascended to the throne. Edward was guided by those over him and moved England in a more Protestant direction. The chief monument of his brief reign was the publication of the *Book of Common Prayer* (originally published in 1549 and revised in 1552) which presented a new order of worship for English churchgoers to follow.

It was during Edward's reign that the Church of England began to move in a more Protestant direction.

Image 10.7: *Portrait of Edward VI*, c. 1550, oil on panel. © Shutterstock.com

Anglican worship was conducted in English, and the *Book of Common Prayer* became a unifying force in England. However, Edward VI's death in 1553 temporarily endangered the church Henry founded. England's move toward Protestantism was almost upended when Edward`s half-sister Mary, Catherine of Aragon's daughter, came to the throne.

Queen Mary I (ruled: 1553–1558) shared her mother's Catholic faith and wanted to reunite England with Rome. Mary retroactively validated her mother's marriage to Henry and repealed the Reformation legislation. In a series of violent acts that continued to prove her intentions, "Bloody Mary" searched out and executed over two hundred eighty Protestant sympathizers, many of them burned at the stake. Many Protestants fled to the European continent during Mary's rule for the sake of protection. Queen Mary I tried to secure her rule through marriage to King Philip II of Spain (ruled: 1556–1598) and the hope of an heir. However, she did not have any children. When Mary died in 1558, her sister Elizabeth, daughter of Anne Boleyn (Henry VIII's second wife), ascended the throne.

Queen Elizabeth I (ruled: 1558–1603) was a very skilled ruler. She strengthened the Church of England and set the nation again on a Protestant course. Although she was not particularly devout or pious, she sought a moderate approach for the Church of England. For example, Church of England services were performed in the native tongue and clergyman could get married. Elizabeth also reaffirmed the church statement of doctrine. These rules provided a somewhat middle ground regarding Christian faith, and they removed any heavy influences of Catholic

Image 10.8: Robert Peake the Elder, *Queen Elizabeth being carried by her courtiers,* c. 1600. © Shutterstock.com

theology or radical Protestantism. In 1571, Parliament made adherence to the church statement of doctrine, entitled *Thirty-Nine Articles*, mandatory and they are still adhered to today by the Anglican Church. These articles also became the basis of creeds throughout the Protestant churches in years to come.

The Catholic Reformation

While Protestantism was spreading rapidly throughout Europe, the Catholic Church searched for a means to counter its momentum and reclaim its position on the continent. The primary Catholic reformer was Pope Paul III. Coming into office in the 1530s, when the Church appeared ready to collapse, Paul hoped to overcome the troubled legacy of his predecessors and restore integrity to the papacy. Realizing that problems within the Catholic Church had to be corrected, he attacked the corruption of the clergy. In pursuing reforms, Paul appointed a commission that pursued such abuses. Their recommendations led him to call a church council. The time when the Catholics could suppress all opposition had passed, and most of the leadership grasped this reality.

Catholic leaders met in a northern Italian city named Trent to discuss a response. The Council of Trent met three times between 1545 and 1563. Devoting much attention to the external struggle against Protestantism, the Council of Trent also sought to eliminate internal abuses by ordering changes in church discipline and administration. To start, it greatly altered the ways in which indulgences were sold. Churches were no longer allowed to seek profit from the sale of their offices, and clergymen were discouraged from pursuing arts and professions thought too secular for a man of God. The new rules placed an emphasis on abiding by stricter rules, and bishops were tasked with maintaining a firm control of the conduct of those under their rank. Church positions were now to be granted to those individuals that were thought to be best qualified for various respective jobs.

The Council of Trent also reaffirmed the basic guidelines of the Catholic faith. Thus, the need to perform good works, live by the laws of the Church, and obey the papacy did not change. Transubstantiation was reaffirmed, tradition was still considered as important as scripture, priests were deemed still necessary as intermediaries between the people and God, and the confirmation of saints and relics was endorsed.

The Catholic Church also reiterated their belief in seven sacraments. These sacraments (baptism, confirmation, Eucharist, marriage, confession, ordination, and extreme unction) became a significant difference between Catholic beliefs and Protestant ones. (Protestant belief held to only two sacraments: baptism and Eucharist). Regarding church government, the Catholic Church still functioned as a hierarchy predicated on a chain of command: from the pope, to the bishops, and so on.

The Council of Trent was important for several reasons. It applied itself to clean up the corruption in the Catholic Church, reaffirmed Catholic beliefs, and started a revolution in education. As Protestantism formed schools to educate people in their beliefs, the Catholic Church matched this effort with educational developments. These moves, coupled with the desire to make converts in the New World, sparked the movement of the Society of Jesus, or Jesuits.

The spirit of reform was reflected in a number of new clerical orders that emerged in the 16th century. Among the reforms was the establishment of a new Catholic order known as the Society of Jesus. Organized along military lines, with their founder, the Spaniard Ignatius Loyola as general and the pope as commander in chief, the Jesuits were an army of soldiers sworn to follow orders and defend the Catholic faith. Ignatius of Loyola was a Spanish nobleman who was wounded in battle in 1521. While recovering in the hospital he read the *Bible* and experienced what he called ecstatic,

Image 10.9: Ignatius of Loyola, c. 1837, engraving. © Shutterstock.com

spiritual visions that changed him forever. Ignatius wrote about his visions in his work, *The Spiritual Exercises* (1548) and sparked a movement that focused on meditations on sin and following the life of Christ. The Jesuit movement was officially founded in Paris in 1534 and began with Ignatius, six followers, and vows of poverty, chastity, and a focus on converting Muslims. As time progressed and with Ignatius' charismatic personality, the group grew and was officially sanctioned by the Catholic Church in 1540.

The Jesuit movement founded schools and colleges, served as missionaries on every continent, and worked their way into government whenever possible. It was the Jesuits who, more than any other group, were responsible for checking the spread of Protestantism after the 1560s. As such, they zealously defended Catholicism in France, drove out Protestants from parts of Europe, and helped Spain and Portugal develop their global, Catholic empires. These divisions between the Catholic and Protestant Churches not only impacted the movement of peoples and spread of education but also increased hostilities between the two and erupted in wars.

Image 10.10: Statue of Matteo Ricci in Macau, China. Jesuit missionaries are known for an emphasis on education, and would learn the language and culture of the area they lived to better teach the Bible. As a result, some Jesuit priests created translation dictionaries. Matteo Ricci, a missionary to China, created one of the most comprehensive Chinese to Portuguese dictionaries of the Early Modern Era.
© Shutterstock.com

Consequences and Conclusions of the Reformation

The Protestant Reformation and the Catholic Counter-Reformation helped create the modern world. By breaking the religious monopoly of European Catholicism, Lutheranism and Anglicanism assisted the growth of Northern European monarchies. Although Luther and Calvin were confident that their readings of the Bible and Christian views were correct, others felt the same and espoused conflicting versions of "true" doctrine. Protestantism then fragmented into different sects, all of which believed in the superiority of their beliefs and practices. As such, this set of developments eventually led to armed conflict between rival factions. Much of the fighting that erupted focused on the religious battle between Protestantism and Catholicism and the political ramifications each of these beliefs instituted.

In total, the fallout from the substantial changes of the Reformation meant several generations of wars among European powers. The fighting was in several different circles, including France with the French Wars of Religion (1562–1598) and the Holy Roman Empire and its final battle, the Thirty Years' War (1618–1648). These wars shaped the Christian church and formation of European nations for years to come.

The French Wars of Religion centered around the Kings of France trying to prevent the spread of Calvinism in their Catholic nation. The Huguenots (French Calvinists) represented only a fraction of the French population but made up between forty and fifty percent of the French nobility, including the House of Bourbon. The Bourbons held the kingdom of Navarre in the southern part of France and were next in line for the throne. The Catholic House of Valois ruled France, and the monarchy felt a threat to their power with the rapid conversion rate of the nobility to Calvinism. As time progressed, military allegiances were formed between the extreme Catholic party, the ultra-Catholics under the leadership of the powerful Guise family, and the Huguenots. The ultra-Catholics desired strict opposition to the Huguenots and obtained the loyalties of the Paris and large northern sections of France. Full-scale fighting broke out in between the ultra-Catholics and Huguenots in 1562 when the Duke of Guise led his soldiers in a massacre of a peaceful congregation of Huguenots in the city of Vassy. The Huguenots banded together into a defensive fighting unit and fought against the ultra-Catholics intermittently for the next decade.

Fighting escalated again between the Huguenots and ultra-Catholics with the St. Bartholomew's Day Massacre in 1572. In an attempt to bring peace between the warring factions, the Valois family proposed a re-conciliatory marriage between the Catholic sister of the reigning Valois king, Charles IX (ruled: 1560–1574) and Henry of Navarre, the Bourbon ruler of Navarre. Henry was the acknowledged political leader of the Huguenots and, thus, many Huguenots traveled to Paris for the event. During the marriage festivities ultra-Catholic fighters, again under the leadership of the Duke of Guise, slaughtered several thousand Huguenots in Paris under the watchful eye of the queen mother, Catherine de Medici. The mass-murder in Paris spread into the countryside and over the course of the next several months; approximately ten thousand Huguenots were killed throughout France. Regular fighting in France continued until the issuance of the *Edict of Nantes* in 1598, which granted substantial protections and rights to Huguenots in Catholic France.

Fighting in the Holy Roman Empire erupted during the early stages of the Protestant Reformation as the German princes fought to maintain control of their states against the powerful Holy Roman Emperor, Charles V. The early conflicts ended with the *Peace of Augsburg* in 1555 which divided the many German states between Catholic and Lutheran and allowed each prince the right to determine the religion of his subjects. However, hostilities continued to burn and the empire fragmented into two hostile alliances: the Protestant Union and the Catholic League.

The Thirty Years' War (1618–1648) began as a religious war and soon devolved into an international struggle transcending religion. It began in the Protestant province of Bohemia when the newly elected Holy Roman Emperor, Ferdinand II (ruled: 1619–1637), tried to impose religious uniformity upon the German states. Bohemia revolted against the tyranny of the emperor and ushered in the first phase of the War. The Thirty Years' War soon pitted the Protestant Union and its allies against the Catholic League's supporters, including the Spanish Hapsburgs. The Hapsburg family at this time controlled both Spain and Austria. The Bohemian phase of the war ended with the battle of the White Mountain in November, 1620, and the conflict left Bohemia in ruins. However, when the King of Denmark Christian IV (ruled: 1588–1648) joined the Protestants in 1625, the Catholic faced a new challenge. His motives were mixed in that he wanted to aid the Protestants for his own territorial and sovereign interests. Christian IV's forces were repelled within a year and Denmark withdrew in 1629.

The third phase of the war opened in 1630 with the entrance of the King of Sweden, Gustavus Adolphus (ruled: 1611–1632). Adolphus combined forces with the German Protestant states and won a key victory against the Catholic League and its allies. However, he was killed in battle and Sweden was forced to withdraw from the war. It was at this time that France entered the war and the hostilities took on new dimensions.

The entrance of Catholic France into the Thirty Years' War under the leadership of Cardinal Richelieu (1585–1642), chief minister of King Louis XIII (ruled:

Image 10.11: In 1618, Catholic representatives from the Holy Roman Emperor Ferdinand II met with Protestant representatives from Bohemia in Prague to discuss issues that had arisen after the repeal of the Peace of Augsburg.
When the representatives could not reach an agreement, the Protestants literally chucked the Catholics out the window. The Catholic representatives survived by, according to the Protestants, falling in a pile of horse manure, or according to the Catholics, by having been caught by angels. The instance is thought to have triggered the Bohemian Rebellion, which fed into the later Thirty Years' War. © Prisma Archivo/ Alamy Stock Photo

Image 10.12: Europe in 1648 after the Peace of Westphalia. *Courtesy of the University of Texas Libraries, University of Texas Austin.*

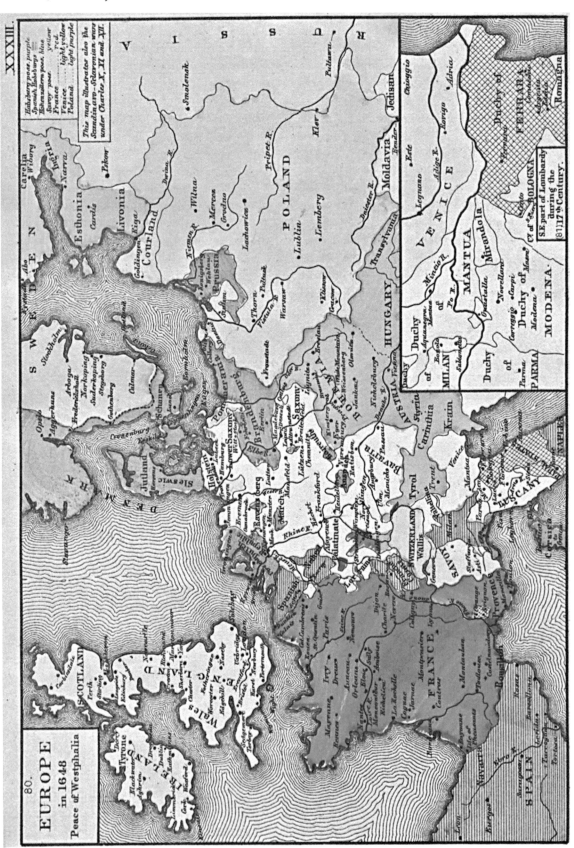

1610–1643), was a political move that changed the course of European warfare. In an effort to stifle the power of the Spanish Hapsburgs, Richelieu decided to side with the Protestants and formed an alliance with Sweden and Germany. His move was a calculated one against the religious definitions of war and a step into the modern era of warfare. Richelieu's alliance forced fighting for another thirteen years and led to a victory over the Catholic League and the Spanish Hapsburgs. Peace negotiations in Westphalia led to the *Peace of Westphalia* (1648) which marked an end to religious warfare. The *Peace of Westphalia* confirmed the *Peace of Augsburg*, in that German princes could choose the religion of their subjects, and it added Calvinism to Lutheranism and Catholicism as a recognized faith. But, the damage of the war was felt by Germans for decades to come. The Thirty Years' War was a brutal conflict that destroyed German land, homes, and men. The empire lost one-quarter of its inhabitants, and its ordained fragmentation set forth by the Peace of Westphalia sealed the divided nation and helped delay its unification for two hundred years.

To properly appreciate the historical influence of this intriguing time-period, you can consider a big picture view of the dramatic influence of several of the dominant figures of the Reformation. Martin Luther came from a tremendous educational experience in the necessities of liberal arts, legal studies, and theology, but his path in life involved much more than being a well-read expert on diverse topics. His intellectual and spiritual world view evolved and matured in a very productive manner. As a result, Luther rather daringly used his capable grasp of theological knowledge, gifted writing skill, strong analytical talent, and a dedicated spiritual faith to drive centuries of tradition into a roller coaster of turbulent changes.

John Calvin left a legacy of extraordinarily well organized, substantial, and legalistic practices that many protestant churches both implemented and wholeheartedly presently live by within their respective greater faith-based communities. At the same time, he maintained a dedicated spiritual faith that fueled these voluminous rules of order. Therefore, Calvin's intellectualism and religious ideas mixed in a transformative manner to greatly add to the tidal wave of change Luther initially brought to the forefront of European society.

There is also, however, a legacy of power, politics, greed, and empire to the Reformation. Monarchs, nobles, and commoners engaged in life or death adventures and conflicts that reshaped villages, cities, nations, and continents. From the Saga of Henry VIII to the Catholic Church implementing notable changes to the Thirty Years' War, the Reformation provided a very tangible record of change. Through the present day and beyond, it gives all students of history a lot to study and build upon.

Index